A
CONCISE DICTIONARY OF
MODERN PLACE-NAMES
IN GREAT BRITAIN AND
IRELAND

A
Concise Dictionary of
Modern Place-Names

IN GREAT BRITAIN AND IRELAND

ADRIAN ROOM

Oxford   New York
OXFORD UNIVERSITY PRESS
1983

Oxford University Press, Walton Street, Oxford OX2 6DP

London Glasgow New York Toronto
Delhi Bombay Calcutta Madras Karachi
Kuala Lumpur Singapore Hong Kong Tokyo
Nairobi Dar es Salaam Cape Town
Melbourne Auckland

and associated companies in
Beirut Berlin Ibadan Mexico City Nicosia

Oxford is a trade mark of Oxford University Press

Published in the United States
by Oxford University Press, New York

British Library Cataloguing in Publication Data
Room, Adrian.
A concise dictionary of modern place-names in Great
Britain and Ireland.
1. Names, Geographical—Great Britain
—Dictionaries
I. Title
914.1'00142   DA645
ISBN 0-19-211590-1

Library of Congress Cataloging in Publication Data
Room, Adrian.
A concise dictionary of modern place names in
Great Britain and Ireland.
Bibliography: p.
1. Names, Geographical—Great Britain. 2. Names,
Geographical—Ireland. 3. Great Britain—History,
Local. 4. Ireland—History, Local. I. Title.
DA645.R66   1983   914.1'0014   83-2472
ISBN 0-19-211590-1

Set by Wyvern Typesetting Ltd.
Printed in Hong Kong

ACKNOWLEDGEMENTS

I AM greatly indebted to a number of people who assisted, some most generously, with background information regarding many of the names in the Dictionary.

First and foremost I should like to thank the librarians, local historians, and other officers of public libraries who at my request supplied information from the resources of the following town and city libraries: Aberdeen, Airdrie, Aldershot, Ballynahinch (South-Eastern Library Service, Northern Ireland), Bangor (Wales), Barnstaple, Bath, Belfast, Birmingham, Boston, Bradford, Bradford-on-Avon, Bridgend, Cardiff, Carlisle, Cheltenham, Cupar, Dumfries, Dunfermline, Edinburgh, Elgin, Falkirk, Forfar, Halifax, Haverfordwest, Huddersfield, Inverness, Leeds, Leicester, Lincoln, Llangefni, Lytham St. Annes, Margate, Matlock, Merthyr Tydfil, Millport, Mold, Neath, Newport (Gwent), Oldham, Peterlee, Plymouth, Reigate, Shrewsbury, Southend-on-Sea, Stockton-on-Tees, Stoke-on-Trent, Sutton Coldfield, Swansea, Truro, Virginia Water, Wakefield, Wallasey, Walsall, Wolverhampton, Worcester, Worthing, and the two London boroughs of Merton and Newham.

I should also like to thank the following public officers for providing information on similar lines: Chief Executive, Castle Point District Council; Public Relations Officer, Hart District Council; Borough Secretary, Hertsmere District Council; Chief Executive, Hyndburn Borough Council; Chief Executive, Shepway District Council; County Archivist, Suffolk Record Office.

For specialist information and guidance I am particularly indebted to the following, some of whom have been of constant assistance throughout my own researches and work on the Dictionary: Professor Kenneth Cameron, Director of Survey, EPNS; Mr Ian Fraser, School of Scottish Studies, Edinburgh; Professor Bedwyr Lewis Jones, Department of Welsh, University College of North Wales, Bangor; Mr Breandán Ó Cíobháin, Ordnance Survey Office, Dublin; Miss Lesley Brown, Librarian, National Coal Board, London; Ms Sally Downes, Assistant Public Relations Manager, The Jockey Club, London.

For 'private' information and help I would very much like to thank James Chaniller of Tangier, Morocco, for information on Frederick William Harris of Treharris, Mrs Sally Evans of Neath, for information on the seven sisters of Seven Sisters, Canon E. T. Davies of Usk, for information on Elliotstown, and Margaret Dickson of Westerfield, Ipswich, who made initial researches on my behalf in the British Library and saw what I was up against.

For permission to quote from various sources I would like to thank: Miss E. C. Carmody, from her father's book *Lisburn Cathedral and its Past Rectors* (1926), Easington District Council, from C. W. Clarke's report, *Farewell Squalor* (1947), Messrs Faber and Faber, from Clough Williams Ellis, *Portmeirion: The Place and its Meaning* (1963), Her Majesty's Stationery Office, from *Local Government Boundary Commission for England, Report No. 2* (1973), and Norman Tildesley, from his book *A History of Willenhall* (Willenhall Urban District Council, Walsall, 1951).

ADRIAN ROOM

Petersfield, Hampshire
April 1983

CONTENTS

INTRODUCTION

MANY of the place-names with which we are most familiar in the British Isles are ancient names, long established to designate a particular geographical object, even where that object today has changed out of all recognition from its original. Thus as we travel north out of London on the A1, following for much of the way the route of the old Great North Road, we pass through or near many places with such historic names: Hatfield, Stevenage, Letchworth, Biggleswade, Eaton Socon, Alconbury, Stilton, Stamford, Colsterworth, Newark-on-Trent, Blyth, Doncaster, Chester-le-Street, Gateshead, Newcastle-upon-Tyne, Berwick-upon-Tweed, finally reaching our destination in Scotland's capital city, Edinburgh. These names, the latter included, in fact provide a microcosm of English place-names of different kinds. Hatfield, for example, has a name meaning roughly 'heather field' that was recorded by Bede (as *Haethfeld*) as long ago as the eighth century, while Biggleswade, recorded in the 'Domesday Book' of 1086 as *Pichelesuuade*, has a name that means 'Biccel's ford', and so is based on a personal name. Eaton Socon, originally just 'Eaton' (*Etone* in the 'Domesday Book') has an old name, commonly found all over the country, to mean 'eastern settlement' (the Old English *tūn* giving modern English 'town'), with the second half of the name, meaning 'soke' (an old administrative district, as in the former Soke of Peterborough) added to distinguish this particular 'Eaton' from the many others. The name of Stamford was recorded as long ago as 922 (as *Steanford*) to mean 'stony ford', and both Doncaster and Chester-le-Street are Roman-based names meaning 'fort on the Don' and 'fort by a Roman road'. The apparent 'newness' of Newark and Newcastle is deceptive, since Newark's name dates back at least to the eleventh century to mean 'new works', i.e. building-work that, at that time, was new in contrast to older building, and the 'new castle' at Newcastle (recorded in Latin as *Novum Castellum* in 1130) was built in 1080 to replace the old Roman fort nearby. And the four river names that appear in the itinerary above, Blyth (the former name of the *Ryton*, on which Blyth stands), Don, Tyne, and Tweed are equally venerable, with the name of the Don related to that of the Danube, and one of the oldest names in the British Isles.

A similar roll of old names can be found on many of the main roads or routes in Scotland, Wales, and Ireland, especially where such names are in a Gaelic or Celtic tongue. We need not doubt that Inverness, Nairn, and Elgin, on Scotland's A96, or Carmarthen, Llandovery, and Brecon, on the A40 in South Wales, or Lurgan, Dundalk, and Drogheda, on the railway running south from Belfast to Dublin in Ireland, are all old and historic names, with Inverness ('mouth of the river Ness') recorded in 1300, Brecon ('territory of Brychan') existing in 1100, and Lurgan an old Irish name meaning 'shin' to describe a long, low hill.

Yet that same A1, as it wends its way north out of central London, passes by places with much more modern names. It begins its route by running by *Angel* Underground Station, then passes through *Archway* to run parallel to the M1 near *Mill Hill* to the east and *Burnt Oak* to the west. It then takes the traveller out of Greater London to *Potters Bar* and, a few miles later, *Welwyn Garden City*. Further north still, it crosses the river *Gwash* near Stamford, and the river *Ryton* at Blyth. It then runs past *Boston Spa* in West Yorkshire to enter Durham as a motorway and continue just east of *Newton Aycliffe*, and some ten miles west of *Peterlee*, until it finally reaches its first sea sea port of Berwick-upon-Tweed, close to the Scottish border. Here the traveller might well pause to pay a visit to *Ladykirk*, a few miles west up the river Tweed, before he resumes his journey on the A1 which, now in Scotland, continues on its way via *Broxburn* to enter Edinburgh through *Joppa* and *Portobello*.

These places, some of them quite well known even to travellers who have never been there, all have names that in most cases have arisen since 1500, and which therefore, in topographical terms, can be regarded as modern and as suitable candidates for entry in this present Dictionary.

It is a regrettable fact that many books on place-names and their origins deal with modern names either sketchily, almost dismissively, or not at all. Those that approach the subject historically, as one must (although not exclusively), usually take the reader down to the Post-Conquest French and Latin names (the latter recorded in official documents by learned scribes) of the twelfth and thirteenth centuries, but barely any further. Little or nothing about modern names will be found in such works as those (listed in the Bibliography, p. 143) by Addison (1978), Cameron (1961), Copley (1971), Gould (1978), and Reaney (1976). Worse still, modern names are mostly omitted from Ekwall (1960), which is rightly regarded by many as the 'bible' of English place-name origins. Where modern names are mentioned, the information is usually brief in the extreme, and often uninformative. Of all the English place-names mentioned above, for example (and originating before 1960, when Ekwall's fourth and final edition was published), only *Ryton* is entered, and the reader who turns to Ekwall to learn the origin of the names of such well-known places as *Burgess Hill*, *Cliftonville* (any of them), *Craven Arms*, *Gerrards Cross*, *Peacehaven*, the *Pennines* (!), *Port Sunlight*, *St. Leonards-on-Sea*, *Saltdean*, *Thornton Heath*, *Virginia Water*, *Waterlooville*, and *Wealdstone*, will be disappointed, since none of these names appears in his book. And although a little information is given for such places as *Morcambe* and *Saffron Walden* (under *Walde*), many well-known names are dismissed simply as 'a late name' (*Devonport*), 'Late names. Self-explanatory' (*Ironbridge* and *Ironville*), and, perhaps least helpfully of all, 'A late place and name' (*Southport*). Even Field (1980) omits almost all these names, and of *Newhaven*, for example, tells us merely that the name means 'newly built harbour'.

Yet these late names, and the many hundreds like them throughout the British Isles, are often extremely interesting, and reveal much about the origins of the place and the social and economic conditions of its time. Who was the 'Burgess' of *Burgess Hill*, for example; why was *Cliftonville* such a popular name; what is the significance of the 'Peace' of *Peacehaven*; how did a port come to be named after a brand of soap; was there a man called 'Thornton' on *Thornton Heath*; how did the American name Virginia come to be given to the Surrey commuter-belt district of *Virginia Water*; why was *Southport* 'south' when it is in the north of England; why was a new harbour built at *Newhaven*? All these are questions that demand an answer.

The aim of this Dictionary is to try to provide some of the answers, and thus to fill an embarrassing gap in British and Irish place-name studies. That many hundreds of modern place-names exist in the British Isles there can be no doubt. A large number of them, for reasons that will be explained, are in Scotland, Wales, and Ireland rather than in England. But they are plentiful enough, and here in this present Dictionary the origins will be found, as far as they can be told, of over a thousand such names. Such a figure falls short, of course, of the actual total number, but at the same time provides a broad enough selection for an objective overview of modern place-names to be made and for certain naming patterns to be clearly discerned. We shall examine these shortly.

Modern Place-Names

The 'watershed' date of 1500 for modern place-names is not entirely an arbitrary one. In the first place it is a date when the 'old' names, from the earliest British names to the post-Conquest Norman ones, had become more or less finally established and, with some variations in spelling and form, fixed as they were to remain from this year on. Such well-known names as London, Birmingham, Edinburgh, Shetland, Fishguard, Snowdon, Belfast, Dublin, and Stonehenge had mostly acquired their present spelling by 1500, or at least a recognizable variant of it. Secondly, it was from 1500 on that political and economic developments would radically alter the status and constitution of all four parts (England, Scotland, Wales, Ireland) of the British Isles. Third, in so far as English names are concerned, the English language had by 1500 passed through its two great formative periods of Old English (usually reckoned as running from the 'beginnings' in 700 to 1100) and Middle English (from 1100 to 1500), and had begun to settle to what linguists now call New or Modern English (from 1500 to the present day), so that significant changes in 'word-based' names are unlikely. For modern place-names, therefore, we are left with a scenario where old names and the English language change little, but where political, religious, social, and industrial conditions change much. It is this second important factor that gave rise to the majority of the place-names recorded in this Dictionary.

Of the four constituent countries of the British Isles, it was Scotland and Ireland that were to acquire the largest number of new place-names in the period after 1500, with Ireland having the historical priority. The cause in both countries, but for different reasons, was the development of new towns and villages, in many cases on the sites of existing settlements.

Ireland had for long been the 'target' for English rulers and settlers ever since the Anglo-Norman king Henry II planned the conquest of that country in the twelfth century. It was the Normans, indeed, who built many of the primitive castles or 'mottes' that were later to become the focal points of English- and Scottish-built settlements. At the same time, many great Norman families such as the de Lacys were granted vast territories of land. These, together with the English territory known as 'the Pale', were the forerunners of the lands that later, under Edward I and Edward III, were confiscated and colonized by increasing waves of English lords and military leaders. The real period of English influence in Ireland, however, dates from 1541, when Henry VIII took the title of 'King of Ireland' and, by conferring earldoms on many of the great lords such as O'Neill, O'Brien, and O'Donnell, aimed to gain supremacy in the country and reduce it to obedience. To this end, many English statesmen decided to 'plant' or settle Ireland with colonies of Englishmen who, at least in theory, were to be cultivators, civilizers, and enlighteners in peace, and soldiers of the king (or queen) in war. Such plantations continued in the reigns of Edward VI, Queen Mary, and Elizabeth I, with Laois and Offaly, for example, shired in Mary's reign respectively as *Queen's County* and *King's County*, and with English names rapidly ousting the old Irish ones. The most far-reaching of the plantation schemes, however, was in Ulster under the reign of James I. Here, beginning in 1609, the possessions of the earls of Tyrone and Tyrconnel were confiscated and their lands apportioned to English and Scottish settlers, as well as to other grantees such as companies from London and Trinity College, Dublin. Scottish settlers were particularly numerous in Down and Antrim, and Scottish noblemen were responsible for the founding and development of such places as *Newtownards* in Down and

Portstewart in Antrim, together with many others elsewhere in Ulster. Plantation continued until the Rebellion of 1641, when the Irish rose against the English settlers in protest at the extensive confiscations in Ulster and the threatened confiscation of Connaught.

This, however, was not the end, for although the attempt of Charles I to 'settle' Connaught failed, Cromwell's men and troops were to follow and forcibly acquire—and rename—many strongholds and settlements, notably in Leinster and Munster.

Many of the English names in Ireland will be found to have originated as the result of a confiscation or a 'plantation'—a much bloodier affair, incidentally, than the peaceful and lawful-sounding term suggests. Today, however, in the Republic of Ireland, the majority of such English names, although by no means all, have reverted to their Irish names, and *King's County, Queen's County, Kingstown,* and *Queenstown* are no longer on the map.

In Scotland the development of new settlements with new names was largely much more peaceful than in strife-torn Ireland, and was mostly for economic reasons. Such development was both industrial and agricultural, and began in earnest in the first half of the seventeenth century, when no less than 64 new burghs of barony were established by landowners in the Lowlands, and especially in Stirlingshire and East Lothian, where coal-mining and salt-mining were expanding. True, not all such settlements arose for economic reasons, and in 1597, for example, the Scottish Parliament had ordered that 'there be erected and builded three burghs and burgh towns in the most convenient and commodious parts meet for the same, to wit: one in Kintyre, another in Lochaber, and the third in Lewis' (quoted in Adams, 1978). These three strategically sited ports were respectively *Campbeltown, Fort William,* and Stornaway.

A unique type of settlement in Scotland, however, was the so-called 'planned village'. These were settlements founded by landowners on their estates between *c.*1735 and *c.*1850, and were designed in particular for agricultural improvement, with carefully laid-out farms and building plots. The planned village movement was not restricted to farming settlements, and in fact the first such village, which was the forerunner of the development, was the fishing village of *Gardenstown,* founded by Alexander Garden of Troup in 1720 in north-east Scotland. It was in this region that the movement had the greatest impact, and today many names of planned villages can be found on the map over a large area between Inverness in the west and Peterhead and Aberdeen in the east. On or near the coast alone here we find (moving eastwards from Inverness) *Campbelltown, Cummingstown, Lossiemouth, Kingston-on-Spey, Portgordon, Macduff, Gardenstown, New Aberdour, Sandhaven,* and *Charles-*

town, while a drive along the A96 from Inverness to Aberdeen will take the visitor through *Fife-Keith*, *Huntly*, *Port Elphinstone*, and *Bankhead*. Later, planned villages with new names (often 'New' names, i.e. 'New' prefixed to an existing name) arose in other parts of Scotland, notably central Scotland from present-day Strathclyde in the west to Fife and Tayside in the east, with other 'pockets' in Dumfries and Galloway in the south and around the Cromarty Firth in the north. There were also planned villages in Skye and the Outer Hebrides—here chiefly as fishing ports. Altogether, it has been calculated that no less than 255 settlements were laid out on new sites or on radically altered old sites, and almost all of these had new names. In some cases where an old name was retained, this was due more to a desire for 'continuity' than a deliberate naming policy. Some towns and villages were almost bodily shifted, name and all, to give their aristocratic owners greater privacy in a new location. An example of such a resiting was the rebuilding of Cullen by the Earl of Seafield in 1822: the present attractive seaside resort, the 'Queen of the Moray Firth', was formerly located over a mile to the south, round St. Mary's Church and Cullen House.

Elsewhere in Scotland, as indeed in England and throughout the British Isles, a number of towns acquired new, specially planned suburbs, many with new names.

Wales, say the guidebooks, is a land of contrasts. And this is certainly true of this small but vital principality's place-names, which range from the old Welsh names, many merely meaningless tongue-twisters to visiting Englishmen, to modern English names, and even several *biblical* names.

The majority of modern Welsh place-names are in the south of the country, where apart from inland spas such as *Llandrindod Wells* and seaside resorts such as *Porthcawl*, the Industrial Revolution brought a wealth of new names from the mid-eighteenth century in the newly arisen iron- and coal-mining settlements. The coal boom in South Wales, with the focal area the Rhondda Valley, was at its height in the eighty or so years following 1850, and it was in this period that many of the modern place-names of Gwent and Mid-Glamorgan emerged. To a certain extent they resemble modern Irish and Scottish names, inasmuch as they are based on personal names. But these are not the names of aristocratic castle-builders and village planners, but mostly those of industrial entrepreneurs—ironmasters and coal-owners. Here in the valleys are *Tylorstown*, *Wattstown*, *Griffithstown*, and *Hopkinstown*, as well as the rather more Welsh-looking *Treharris* ('Harristown'), *Treherbert*, and *Tretomas*. True, there are aristocratic names (*Beaufort*, *Dukestown*, *Princetown*, *Fleur-de-Lis*), but these are rather by indirect association and patronage than through direct royal or noble involvement. Some of the recent names are English translations from the Welsh, such as *Middletown* and *Newchurch;* other English names, although today having Welsh equivalents, have always been English, such as *Port Talbot* and *Pembroke Dock*. However, many of the apparently modern English names in South Wales have long existed, with the important Gwent *Newport* dating back to the thirteenth century as a name (and to the twelfth century as Latin *Novus Burgus*) and the smaller Dyfed *Newport*, formerly in Pembrokeshire, recorded as *Nuport* in 1282. (Much of Pembrokeshire and the Gower Peninsula, still known as 'Little England Beyond Wales', has been English-speaking since the twelfth century.)

We shall be considering the biblical names separately (see p. xxii), but suffice it to say here that they mostly arose in the first half of the nineteenth century as a direct result of the Methodist revival. Among them are several places named *Bethel, Bethesda, Carmel, Hebron, Saron,* and even a small village in Clwyd called *Sodom*.

Apart from the recent revival of ancient names for the new Welsh counties (*Clwyd, Dyfed, Gwent, Gwynedd,* and *Powys*), there are also a number of modern Welsh names, among them the famous record-breaking Anglesey village of *Llanfairpwllgwyngyllgogerychwyrndrobwll-llandysiliogogogoch,* an early nineteenth-century compilation.

Most of the modern place-names in England itself are those of newly-developed places of various types, unlike the more specialized settlements of the Celtic countries. Among them are industrial towns and cities such as *Nelson, St. Helens, Spenborough,* and *Queensbury* in the Midlands, suburban developments, some of them approaching the Scottish 'planned village' in origin, such as *Akroydon,* Halifax, *Carrington,* Nottingham, *Charlotteville,* Guildford, *Egremont,* Wallasey, and *Vauxhall,* Birmingham, seaside resorts and ports such as (down the west coast) *Maryport, Morecambe, Fleetwood, Blackpool, Southport, New Brighton, Avonmouth, Westward Ho!,* and *Newquay,* (down the east coast) *Robin Hood's Bay, King's Lynn, Southend-on-Sea, Cliftonville,* and *Broadstairs,* (along the south coast, west to east) *Plymouth, Torquay, Highcliffe, Southsea, Peacehaven, Newhaven, St. Leonards,* and *Littlestone-on-Sea,* and, the newest of modern names, the administrative districts and counties introduced in 1974 as the result of the reorganization of local government boundaries, such as the counties of *Avon* and *Tyne and Wear* and the districts of *Castle Point,* Essex, *Rushmoor,* Hampshire, *Dacorum,* Hertfordshire, *Gravesham,* Kent, *Hyndburn,* Lancashire, *Breckland,* Norfolk, *Babergh,* Suffolk, and *Thamesdown,* Wiltshire.

Of all English cities, though, it is London, as might be expected, that has the greatest density of modern place-names. Many of them arose as 'random' names, simply borrowed from some local landmark with the development of a district, or transferred from the personal name of an industrial entrepreneur. Others, such as the new administrative districts, were 'planned' names, carefully chosen for a new industrial or residential development. Others again derive from railway stations built in the nineteenth century, both for suburban 'overground' lines and the London Underground railway. Even on a single-sheet plan of London, one cannot help noticing the obviously modern names of different types: *Shepherds Bush, Olympia, Golders Green, Camden Town* (but not, unexpectedly, Kentish Town, an old name), *King's Cross, Waterloo, Mayfair, Isle of Dogs* (with *Millwall* and *Cubitt Town*), *Crystal Palace, Herne Hill, Tulse Hill, Gipsy Hill, Mill Hill, Dollis Hill, Archway, Maida Vale, Marylebone* . . . The list seems endless.

Of course, such names exist generally throughout the British Isles, and London by no means has an exclusive monopoly of these: Dublin, Belfast, Edinburgh, and Cardiff also have their residential developments, industrial estates and administrative districts with new names. It is simply the size of London, and especially Greater London, that gives it the lion's share of modern place-names.

A special economic development of the twentieth century throughout Great Britain has been the 'New Town' movement. Since 1946 thirty-two new towns have been designated (21 in England, two in Wales, five in Scotland, four in Northern Ireland) to encourage the gradual dispersal of industry and population away from crowded cities to new areas. Many of them arose round an existing town or village, and retained the name. 'New Town' does not therefore automatically mean 'new name'. But some new towns did receive new names, or at least ones modified from the existing town or village. Among them are *Welwyn Garden City, Newton Aycliffe, Peterlee,* and *Telford* in England, *Cwmbran* and *Newtown* in Wales, the latter, paradoxically, also being an 'old' town, *Glenrothes* in Scotland (but not the new-sounding Livingston or Irvine), and *Craigavon* in Northern Ireland. Such well-known English new towns as Milton Keynes, Stevenage, and Washington all have old names, despite the resemblance of these names to those of people. (The last did, however, lend its name to the ancestors of George Washington, who held an estate here.)

As mentioned, especially with reference to names in Ireland, Scotland, and Wales, many places are based on a personal name of some kind, whether a lord, a military leader, an industrialist, or a proprietor. This basing of a place-name on a personal name is nothing new, and indeed many of the oldest names in Britain are so based. In England, the oldest place-names are the Celtic or so-called British ones, dating back to pre-Roman times, and many of them can be found in Cornwall, where they often embody the name of a saint: Lanivet means 'church of Nivet', for example, and Lanhydrock 'church of Hydroc'. (In this sense, the

Cornish *Lan-* corresponds to Welsh *Llan-*.) London itself is a Celtic name possibly based on that of a person, one Londinos. Next chronologically came the Anglo-Saxon or Old English names and here many names ending in *-ing* or *-ingham* are based on a personal name, among them many Sussex names, such as Cocking (named after one Cocca), Oving (Ufa), Worthing (Wurth), and, in England as a whole, such important names as Birmingham (Beorma), Nottingham (Snot), and Buckingham (Bucc). Personal names are similarly found in Scandinavian or Viking names, and these frequently end in *-by*, such as Formby (named after one Forni), Grimsby (Grimr), Corby (Kori), and Granby (Grani). All these names are of pre-Conquest vintage. Finally, the Normans were to introduce many French personal names, with several of them being the names of manor-holders and appearing as the second word in the place-name. Examples, where the second half of the name even looks French today, are Sampford Courtney, Compton Verney, Manningford Bohun, Swaffham Bulbeck, and Carlton Colville.

Although not in a majority, many modern place-names (just over a quarter of those in this Dictionary) are directly derived from personal names, and a great many more indirectly incorporate a personal name.

Where direct derivations are involved, the personal name can appear as a Christian name or forename, as a surname, as a title (such as that of an earl or marquis), or even as the name of a close relative of the person concerned. When used for a place-name, a personal name can be used 'neat' or with the addition of a prefix or suffix. In a few cases it may be shortened in some way. A very common suffix for a modern place-name is 'town', whether joined to the personal name or given as a separate word. Examples are *Agar Town, Angell Town, Archiestown, Bagenalstown, Dufftown, Hilltown, Lennoxtown,* and *Somerstown*. In Scotland this suffix may be replaced by 'toun' or 'burgh' as in *Dennystoun, Gordonstoun, Colinsburgh, Helensburgh,* and *Leverburgh*. In any part of the British Isles one may find the suffix *-ville*, such as *Charlotteville, Jemimaville* (both names after wives, incidentally), *Pentonville, Pittville,* and *Thornville*. In the last name the original surname was Thornton. In Ireland the prefix 'Newtown' is frequently found, as with *Newtownbarry, Newtown Forbes, Newtownhamilton,* and *Newtownstewart*. (In many sources the prefix is detached, and *Newtown Barry* and *Newtown Hamilton* are found, for example.) A more specialized prefix is 'Port', and it is noteworthy that almost all names so prefixed are elsewhere than in England, among them *Port Allen, Portarlington, Port Dundas, Port Ellen* (a wife's name), *Port Montgomery, Portstewart, Port Talbot,* and *Port William*. Otherwise the prefix or suffix can simply indicate the nature of the place, as *Bedford Park, Bettyhill, Blundellsands, Connah's Quay,* and *Drake's Island*. A more extreme example of this is *Via Gellia* to suggest a Roman road, based on the surname Gell. Among 'neat' personal names are *Anglesey* (a title), *Ansdell* (a surname), and *Moira* (a title). Some women's names have already been quoted, and there are more than a few places named after a wife or other relative called Mary, as *Maryland* and *Maryport* (both wives). *Maryhill*, however, does not indicate a settlement on a hill but represents the full name of the proprietress, Mary Hill. *Renton* is a maiden surname.

All these names, and many more, represent a wide range of landowners, founders, planners, builders, sponsors, entrepreneurs, and other noted local figures. As may be expected, some geographical areas provide a greater unity of name, so that in South Wales, for example, can be found a number of place-names based on those of colliery owners or mining pioneers, among them *Markham*, *Phillipstown*, *Tallistown*, and the previously mentioned *Treharris* and *Tretomas*. An interesting personal name borrowing is here as *Trealaw*, the Welsh bardic name (Alaw Goch) of coal-owner David Williams.

In some cases the place-name is based not on an individual personal name but a group name, so that *Charterville* was founded by the Chartists, *Draperstown* was named after the London Drapers' Company, and *Quakers' Yard* arose as a burial place for Quakers. Less formally, *Gipsy Hill* in London was named after the gypsies that inhabited the area. Such names are not, of course, based on actual personal names, but the people who belonged to the various groups were directly connected with the place named after them.

There are place-names named after an individual who was not directly connected with the settlement. *Hallsville*, for example, was named after a railway company director, and *Peterlee* was named after a mining trades union leader who died thirteen years before the new town that bears his name was designated. Such names—*Telford* is another—are really commemorative, and are given as a form of tribute, official or unofficial, to the person concerned. Among other such names are *Halse Town*, *Mount Batten*, *Mount Vernon*, *Pulteneytown*, *Rosherville*, *Smithborough*, and *Wilsontown*.

Truly commemorative or complimentary names are those deriving from royalty, with the place embodying the name of a sovereign or prince, or else the actual royal title 'King', 'Queen', 'Prince', 'Regent' and the like. They range from the modest *Albert Village*, named after Prince Albert, consort of Queen Victoria, to *Victoria* itself, and also include, by name, *Charleville*, *Jamestown*, *Maryborough*, *Philipstown*, *Port Clarence*, and *Port Mary* and, by title, *King's County*, *Kingstown*, *Queen's County*, *Queenstown*, *Princetown*, *Regent's Park*, and 'Royal' names such as the *Royal Military Canal*. There is even a *Virginia* to refer to Queen Elizabeth I, the 'Virgin Queen', although *Virginia Water* has a remoter link with this same monarch.

Place-names that end in 'Regis', such as Lyme Regis and *Bognor Regis*, not all of them modern, form a special category and are considered separately in Appendix I, p. 139.

A final type of name based on that of a person is the place that was not so much deliberately named after (and even by) a particular individual but which gradually came to acquire a family name, usually because the family, or its head, owned a local territory such as a hill, a green, a park, or just land in general. In some cases the owned object is simply a cross or other man-made monument. In others the territory is a whole settlement. In the case of a green, for example, the name itself may well date back to medieval times but then came to denote the settlement built by the green in modern times. Among such examples appear to be *Acocks Green*, *Balls Green*, *Bucks Green*, *Furner's Green*, *Golders Green*, *Jenkins' Green*, and *Palmers Green*. One is obliged to say 'appear' since in many cases early records of the family name have not been found, and doubt still hangs over the precise origin of many such names. It is thus still not absolutely clear who the 'Dollis' of *Dollis Hill* was or the 'Saunders' (who may have been Alexander) of *Saundersfoot*. The names are usually regarded as modern rather than 'ancient', however, and others of the type include *Arnos Grove*, *Barnes Cray*, *Clay Cross*, *Colindale*, *Heronsgate*, *Hunter's Quay*, *Lowthertown*, *Ponders End*, *Potters Bar*, *Shepherds Bush*, and *Shottermill*. All these places *may* denote, respectively, the grove, river (named Cray), cross, dale, gate, quay, settlement, section of a parish ('end'), gate ('bar'), bush, and mill owned or operated, as appropriate, by persons named Arnold, Barne, Clay, Collin, Heron or Herring, Hunter, Lowther, Ponder, Potter, Shepherd or Sheppard, and (possibly) Shotover.

We can now consider those modern place-names that derive from an important building around which a settlement grew up. Such a building, often originally existing in isolation, may have been a castle, manor house, church, inn, farm, or, in more recent times, railway station.

Many of the castles or forts that formed the nucleus of a later town or village were those built in Ireland and Scotland during an actual or potential time of war with English forces. Several Irish castles are in turn named after the family who owned them, such as *Castle Bellingham*, *Castleblayney*, *Castlecaulfeild*, *Castlegregory* (the last from a Christian name, not a surname), and *Castletownshend*. In Scotland castles, and certainly the better known ones, were named by way of compliment to a member of royalty or the aristocracy, so that we find *Fort Augustus*, *Fort George*, and *Fort William* named respectively in honour of William *Augustus*, Duke of Cumberland, King *George* II, and King *William* III. Not all castles are named after the family or individual who owned them, however, and we also thus find place-names such as *Newcastle* and *Southsea*: the former was one of the many 'new castles', the latter a 'south sea castle'.

Castles and forts, as well as being defensive buildings, are also dwelling-places, of course, and the precise point in history at which a stout-walled structure designed to keep out the enemy became an ornate family residence is difficult to determine. Many grand houses of the sixteenth century and later are still named 'Castle' even though no enemy has ever assailed them, or was ever expected to. Even *Castlecaulfeild*, already mentioned, may be regarded as primarily a residence, since it was not a true castle but an Elizabethan-style mansion built in the early seventeenth century. Certainly *Castle Howard*, built in England a few years later, was not designed to keep the enemy at bay but to serve as an imposing seat for the Howard family. It follows that a settlement named after a castle may not necessarily have arisen round a fortress. An Englishman's 'Castle'—and very often that of a Scotsman, Irishman, or Welshman—is very often his home.

Just as in medieval times a village or hamlet arose round a manor house, itself known by the name of its owner, the traditional 'lord of the manor', so in modern times settlements and districts have arisen around a noted dwelling-house. The difference, however, is that modern seats and residences are very often not named after the family who has made their home there, but either descriptively or topographically, to point to their location. A descriptive house name may be direct, as *Rockvilla*, *Seaview*, or *Anerley* (Scottish 'lonely', 'isolated'), or more allusive, as *Bellamour* ('fine love') or *Branksome*, apparently after a fictional place in a work by Walter Scott. Topographical names include *Highcliffe*, *Spring-head*, and *Tollcross*. All these are now names of villages or districts, as those house names that do derive from their owners, such as *Seaforde* (Colonel Forde), *Wentworth* (Mrs Wentworth), and *Blairadam* (William Adam). Many house names, even those of the more modest 'semis' of today, are convoluted in origin, and this applies to such modern derived place-names as *Strawberry Hill*, which is a blend of a field name and the nickname of a house (Chopped Straw Hall). In traditional manner, there are houses with transferred names, even from overseas, as the *Etruria* that gave the present place-name. A modern place-name may thus be the result of a house name that is itself a transferral, and a good example of the complexity of the process can be instanced by the district of Crosby, Merseyside, known as *Seaforth*. This derives from Seaforth House, whose owner named it after his wife who was a member of the Mackenzie clan whose head was Baron Seaforth. The Baron took his own title from Seaforth in Scotland. So we find place-name to title to house to place-name, a full-circle triple transferral. Indeed, the majority of modern place-names are transferred names of one sort or another, a feature that we shall be examining later.

If not castle or house, then it may well have been a church, chapel, or abbey that was the focal building round which a village or town grew up. The modern settlement name may be simply *Churchtown* or more specifically indicate the dedication of a particular church, as *St. George*, *St. Helens*, and *St. Leonards-on-Sea*. Very often the church, chapel, or abbey existed long before the settlement arose, and in more than a few cases may have disappeared altogether or have been replaced by a more modern building. This is true of *St. Leonards*, where the original church was washed away in the early fifteenth century, and of *Abbey Town*, where the original twelfth-century abbey was rebuilt in the late nineteenth century. In *Abbeyleiz* there is no abbey at all. At *St. Budeaux*, however, it is the name that has changed rather than the church (even though the building itself may today bear little resemblance to the original).

In many English villages, the pub is never far from the church, and the inn has for many centuries long been one of the focal points of an English settlement. A considerable number of modern place-names are direct transferrals of the name of the inn where they grew up, so that we find places named *Bay Horse*, *Black Dog*, *Craven Arms*, *Crosskeys*, *Halfway*, *Nelson*, *New Invention*, *Royal Oak*, *Six Bells*, *Triangle*, *Waterloo*, and *Welsh Harp*. The prominence of the inn has often been enhanced by its pictorial sign, and it may well have been the visual impact of the sign, together with its distinctive name, that attracted the attention of builders who raised settlements round *Beeswing*, *Old Swan*, *Tumble*, and *Woolpack* (which may have been 'Woolsack'), as well as the inns already mentioned. An inn, of course, will only be set up where it is likely to attract custom, and such a site may in itself, as a new road or a new bridge, prove an advantageous point for a settlement to arise. After all, people like to live where they can obtain food, drink, and convivial company (an inn), and a means of communication with other places (a new road, bridge, or rail link). In a few place-names, the actual word 'Inn' has been preserved, as in *Tram Inn*. Inn names have provided some of the more colourful modern place-names, with others being *Normandy*, *Nunhead*, *Three Cocks*, and *Swiss Cottage*.

A more sophisticated version of an inn is a hotel, and this establishment has also provided some recent place-names, such as *Cliftonville*. These will be among the later place-names, probably dating from the second half of the nineteenth century. But it is just as difficult to determine when 'inn' became 'hotel' as it is to decide when 'castle' became 'residence', although it is certainly true that many English inns date back to the fifteenth century, if not before.

Somewhat less frequently, a settlement may grow up round a farm, as the Hampshire town of *Eastleigh* did, and possibly the Scottish village of *California*. The name of the *Isle of Dogs* was first recorded in the late sixteenth century as that of a farm, although this may well in turn have taken its name from the 'Isle' (actually land on a bend in the river Thames). Many farms, however, have necessarily remained isolated rural dwellings, surrounded by the fields and lands that justify their existence.

Among the more remarkable modern place-names are those of Welsh villages and hamlets with biblical names, as mentioned above. Such settlements took the name of the Nonconformist chapel that was the focal point of the community, with the chapel itself taking a name from the Bible, in many cases from the Old Testament, that was 'meaningful' in religious and moral terms. Nonconformity in Wales dates back to the seventeenth century, although even by the end of that century there were hardly more Nonconformists than 5 per cent of the population. It was the coming of Methodism in the first half of the eighteenth century that really fired the enthusiasm of the indigenous population, and in particular the 'revivalist' communities who were to form the Calvinistic Methodist church, and it would not be long before chapels came to be dotted liberally in almost all parts of the country. The driving force behind the 'Methodist Revival' in Wales was as much social and political as religious, since it was 'us' against 'them', otherwise the Welsh-speaking peasantry—later, miners and industrial workers—against the English-speaking landowners, the radicals against the Tory gentry, 'Chapel' against 'Church'.

At first, many chapels were not given particular names. Later, and certainly by the early years of the nineteenth century, names came to be given that were significant to the people who worshipped in the individual chapels. The names were largely popular explanations of the biblical names, and such interpretations can be found in a number of contemporary scriptural commentaries and dictionaries, notably in the *Geiriadur Ysgrythyrol* ('Scriptural Dictionary') by Thomas Charles published in Bala in 1805–11. (In the chapel name entries in the present Dictionary, the popular interpretations of the names are largely as given by Charles, translated from the Welsh.)

Many of the names came to be repeated several times in different villages, with *Bethel*, *Carmel*, *Hebron*, and *Salem* being specially popular. The popular meanings are, of course, always favourable, with these particular four, for example, meaning respectively 'house of God', 'God's vineyard', 'fellowship', and 'peace' (*Salem* taken as a variant form of 'Jerusalem'). The single exception is the surprisingly named *Sodom*, but this was almost certainly not a true chapel name in origin but a nickname. Most of the chapel settlements have remained small, but one,

Bethesda, grew into a slate-quarrying town in the latter half of the nineteenth century. On the other hand, the small hamlet of *Bethlehem*, between Llandovery and Llandeilo, in Dyfed, gained fame in the twentieth century for its ability to provide an appropriate postmark for Christmas cards.

Most chapel names originated in the nineteenth century, as also, of course, did places named after railway stations. In a way, the two buildings are similar, since each serves as a kind of 'community centre', a place where people gather for a common purpose. Moreover, a railway station provides people with an efficient way of travelling to other places, and therefore is a useful location near which to make one's home. If you cannot live in a town, you can at least live near a building that will provide you with a means of communication with that town. Hence stations can become centres of population, and, conversely, centres of population can attract a railway. In either case, the station will have to have a name. Where the settlement or district is already established, the station will usually, and logically, take the already existing name, and in the process reinforce it. This happened in London with the coming of the various suburban railway companies and in particular the coming of the Underground. A district named, say, 'Oakwood' becomes much more prominently 'Oakwood' (even with the name publicly displayed for all travellers to see) when a station of the name is built. On local maps and street plans, too, the name is repeated to enhance the importance of the place. Where, however, a station is built outside an existing district or town—for example, at an intermediate point on a newly constructed railway line linking two established towns—it will take either a local minor name, such as a field name, or else perhaps have a name devised specially for it. Travelling today by train from London to Brighton (on British Rail's route 186), one passes through towns and residential districts that have grown up around stations built in rural Surrey and Sussex in the mid-nineteenth century and named after local topographical features, such as *Redhill*, *Three Bridges*, *Haywards Heath*, *Burgess Hill*, and *Hassocks*. By a similar process, although in an urban setting, the name of the London mainline station from which the traveller to Brighton departs, *Victoria*, has spread to the surrounding district, where also are found Victoria Street and Victoria Square, as well as Victoria Underground station.

A railway with its stations is a commercial enterprise, and several places take their modern name from an industrial concern of some kind, such as an ironworks, a colliery, or a brewery. Such a name may be quite basic, simply stating the type of enterprise, as the two places entered in the Dictionary by the name of *Furnace* or the village and town respectively of *Ironville* and *Coalville* (although the latter directly originated in a house name). In other cases the place may be named after the firm, itself embodying a family name, such as *Coryton, Dormanstown, Shortstown* or *Vickerstown*. Again, the place may have assumed what is virtually a trade name, as is the case with *Port Sunlight* and *Vulcan Village*. *Fleur-de-Lis* also appears to be in this category. Collieries, as we have seen, are often named after their owners.

Among other 'building' names can be included *Crystal Palace* and *Olympia*, both famous exhibition centres, and *St. James's* and *Spital*, both originally named after a hospital.

There are several smaller man-made landmarks or vaguer constructed units that can give their name to a settlement. This can be a bridge (*Archway, Bridgend, Bridgeton, Coatbridge, Ironbridge, Ponthir, Pontypool, Whaley Bridge*), a monument (*King's Cross, New Cross, Seven Dials*), a boundary mark (*Four Marks, Wealdstone*), a gate (*Forest Gate, Landport, Parkgate, Pease Pottage*), a row of houses or other buildings (*Forest Row, Southbourne*), as well as such objects as a crossroads (*Cross Town*), a signpost (*Handcross*), a wall (*Millwall*), a military camp (*North Camp*), a well (*Tobermory*), or an artificial lake (*Virginia Water*).

A final object, part 'man-made', part natural, that can give its name to a modern settlement is that of a field. Many fields came to be enclosed only as late as the eighteenth or even nineteenth century, and from this time came to be marked on the map as a toponymical unit. There were much earlier fields, of course, but even they had their names recorded rarely before the sixteenth century. This means that for purposes of this Dictionary many field names themselves can be regarded as modern names, with the settlements named after them later still. *Hassocks*, just mentioned, originated in a field name, as also did *Whyteleafe*, first recorded (in a more conventional spelling) only as late as 1839. On the whole, though, field names are often regarded as too 'minor' to be transferred to a town or district, so are thinly represented in the present collection. However, one sizeable industrial town that owes its origins to a field name is *Maesteg*, Wales.

Passing now from man-made objects to natural features, we come to names derived from one of the most important and vital elements of the countryside—the river. It is hardly surprising that settlements should grow up by a river, at a point where it can be crossed by bridge or ford, at a point where it can be used for communication, as a port of some kind, or at a point where it can be exploited in some other way, as for provision of a water supply, or for irrigation or drainage. In peacetime, rivers play a key role in the economy of a country: in time of war they can be used as a natural defence against a real or potential enemy. At the mouth of a river, many famous and important ports, cities, and resorts have arisen, and one has merely to trace the coastal outline of Britain on the map to find many names incorporating the name of the river and the word 'port' or 'mouth'. Inland, a large number of places have a similarly composed name, although the second element here will be 'ford', 'bridge', '-ton', and the like. Most such names are longstanding ones, but among modern river-based names are *Ammanford, Avonmouth, Banbridge, Clydebank, Derwentside, Inverclyde, Spenborough, Strathkelvin, Tameside,* and *Thamesmead*. In some cases, 'neat' river names have been used for the new counties and administrative districts established in England in 1974, among them being *Avon, Brent, Hart, Kennet, Rother, Swale,* and *Wyre*. There is even a district named *Three Rivers*. One of the most common river names in Britain is 'Avon', and this is used in more than a few modern names, including *Avonmouth, Avonwick, Northavon,* and *Wychavon*, as well as the name of the county of *Avon* itself. Among modern names of the 'Town-on-River' type are *Stourport-on-Severn, Stratford-on-Slaney,* and *Thornaby-on-Tees*. The first of these three rather unusually contains the name of two rivers, the Stour and the Severn.

Several river names are modern in their own right. These are the ones technically known as 'back formations', and we shall be considering them in due course.

A host of other natural features have lent their names to places in modern times, and they include hills (*Box Hill, Forest Hill, Hindhead, Hugh Town, Mill Hill, Newtownards*), woods (*Colliers Wood, Northwood, Norwood, Wood Green, Wormwood Scrubs*), moors and heaths (*Boxmoor, Forest Heath, Haywards Heath, Rushmoor, Thornton Heath*), headlands (*Peterhead, Thorpeness, Whitehead*), and, off the coast, sandbanks (*Cowes, Hoylake*), and prominent rocks (*Greatstone-on-Sea, Littlestone-on-Sea*). Among other names of this type are *Fylde* (a plain), *Langbaurgh* (a ridge), *Greenacres* (a common), *Saltdean* (a cliff-gap), and *Welshpool* (a lake). Of all natural features serving as prominent local landmarks, however, it is the tree that has given its name the most extensively to modern places, whether as a single tree or a group. The name may be purely descriptive, as *Broad Oak, Crowthorne, Fair Oak, Knotty Ash, Mountain Ash*, or refer to a specific incident or custom associated with a particular tree, as *Burnt Oak, Gospel Oak, Honor Oak*. Names derived from groups or clumps of trees include *Five Ashes, Four Elms, Nine Elms, Three Oaks*. (Sevenoaks in Kent, although in this category, is an old name dating back to at least 1200.) It is perhaps not surprising that of these twelve tree names, half refer to the oak, one of the sturdiest, longest-lived, and most distinctive of English trees.

We mentioned earlier that many modern names are secondary ones, derived from already existing names, and we saw that this was certainly true when applied to place-names transferred from personal names. Nowhere is this more evident than in the very many modern names transferred from other places, so that many present-day towns, villages, and other settlements and districts have names that are direct transferrals from existing place-names, often with a straightforward distinguishing prefix or suffix added, but also 'neat' in the original form. Thus *Angmering-on-Sea* is named after the nearby village of Angmering, *Ash Vale* is named after Ash, *Barkingside* after Barking, *Bathford* after Bath, *Devonport* after the county of Devon in which it is located, *East Guldeford* after Guildford, *Ellesmere Port* after Ellesmere, *Gowerton* after the Gower Peninsula, *Pembroke Dock* after Pembroke, *Waltham Forest* after Waltham-stow and Epping Forest (a hybrid name), and *Welwyn Garden City* after Welwyn. Even more obviously, such transferrals can be seen in many names prefixed 'New', and named after a nearby place that is the 'Old' name (and on occasions even acquires this prefix with the rise of the 'New' settlement). Examples are legion, but we may cite *New Deer, New Elgin, New Keith, New Pitsligo,* and *New Tredegar.* Not all 'New' names are local transferrals, however, and many such places assume the name of a more or less distant place—even one abroad—that they aim to resemble in some way. Examples are *New Birmingham,* Ireland, after Birmingham, England, *New Brighton,* Clwyd, Hampshire, and Merseyside, after Brighton, East Sussex, *New Geneva,* Ireland, after Geneva, Switzerland, *New Holland,* formerly north Lincolnshire, after Holland, south Lincoln-shire, and *New York,* Lincolnshire, possibly after York, Yorkshire. Among 'neat' borrowings of this type are *Acton,* Ireland, after Iron Acton, England, *Dresden,* England, after Dresden, Germany, and *Etruria,* England, after Etruria, Italy. The first of these last three names was transferred for reasons of family ties; the other two names were imitative, for the particular reputations of the overseas places (in this case, their fine pottery). Further imported names of this type are *Dunkirk, Flushing, Fulneck,* and *Patna,* with the connection varying from a personal tie (Patna) to a 'home-from-home' link for emigrants (Flushing, Fulneck). One of the more celebrated transfers within England, but from north to south, was that of *Richmond,* Greater London (formerly Surrey), which name was borrowed by Henry VII from Richmond, North Yorkshire. In a few cases a borrowed name did not replace an earlier one, as here (Richmond was formerly Sheen), but was simply added to it. This happened with *Londonderry,* where the name of the English capital was added to the old Irish name of *Derry.* In a sense, a similar borrowing took place with all the resorts that added 'Spa' to their names, since this originated in the Belgian town of Spa, whose mineral springs became famous in the sixteenth century although known to exist long before this. However, the name became a common noun, so lost its original 'name' status, and a town such as Cheltenham Spa has a suffix that really means 'having mineral springs such as Spa has'.

It may be argued that such borrowings do not constitute 'new' names since the names themselves already exist. But even an unchanged borrowing such as *Dresden* is an entirely new use of the name, and the place is therefore, as the English district of Longton in Staffordshire, a place with a modern name. The name is old, but the usage is new.

A special though much more limited class of transferred place-names is that of commemorative battle names. These are the names such as *Balaclava, Portobello,* and (above all) *Waterloo,* given to mark a victory in war. Many of the places called *Waterloo*—Mason (1977) lists eleven in England, Scotland, and Wales alone, as well as Waterloo Cross, Waterloo Port and *Waterlooville*—originated as the name of an inn or house. Even so, the name spread sufficiently for it to apply to a settlement or inhabited area of some kind. (Probably the best-known *Waterloo,* not in fact listed by Mason, is the London one.) At least such names can be dated with confidence: *Waterloo* must have been shortly after the victory of 1815, *Balaclava* after that of 1854, *Portobello* after an earlier victory in 1739. Similar names are those of *Blenheim Park* (victory of 1704), *Louisburgh,* Ireland (1758), *Maida Vale* (1806), and *Sebastopol* (1854, the same year as *Balaclava* in the Crimean War). Battle names more recent than the nineteenth century are rare, although *Enham Alamein,* formerly Knight's Enham, changed its name after World War II to commemorate the victory of El Alamein in 1942.

We now come to a particularly interesting type of river name, the so-called 'back formation'. These are rivers having a name that is derived from a town or village standing on it or near it, such as the *Chelt,* on which Cheltenham stands, or the *Ems* that flows through Emsworth. Normally, of course, one expects a town or village to be named after the river, not the other way about, and usually this is so. We thus find Doncaster on the Don, Weybridge on the Wey, and Wilton, Wiltshire, on the Wylye (with the county name deriving from this town). For this reason it may be supposed that Cambridge is so named as it is on the *Cam,* Chelmsford because it is on the *Chelmer,* and Yarmouth because it is on the *Yar* (or *Yare*). But things are not so simple, and it is precisely because of this mistake that an older name of a number of rivers was changed to 'derive' from that of the town. Chelmsford, for example, looks like meaning 'place at a ford over a river called the Chelm (or something similar)'. But in fact the name Chelmsford means 'ford of Ceolmaer', the latter being an Anglo-Saxon personal name. This can be established from old forms of the name. The river that is now the *Chelmer* must some time before the sixteenth century have had another name. (In many cases we know what the former name was: for the *Arun* of Arundel, for example, it was the Tarrant, and for the *Eden* of Edenbridge it was something like the 'Hedgecourt River'.) Such errors, where the first half of a name was misunderstood as that of the river on which the place stood, are mostly first recorded in the sixteenth century, and are frequently the 'scholarly' attempts of antiquarians and mapmakers to explain a name or propose a new etymology for a place. It is likely, of course, that such formations were in existence some time before they were recorded, so in this sense they may not be properly 'modern' (or post-1500) in our definition of the term. However, most back formations do seem to have occurred, and been first recorded, well within the modern period. The story behind the *Cam* of Cambridge, mentioned above, is actually rather more complicated than it seems, since the river name is really a modification of its earlier name of 'Granta', from the original name of Cambridge, which was something like 'Grantachester' (in other words, similar to the village near Cambridge that today is called Grantchester, also on the Cam—which here is called the Granta!).

In fact places with names ending in '-ford' have a river-name as the first element much less frequently than might be supposed, so that although Crayford is on the Cray and Dartford on the Darent, many other such names have a river-name that is a back formation. Examples are the river *Alre* of Alresford, the *Box* of Boxford, the *Crane* of Cranford, the *Dorn* of Dornford, the *Ore* of Orford, the *Roach* of Rochford, the *Rom* of Romford, the *Stort* of Bishop's Stortford, and the *Thet* of Thetford. Similar back formations are the *Batherm* of Bampton, the *Brain* of Braintree, the *Chess* of Chesham, the *Deben* of Debenham, the *Kym* of Kimbolton, the *Mole* of Molesey (and possibly the *Mole* of Molton), the *Nar* of Narborough, the *Pang* of Pangbourne, the *Penk* of Penkridge, the *Ter* of Terling, and the *Wandle* of Wandsworth. In a few cases the entire name of the place has been taken over by the river, as with the *Evenlode* of the Gloucestershire village so named, the *Stiffkey* of the Norfolk village, and the *Thurne* of another village in Norfolk. That *Plymouth* is a modern name can be attested by the fact that it is named after the river *Plym*, a back formation from Plympton. This, however, is one of the earlier back formations, recorded in the thirteenth century. Finally, it may well be that the name of the river *Isis* is a special type of back formation—not from some place on the river but from an early name of the river itself, this being the Thames.

When considering transferred place-names above, we mentioned that many places acquire a distinguishing prefix or suffix to differentiate the new place from the old. *Angmering-on-Sea* is thus the 'new' Angmering (on the sea coast) as distinct from the 'old' Angmering inland. Such added elements designed to distinguish have long been a feature of place-names, especially when there are several places with the same name. Of the scores of places named Newton, for example, there are actually more bearing a suffix than having the 'neat' name alone, these ranging from Newton Abbot to Newton Wood (at least, in Mason, 1977), via such variations as High Newton-by-the-Sea (and Low Newton-by-the-Sea), Newton-le-Willows, Newton of Falkland, and Newton-on-Rawcliffe. Among modern place-names so distinguished are *Georgeham* (as distinct from other places called Ham), *Kirk Ella* (which is not the same place as West Ella), *Plaistow New Town* (not the same as Plaistow), *Port Glasgow* (not Glasgow itself), *Queen's Nympton* (not to be confused with King's Nympton), *Saffron Walden* (not Little Walden), *Thornton-le-Fen* (not any other Thornton), and *Westmeath* (not Meath itself). Of course, many place-names beginning 'New' will have acquired this prefix not simply to describe (and even advertise) a new settlement, but also to differentiate it. *New Aberdour* is not the same as 'Old' Aberdour, *New Bradwell* is not the same as Bradwell, *New Elgin* is different from 'Old' Elgin, and so on. In some cases, the differentiation is a gradual process, even a complex one, as with *Shillingstone*, which took the prefix 'Shilling' when originally named 'Okeford' to distinguish itself from Child Okeford and Okeford Fitzpaine, at the same time substituting '-tone' for 'Okeford'.

As can be seen from these few examples, the distinguishing added element can be one of a variety of types, referring to a church (*Georgeham*, *Kirk Ella*), a geographical location (*Thornton-le-Fen*, *Westmeath*), a local product (*Saffron Walden*), a commercial feature (*Port Glasgow*), a commemoration or incident (*Queen's Nympton*), and a relative dating (*Plaistow New Town* and many places starting 'New').

All such names are modern names, evolving from older names. Similar modern names, although much less numerous, are those that are translations in some way of an older name. In the British Isles this usually implies an English translation of a Celtic or Gaelic name (Irish, Welsh, or Scottish) or the reverse, although a translation from one Celtic language into another is theoretically possible. Two Welsh villages named *Newchurch* have names translated from their Welsh equivalents, and *Middletown*, in Wales, is a translation of Welsh *Treberfedd*. The Scottish village of *Broadford*, on the Isle of Skye, is a name translated from the Gaelic, and in Ireland the village of *Blessington* was a (mistaken, as it happens) translation of the Irish original. Sometimes the 'translation' is the result of a coincidental resemblance of a word in one language to that in another, so that Welsh *Pwll y Tarw* should have become 'Bull Pool' (from *pwll*, 'pool' and *tarw*, 'bull'), but it was the word *pwll* that was taken to mean 'bull' and the place ended up as *Bull Bay*.

An extension of the translation is the 'adaptation', when a name in one language is assimilated to a version in another language, usually English, in which it is felt to be more meaningful. There are two striking examples of this. The first is the Irish name *Páirc an Fhionnuisce*, 'park of clear water' ('Clearwater Park', as it were), which became the famous *Phoenix Park* in Dublin. This anglicized version of the Irish is even commemorated by a column in the park having a phoenix at the top. The other example is the Irish village and port of *Groomsport*. This is not named after a groom or grooms, or a man named Groom, but is, again, an anglicized version of the original name, *Port an ghiolla ghruama*, 'port of the gloomy individual', or 'harbour of the gloomy servant'. In similar fashion the Welsh name of *Abermawddach*, 'mouth of the Mawddach' was corrupted—deliberately, it seems—into the English simplified version of *Barmouth* (with the 'mouth', incidentally, not translated from the 'Aber-' of the original name but modified from the river name Mawddach). A more unusual adaptation is the name of *The Trossachs*. These Scottish mountains appear to have acquired their name as a Gaelic version of the Welsh *Trawsfynydd*, 'cross hills'. Another Scottish name, *Hopeman*, seems to have been adapted from a French name *Haudmont*, with the second syllable, pronounced 'mon', understood as 'man', as one might expect in Scotland.

Many modern names fall into a rather more nebulous category. These are the names that for one reason or another have changed, either as the result of a deliberate renaming or by a natural, gradual process.

Among the deliberate renamings a special category is the 'undesirable' name. A name that has undesirable or unfortunate associations is changed or improved to one that is more acceptable or less offensive. Thus 'Little Hell' was renamed *Belmont*, 'Fiendsfell' was renamed *Cross Fell* (a favourable religious name substituted for an evil one), 'Nackershole' became *Crownhill*, 'Shittleworth' became *Littleworth*, 'Tyburn' (with its associations of the gallows) became *Marylebone*, 'Middle Shitlington' became *Middlestown*, 'Nether Shitlington' became *Netherton*, and 'Over Shitlington' became *Overton*. In almost all these cases the original name did not have the undesirable sense it seemed to have. The three 'Shitlingtons', for example, had a name that simply meant 'Scyttel's farm', this being a personal name, and 'Shittleworth' might just as well have been 'Shuttleworth' (and so quite acceptable), since the name means simply 'shut enclosure'. But the man in the street (or down on the farm) was not to know this, and the unpleasant sounding name came to be changed. Similarly, 'Little Hell' was very probably only a form of 'Little Hill', and so perfectly innocuous.

Such renamings were deliberate, but subconsciously done, and it is impossible to say when the 'new and improved' name finally took over from the undesirable one.

Deliberate and formal renamings were sometimes made, in more recent times, by the Post Office, on the grounds that the original name was misleading in some way. Thus 'Macherie' was changed to *Cairnryan*,

'Cambridge Town' was changed to the less misleading *Camberley*, 'South End, Frimley' was changed for similar reasons to *Frimley Green* ('South End' could be anywhere, including Southend), and 'Longgrove', an English village near the Welsh border, had its name 'welshified' to *Llangrove*, thus incidentally changing its meaning from 'long grove' to 'church grove'.

Other changes were more subtle, with many still not fully explained. At some stage, for example, 'Chalcot' became *Chalk Farm*, although there does not appear to have been a farm of this name in this present district of London, and 'Hanging Stoke' became *Limpley Stoke*, with the first part of the name still not satisfactorily explained. On the other hand, some names are known to have changed or altered as the result of a copying error. The Cornish river 'Cohor' is today the *Cobor* because some writer mistook the *h* for a *b*, and what today should be 'Sypenham', or something similar, became *Sydenham* when the *p* of the original name was mis-copied as a *d*.

Among other changes are such gradual ones as 'Kirkby' to *Kendal*, when, as we have seen before, a distinguishing element was added, then subsequently dropped. 'Kirkby' became 'Kirkby Kendal' (to be distinguished from other places called 'Kirkby'), then finally *Kendal*. 'Thele' became first 'Stanstead Thele' then *Stanstead St. Margarets*.

An apparent change from a favourable name to an unfavourable one, unusually, can be seen in *Sodom*, the Welsh village that may originally have been 'Salem'.

A large number of modern place-names are obviously descriptive, unlike many old names, whose original meaning has frequently been obscured over the years. Thus there can be little doubt about the nature of such places as *Bridgend*, *East End*, *Fairlands*, *Green Island*, *Hightown*, *Littleton*, *Longtown*, *Millport*, *Newborough*, *Newhaven*, *Newmarket*, *Newquay*, *New River*, *Newtown*, *Northchapel*, *Park Village*, *Pilgrims' Way*, *Riverstown*, *Sunk Island*, *Three Rivers*, *Union Canal*, *West End*, and *Whale Island* (unless it is supposed that the last is so named for its connection with a real whale, instead of simply having the contours of one). Nor need one be surprised to find a beautiful island in *Belle Isle*, a fine view from *Belle Vue*, wide steps in the cliff at *Broadstairs*, a stream entering a harbour at *Burnhaven*, a spot to recover one's breath after a hill-climb at *Rest and Be Thankful*, or a sandy harbour at *Sandhaven*. It is to be expected that *Eastville* should be east of *Westville*, that the *Hog's Back* should be a long ridge like the back of a pig, and that *Summertown* could well turn out to be a pleasant place in summer. Any name beginning 'Port' clearly indicates a present or former port (although not necessarily on the coast), and it would be surprising to find that no coal has ever been mined in or near *Coalville*. It may require local knowledge, however, to appreciate that eel pies were eaten on *Eel Pie Island*, and that *Park Royal* was an area of land (not actually a park) selected for an annual show by the *Royal* Agricultural Society. Even so, these are also descriptive names. Since modern names, by definition, are mostly expressed in Modern English, with recognizable words and names, there is less chance that the name will have become corrupted or assimilated to some other form. Even so, there are snares, since there does not appear to have been a stone harbour that gave *Stonehaven* its name, and the river *Swift* is not fast-flowing but slow. And as mentioned at the beginning of this Introduction, it should certainly not be assumed that any name beginning 'New' is automatically a modern one.

A special feature of the new names chosen for the non-metropolitan administrative districts in England when many local government boundaries were changed in 1974 is that in many cases old names were introduced. Often these were 'Domesday Book' names dating back to 1086, and originally used of an old district such as a hundred or a wapentake that approximated in area to the new district. We thus find the re-emergence of such ancient names as *Babergh, Broxtowe, Carrick, Craven, Dacorum, Elmbridge, Gedling, Gravesham, Kerrier, Rushcliffe, St. Edmondsbury, Shepway, Spelthorne,* and *Uttlesford*. It is significant that the use of such names was recommended by the report of the Local Government Boundary Commission for England in 1973. In this the guidelines for selecting a new name were stated in a letter to the Commission from the Secretary of State for the Environment, and were as follows:

'Bearing in mind that the objective is to select a name for a local government unit and that existing place names, whether or not adopted for local government purposes, will continue to apply to towns and localities within the district, the Commission should have regard to the following considerations when reviewing suggestions for the naming of the non-metropolitan districts:

(*a*) local wishes should be followed as far as possible and there should be a strong presumption in favour of a name generally acceptable within the area;

(*b*) the name should be relevant to the geographical, historical or traditional background of the district concerned;

(*c*) the names should be simple and straightforward; hybrid, concocted or double-barrelled names are best avoided;

(*d*) districts in the same county should not have names so similar as to give rise to confusion between them; and

(*e*) the implications should be considered if the name suggested for the district is already in use at parish level.' (*Local Government Boundary Commission for England, Report No. 2,* 1973).

It is clear that many local authorities followed the 'geographical, historical or traditional' recommendation in section (*b*), therefore, although some 'hybrid' names did emerge, among them *Castle Point* in Essex (from Hadleigh *Castle* and Canvey *Point*) and *Wychavon* in Hereford and Worcester (from the old name of Droit*wich* and the river *Avon*).

In view of increasing 'nationalist' sentiment in the twentieth century, it was also no surprise that four of the new counties formed in Wales that same year (1974) should assume the names of ancient kingdoms, these being *Dyfed*, *Gwent*, *Gwynedd*, and *Powys*. (Glamorgan was not renamed 'Morgannwg', after the eighth-century Welsh kingdom, but was redistributed as West Glamorgan, Mid Glamorgan, and South Glamorgan. There is little doubt, however, that many Welshmen bitterly regretted the disappearance of the former county names, even in their anglicized form: with the stroke of a pen the names of Denbighshire, Caernarvonshire, Flintshire, Merionethshire, Cardiganshire, Radnorshire, Carmarthenshire, Pembrokeshire, Brecknockshire, and Montgomeryshire were wiped off the map, although a few of these remain as administrative district names.)

In Ireland, many old Irish place-names were readopted from *c*.1920 in places that, sometimes even for centuries, had borne an English name. Classic examples are *King's County* and *Queen's County*, *Kingstown* and *Queenstown*, which in 1920 reverted to the names they had not borne for 364 years, respectively Offaly and Laois, Dun Laoghaire and Cobh. Similarly, *Maryborough* and *Phillipstown* took the old names of Port Laoise and Daingean, after exactly the same period under these English names. Other reversions occurred elsewhere, such as *Terenure*, now a suburb of Dublin, which for a time was known as *Roundtown*.

A few apparently ancient names are in fact antiquarian inventions, often made as late as the sixteenth century. In this category are rivers such as the *Adur*, *Anton*, *Avoca*, and *Gwash*, Roman roads such as *Akeman Street* and the *Via Devana*, old forts such as the Iron Age fort of *Cissbury Ring* and the Roman forts of *Melandra Castle* and *Templeborough*, and even well-known towns such as *Morecambe*. Some of these were doubtless genuine attempts to give a place its rightful original name, but others seem to be more fanciful. The *Adur* derived its name as the result of an incorrect identification of a river mouth, and *Morecambe* (as applied originally to the bay, not the resort) was an attempt to locate a place called *Morikámbē* on a map drawn by Ptolemy in the second century. *Melandra Castle* and *Templeborough* (at first *Templebarrow*) appear to be names that are either arbitrary or vaguely descriptive. *Akeman Street* is a genuine old name for the Roman road that leads to Bath, since this town was once known as *Acemannes-ceaster*. The name is spurious, however, for the Roman road so called in East Anglia. But possibly the most remarkable name is that of the *Pennines*, which looks so genuinely British (or Celtic). The name was invented only in the eighteenth century by the literary forger Charles Bertram. Before his time, there was no single general name for the range of hills.

Finally, in considering the origins of modern place-names, mention should be made of two names of literary origin, one in Ireland and one in England. The former is the village of *Auburn*, whose name derives from a line in a poem by Oliver Goldsmith. The other, more unusually in view of its orthography, is that of the title of a novel—Charles Kingsley's *Westward Ho!* The little Devon resort must have attracted more than a few visitors by its curious name alone. Almost in the same literary category are the *Gog Magog Hills* near Cambridge, named after a mythical giant, and *Robin Hood's Bay* in North Yorkshire, named after the legendary outlaw. It is possible, too, that *Rob Roy Town*, a former district of London, may have a name that refers, even indirectly, to Robin Hood's Scottish equivalent, the (historical) outlaw who features in Walter Scott's novel.

Apart from such obviously modern place-name elements as 'town' (*Abbey Town, Agar Town*) and 'village' (*Abbey Village, Albert Village*, and the like), one peculiarly modern suffix is '-ville'. In the thousand-plus names entered in the Dictionary, this suffix occurs a total of 25 times, four of these (*Eastville, Frithville, Langriville*, and *Westville*) being located within a few miles of one another in Lincolnshire. In their formation, these Lincolnshire '-ville' names are exceptional, since most names with this suffix have a personal name as their main element, as *Charleville, Charlotteville, Hallsville, Jemimaville, Lowtherville, O'Connorville, Pentonville, Pittville, Ripleyville, Rosherville*, and *Thornville*, the last name deriving from Thornton. Of the remaining '-ville' names in the selection, there is an equal division between names that have a place-name element (*Bournville, Cliftonville, Langriville, Waterlooville*, respectively from the Bourn or Bournbrook, the Clifton Hotel, Langrick, and Waterloo) and those that begin with a standard word (*Coalville, Frithville*, 'frith' being 'wood', 'scrub', *Ironville*, and *Woodville*). *Charterville* is a 'group' name referring to the Chartists.

How did the '-ville' suffix come to acquire such popularity? It has special associations with the nineteenth century, and indeed all but three of the above 23 names originated then. The earliest name in the sampling is that of *Charleville* (moreover, the only Irish place-name included here). This dates from 1659. *Thornville* is the next oldest, dating from 1771, and this is followed by *Pentonville*, apparently so known from *c.*1790. The rest, as mentioned, are nineteenth-century names, with the most recent being *Charlotteville*, which dates from no earlier than 1892. As for its origin, we may have to look to either America or France. America has a large number of '-ville' names (Charlottesville, Fayetteville, Gainesville, Huntsville, Janesville, Steubensville, and Zanesville among them), and it could be that such names had something of an indirect influence on many of the later British names (although hardly the Irish name, which pre-dates all of them). The influence rather seems to be in the many French names ending in the suffix, whose own 'foreignness' was thought to give the names something of an exotic air. It is significant, too, that some of the names originated as a house name (*Cliftonville, Coalville, Thornville*), with 'ville' here obviously intended to suggest 'villa'. Furthermore, many of the French places ending in '-ville' best known to Englishmen were, as they still are, seaside resorts, and this has the right association for such English resorts as *Cliftonville* (which see, in this connection), *Lowtherville* (part of Ventnor, Isle of Wight), *Pittville* (a district of Cheltenham Spa) and *Rosherville* (originally a pleasure garden near Gravesend).

There are other names with the suffix not included in the Dictionary, of course, but one or two names ending in '-ville' are genuinely old names. Among them is Wyville, Lincolnshire, which despite the other Lincolnshire '-ville' names dates back to the 'Domesday Book' of 1086, where it was recorded as *Huuelle*, this apparently meaning 'holy place by a stream' (the '-ville' in the name corresponds to modern English 'well').

Apart from names prefixed with 'New' or 'Port', which range throughout the whole modern place-name period, from 1500 to the present day, '-ville' is the most specific and suggestive, as distinct from directly descriptive, of regularly occurring elements. (For the seaside suffix '-on-Sea' see Appendix II, p. 141.)

Topographical Sources

Where does one find modern place-names recorded in their earliest forms, and where are their first appearances to be tracked down?

For the original forms of the old names, we must go back to the early texts, such as Bede's *Historia Ecclesiastica Gentis Anglorum* ('Ecclesiastical history of the English people'), completed in 731, *The Anglo-Saxon Chronicle*, first compiled in the ninth century, the 'Domesday Book' (*par excellence*) of 1086, and the various historical documents known as Pipe Rolls (from their pipelike shape), Feet of Fines (the bottom parts of indentures preserved in records), the Book of Fees (recording property held by tenants), and the like, as well as more specialized local records.

For modern names we need similar authentic and reliable records. There are many to choose from, of course, since with the invention of printing and general increase in scholarship many accounts of Britain and the British Isles came to be written. Of the hundreds of topographical sources available, there are five that have traditionally come to be regarded as the most valuable for place-names since 1500. In chronological order (of writing, but not necessarily of publishing), they are as follows:

1. *The Itinerary of John Leland in or about the years 1535–43*. This rambling work by John Leland (?1506–52), the first of the modern English antiquarians, was the result of his tour throughout England, made with the aim of producing a great work on the 'History and Antiquities of this Nation'. It was first published at Oxford in 1710, with a good modern edition, edited by Lucy Toulmin Smith, published in London in 1906–7 and reprinted in 1964. The *Itinerary* covers many place-names in England and Wales, but was largely based on the writings of earlier antiquarians.

2. William Harrison's *Description of England*, included in Holinshed's *Chronicles* of 1557. William Harrison (1534–93) was a social historian, and his *Description* amounts to a detailed survey of life in Elizabethan England.

3. William Camden's *Britannia*. This great and important work, subtitled *a chorographical description of the flourishing Kingdoms of England, Scotland, and Ireland from the earliest antiquity*, was published in Latin in 1586 with a sixth and enlarged edition appearing in 1607. This was translated into English by Philemon Holland, a classical scholar, and published in 1610. Meanwhile Camden had himself published in English, in 1605, his *Remains Concerning Britain*, a book of collections from his *Britannia*. This latter work is the first comprehensive topographical survey of Britain, and William Camden (1551–1623) was the greatest antiquarian and historian of his time, 'Queen Elizabeth's first historian', as Hugh Trevor-Roper called him in his biography of him (1971). The *Remains* has been republished in a variety of editions with the most recent being that of 1974 by EP Publishing. There is little on place-names in *Remains*, however, and for these we need to go back to the original work. William Camden's own name deservedly appears as a place-name in the present Dictionary (see *Camden Town*).

4. Michael Drayton's *Polyolbion*. This unusual work, whose Greek title means 'much blessed', is a set of thirty 'Songs', each 300 to 500 lines long, in which the author aims to record the beauties and glories of Elizabethan England, with its fine and varied countryside, ruined abbeys and spoiled forests, histories and legends, and its wealth of saints and hermits, birds, fishes, and plants. The first and main part appeared in 1612, although Drayton produced a second part ten years later. Michael Drayton (1563–1632) was primarily a poet, although this, his most ambitious work, in the end amounts to simply a vast catalogue in verse. He starts his itinerary in south-west England, travelling up to Chester, then down through the Midlands to London, up through East

Anglia to Lincoln, and then on through Lancashire and Yorkshire to Northumberland and Westmorland. Throughout the work there are several hundred place-names, especially those of rivers and streams, some apparently invented by Drayton himself (as the river *Adur*). The *Polyolbion* has been published several times since the original version, with a scholarly edition produced, as part of Drayton's collected works, in 1962.

5. Daniel Defoe's *Tour through the Whole Island of Great Britain*. This work by the famous author of *Robinson Crusoe* is an entertaining guidebook, appearing first in three volumes in 1724–7. Defoe had travelled extensively in the course of his duties as a pamphleteer and intelligence agent, paying several visits to Scotland, and these travels formed the basis of the informative and observant account of his journeyings. The *Tour* has been published several times, but in some of the later editions, such as the Penguin one of 1971, the text has been abridged and the place-name spellings modernized.

There are many other early topographical works of a general or local nature, of course, ranging from local surveys and histories to general accounts of roads and rivers, and leading to the many road books, guidebooks, gazetteers, directories, and the like of the present day. Readers anxious to sample the vast choice of works available could do no better than study the titles of nearly 14,000 books listed in John Anderson's *The Book of British Topography* (see the Bibliography). This work, subtitled *A Classified Catalogue of the Topographical Works in the Library of the British Museum relating to Great Britain and Ireland*, was first published in 1881 and contains many valuable place-name sources, a number of which were used in the compilation of material for this present Dictionary. (The small number of titles featuring in various entries is merely a fraction of the books actually consulted.)

For a useful bibliographical guide to books on place-names in Ireland, readers should consult, if possible, the publication *Books Relating to Ireland: History and Topography*. This was published in 1960 in Dublin as Catalogue 14 by Hodges Figgis & Co., and, although intended as a stock list of new and second-hand books held by the company, contains the titles of over 1300 books on Ireland, as well as 65 atlases and maps, many of which will be of great interest and use to the place-name researcher in that country.

Apart from such works as the five mentioned above, there are also important maps that record the early forms of modern place-names. Here the two great individual map-makers are Christopher Saxton (*fl.* 1570–96) and John Speed (?1552–1629). Saxton was commissioned in c.1574 to survey and draw maps of every county in England and Wales. The maps were completed in 1579, in which year they were published.

This was the first survey of English counties, and all subsequent maps, even those of Speed, were based on them. Speed not only made various maps of English counties but was also encouraged by Camden and others to write his *History of Great Britain*. Both this and an atlas of maps—the latter being far more valuable to the place-name student than the book—appeared in 1611. An expanded edition of the book, entitled *The Theatre of the Empire of Great Britain, presenting an exact geography of the Kingdom of England, Scotland, Ireland and the Isles adjoining*, appeared in 1627. Similar, more specialized works, appeared separately for Scotland, Wales, and Ireland.

In more recent times, an invaluable source of modern names exists in the one-inch (and also six-inch) maps published by the Ordnance Survey. The Ordnance Survey was founded in 1791 and produced its first 'inch-to-a-mile' map to satisfy military needs during the Napoleonic Wars. When the Wars ended in 1815, however, its maps came to be used for more general (and peaceful) purposes, and in 1840 it completed the production of one-inch maps for the whole of England except the six northern counties of Yorkshire, Lancashire, Durham, Westmorland, Cumberland, and Northumberland. At the same time, Ireland was surveyed at six inches to the mile, and this scale was used in 1840 for maps of the six northern counties and Scotland. By 1896 the whole of the cultivated area of England had been mapped on a scale of 25 inches to a mile (1:2500). These nineteenth-century large-scale maps are a unique source, through their various revisions and up-datings, of the gradual appearance and increasing importance of the names of industrial settlements and residential districts. A composite reprint of the first one-inch Ordnance Survey maps of England and Wales was published by David & Charles in 1971. Although at times the quality of reproduction makes place-names difficult to decipher, especially in heavily hachured mountainous sections, the reprints (a total of 97 sheets) are an important source of modern place-names, and graphically illustrate the transformations that have occurred over the past century in industrial and coastal areas.

The best and most informative sources for modern place-names, of course, are those books that give their origins. Many of these are listed in the Bibliography, where it will be seen that hardly a county of England, Wales, and Scotland (we are speaking here of the old, pre-1974 counties) is not represented by a place-name source-book. It goes without saying that the specialized publications, by counties, of the English Place-Name Society are of extreme importance here, since they give the origins of virtually all major and minor names in a specified area, including the street names of towns. Even so, not all counties of England have yet been covered (in 1981 the volumes for Kent, Leicestershire and Rutland,

Lincolnshire, the City of London, Shropshire and Staffordshire were still in preparation), and regrettably there is no similar body producing source-books on the place-names of Wales, Scotland, or Ireland. For all places not covered by the EPNS, therefore, we must turn to other authorities and sources. Some of these are not always reliable, although in general it is likely that information on the origin of recent names, simply because it *is* recent, will be more dependable than some of the etymologies given for the old names. Of those books listed in the Bibliography, the following are among the most dependable or informative, and were extensively used in the compilation of material for the Dictionary:

1. For local topographical sources, as mentioned, Anderson (1881).

2. As gazetteers, Brabner (1894–5), *Cassell* (1893–8), Davies (for Wales) (1975), Groome (for Scotland) (1882), Hudson (especially for minor places and districts) (*c.*1960), Mason (easily the best and most detailed) (1977), Munro (for Scotland) (1973), *Ordnance Survey Atlas* (the most up-to-date) (1982), *Postal Addresses* (for officially approved Post Office names) (1976); Brabner covers only England and Wales, *Cassell* covers the whole of the British Isles, Hudson and Mason cover England, Wales, and Scotland, as does the *Ordnance Survey Atlas*; *Postal Addresses* covers the whole of the British Isles, as well as Guernsey, Jersey, and the Isle of Man.

3. For good background on the origin of place-names, Addison (1979), Cameron (1969), Copley (1971), Gould (1978), Reaney (1976), Stokes (1948), all on names in England, although Gould also mentions Celtic names.

4. For specific origins of place-names in one or more of the five constituent countries of the British Isles, Davies (Wales) (n.d.), Ekwall (England, and in a class on its own) (1960), Field (somewhat restricted coverage, but the whole of the British Isles) (1980), Johnston (Scotland, and having a tendency to see all names as basically Celtic, but of good value if used with care) (1934), Jones (Wales) (1979), Morgan (Wales, and particularly good on the later names) (1887), Nicolaisen (Scotland, concentrating mainly on the Celtic names) (1979); Joyce (1875) and O'Connell (1979) are good on Irish names, but have little time for English names in Ireland: with the 'really modern English names, imposed by English-speaking people, such as Kingstown, Castleblakeney, Charleville' Joyce declares that he will 'have nothing to do', adding incorrectly, as the present Dictionary shows, that 'they are much less numerous than might be at first supposed'.

5. For specific origins on a local basis, and approaching the thoroughness, though not always the scholarship, of the EPNS publications, Field (Greater London) (1980), Glover (Kent) (1976),

(Sussex) (1975), Harris (Greater London, based on the Underground station names) (1977), Mills (Lancashire) (1976), Smith (London street-names) (1970); for thematic name origins, best are Ekwall (rivers) (1928) and Gelling *et al.* (towns and cities in Great Britain) (1970); Darley (1978) is good on names of planned villages, and *Place Names on Maps* (1973) is useful for the roots and elements of Celtic names in Wales and Scotland.

6. For good topographical, historical, and local information, there is little to beat the *Shell Guides*: England (Hadfield, 1981), Scotland (Macnie and McLaren, 1977), Wales (Vaughan-Thomas and Llewellyn, 1977) and Ireland (Killanin and Duignan, 1967); almost in the same category are the road books published by the Automobile Association: England and Wales (1963), Ireland (1962), and Scotland (1960), and the newer versions of these such as those edited by Russell Beach (see under his name in Bibliography).

7. For information on the many titled and other prominent families and individuals who gave their names to places, the *DNB* (1885–1901).

Finally, for a unique topographical, historical, and factual record of all parts of the British Isles in the first half of the nineteenth century, the *Topographical Dictionaries* of Lewis: England (1849), Ireland (1837), Scotland (1846), Wales (1849). (The dates are those of editions used for this Dictionary; there are others earlier and later.)

Outside the Bibliography, and apart from the many sources listed in Anderson, much useful and interesting information on modern place-names can be found in such authoritative publications as the *Victoria History of the Counties of England* (first published in the early twentieth century and reprinted since, although not yet complete for all counties), Kelly's Directories, the *Shell* county guides (again, not all counties are covered), the longer established guides for all parts of the British Isles, in particular the *Blue Guides* published by Benn, the *Red Guides* by Ward Lock, and the *Little Guides* by Methuen, county guides by Arthur Mee in *The King's England* series published by Hodder & Stoughton, and a whole range of journals, magazines and brochures, notably the journal *Notes & Queries*, county magazines such as *Lincolnshire Life*, *Hereford County Life*, and *The Hampshire County Magazine*, and the many town and district guides published locally. There are also more specialized journals and publications dealing wholly or partly with place-names, among the best known being the *Journal* of the EPNS, published annually, *Nomina*, a 'journal of name studies relating to Great Britain and Ireland published by English Name Studies', also annually, and *Names*, the quarterly journal of the American Name Society (which is by no means restricted to names in America).

SCOPE AND ARRANGEMENT
OF THE DICTIONARY

THE 'watershed' date for modern place-names has been fixed as the year 1500, as explained in the Introduction, and most of the names in the Dictionary are of places that have arisen since then. In some cases, however, names are included that existed in some form or other before this date. These mainly come into one of four categories:

1. Names that were first recorded since 1500, but which may well have existed some time before this. Some 'back formation' river names are of this type.

2. Names that in their modern form are based on an old form. Obviously, the revived names of former hundreds as used for modern administrative districts come into this category, but the places are new, and the names sufficiently 'ancient', and in many cases disused, for them to be included.

3. Names that are old in origin, but which designated originally quite a different geographical or man-made object to the one they designate today. An example is the name of *Bournemouth*, which originally simply designated the mouth of a river. Today the name is used for the flourishing town and resort in Dorset that grew up recently (in historical terms) on the site of this river-mouth. Other places named after rivers or their mouths are not included in most cases since the places have long existed as settlements. Such old names are Charmouth, Dartmouth, Weymouth, and Exmouth, all on the south coast and all of 'Domesday Book' vintage, at the latest.

4. Names that are basically old, but which have come to be known in their modern form accompanied by a recent addition such as a distinguishing prefix, suffix, or other word. An example is *Bognor Regis*, which only recently added its 'royal' suffix. Another is *Thornaby-on-Tees*, which added its river suffix in modern times.

The entries run in alphabetical order, and comprise the following components:

1. *The place-name itself*, followed by its geographical or administrative status and its location. The 'status' (town, village, river, etc.) is certainly not an official one, and is intended to indicate the approximate size or importance of the place. In particular, many places given as a 'village' are (or were) more accurately a hamlet, parish, settlement, ward, or the like, or what many gazetteers simply call a 'locality'. The aim is merely to indicate that a community of some sort lives (or lived) in the place, and that it is a relatively small one. Many villages, of course, become districts

of a town when a nearby urban development expands and absorbs them. In many entries, therefore, the description 'district of . . .' followed by the name of a town very likely means that the place concerned arose as a separate village or other settlement. As far as the location is concerned, this is given in the form of (a) the county (or region, in Scotland) in which the place is located, and (b) the constituent country of the British Isles in which that county or region is located (England, Scotland, Wales, Northern Ireland, or Ireland). Many places in London are officially in Greater London. Of districts in London 'proper', an approximate geographical location is further given, such as '*Queensbury*, district of north-west London'. Again, such a location is not an official one, and may not correspond to a Post Office district, for example. The location of districts in cities other than London is not given. For names that are modern but which are no longer used, the qualification 'former name of . . .' is given, followed by the modern name of the place. For villages in Scotland, and sometimes in Wales, a more precise location is given than simply the name of the region or county. This is because of the large area of many Scottish regions, and the multiplicity of identical names in Wales. Such a location gives the name of a town near which the village is situated, such as '*New Pitsligo*, village (near Fraserburgh), Grampian'. The town mentioned in such cases is not always the nearest in terms of miles on the map.

2. *The entry proper*. This gives, as far as it has been possible to establish it, the origin of the name, together with the relevant dates and historical or other information. By 'origin' is usually meant the immediate source of the name, although in some cases the name is taken back to its ultimate source. As stated in the Introduction, many modern names have transferred not once but several times, and the fascinating exercise of tracing a name back as far as it can be traced is not one that is usually carried out in an entry. An exception may be made, however, where the name is unusual or interesting, as *Virginia Water*, which traces its name back via a lake (Virginia Water) to a man who had been governor of an American state (Virginia) that was itself named in honour of an English queen (Elizabeth, the 'Virgin Queen') whose nickname derives from an ordinary word—at which point the category of 'name' is lost. A similar 'retrack' can be made for the London district of *Waterloo*, which goes back via station, bridge, and battle to the small town in Belgium so called, its own name perhaps meaning 'water marsh' (or 'water wood' or 'water ditch'), a fourfold transfer. The entry will also give the first recorded forms of the modern name, as far as they are known. The unusual and apparently erratic spelling of many of the names, even in the sixteenth and seventeenth centuries, is simply because English orthography had not stabilized at that stage, and what people wrote depended very much

on how they pronounced the word, where they lived (and whether they spoke a dialect or not), and on their general level of literacy. It should not be thought that such spellings are 'wrong': to the people who wrote 'Herynsgarste' (for modern *Heronsgate*) and 'Erleswode' (for our *Earlswood*), the forms were as accurate as many of our forms of the same name are corrupt. (See *Llangrove* for an example of an apparently deliberate corruption, made through ignorance.)

3. *A cross-reference system*. Where a name occurs in an entry in bold type, this means it has its own entry. The system does not apply to the heading of an entry, since this would involve constant cross-referral in the case of names of Welsh counties, for example. Some of the more important but now disused names have a separate entry in the form of a cross-reference, for example '**Henderskelfe** see **Castle Howard**'.

4. *Bibliographical references*. Where a reference is made to a work listed in the Bibliography it is referred to by the surname of the author, or short title of the work, together with the year of publication (the latter given to identify the particular work of a multiple author, or a work by an author having the same surname as another listed). Thus 'Taylor (1896)' refers to Isaac Taylor's *Names and their Histories*, and 'Davies (1959)' refers to *Flintshire Place-Names* by Ellis Davies, as distinct from a work by any of the other authors named Davies listed. Where a single author has two works published in the same year, it should be obvious from the context which is meant. Thus 'Field (1980)' in the entry for *Morecambe* must refer to this author's *Place-Names of Great Britain and Ireland*, not his *Place-Names of Greater London* published that same year. A list of short titles of works is given at the head of the Bibliography (p. 143). A reference to any work or publication not listed in the Bibliography is always given in full.

The main text of the Dictionary is followed by two Appendices, the first on 'royal' place-names and the second on 'seaside' names.

SPECIALIZED TERMS

SOME specialized historical and linguistic terms are used in the Dictionary, and brief definitions of these terms are given below.

administrative district: As used in the Dictionary, mainly in the entry headings, this means a new district, sometimes with a new name and new boundaries, established from 1974 within the counties of England and Wales and the regions (formerly counties) of Scotland for the purposes of local government.

back formation: The name of a river or stream formed from a town or village standing on it or near it (see Introduction, p. xxvii).

burgh of barony: A Scottish town or other settlement granted a charter by a baron and having special trading privileges.

chapel-of-ease: A chapel for worshippers at some distance from the parish church.

feu: In Scotland, a right to land, property, etc. granted on perpetual lease in return for a stipulated annual payment.

free port: A port where no duties are levied on articles of commerce.

hundred: An ancient division of an English shire or county having its own court and traditionally supposed to contain a hundred families. Hundreds had become established administrative units by the tenth century, and existed on a decreasingly important scale down to the nineteenth century. See also Introduction, p. xxxii and compare *wapentake* and *ward*, below.

liberty: In England down to 1850, a district within a county that is exempt from the jurisdiction of the sheriff (the chief officer of the Crown) and has its own Justice of the Peace. In many liberties the jurisdiction was held by a single lord, especially where the liberty contained several manors.

township: A division of a parish having its own community and, often, its own church.

wapentake: In the areas of Danish settlement in England (the 'Danelaw'), the equivalent of a *hundred* (see above). Wapentakes were mainly in north-east England, from Northumberland in the north to Essex in the south. The word literally means 'weapon-taking', since assent at a meeting was made by brandishing a weapon.

ward: The equivalent of a *hundred* (see above) in the extreme northern counties of England. The word can also refer to the administrative division of a town or city.

A

Abbeyleix, village, Laois, Ireland.

The village was built by the 1st Viscount de Vesci in the mid-18th century and named after a vanished abbey founded 1194 by Conor O'More of Leix, with Leix being a variant form of Laois. The Irish name is *Ministir Laoise*, 'monastery of Laois'.

Abbey Town, village, Cumbria, England.

The village was originally named Holme Cultram, this being a settlement of cottages around the abbey, founded c.1150 by Prince Henry of Scotland and rebuilt in the 1880s. The earliest recorded form of the name is in the Public Record Office's Parliamentary Surveys deposit for 1649, as *the towne of the Abbey, Abbey Towne*.

Abbey Village, village, Lancashire, England.

The village consists of cottages originally built for the workers at Abbey Mill, a cotton mill built c.1840 and named after Stanlow Abbey. This abbey held land in the township of Withnell within which the present village stands.

Aberlour see **Charlestown (of Aberlour)**.

Aboyne see **Charlestown** (Grampian).

Acocks Green, district of Birmingham, West Midlands, England.

The name derives from the family of a Richard Acock who lived here in the 17th century.

Acton, village, Armagh, Northern Ireland.

The village was founded in the 16th century by Sir Toby Poyntz (compare **Poyntz Pass**), who obtained it as part of the forfeited estate of the O'Hanlons and named it after his family's native village in England, Iron Acton, Gloucestershire.

Addiewell, village (near Bathgate), Lothian, Scotland.

The village arose round a chemical works founded in 1866 as an offshoot of those at Bathgate. The name seems to derive from a well belonging to a man named Adam.

Adur, river and administrative district, West Sussex, England.

The name was coined by some antiquarian who identified Portus Adurni, in fact the Roman harbour at Portsmouth, with the mouth of the Adur. Michael Drayton quotes the name in his *Polyolbion* (1612) and he himself may have actually coined the name. An earlier name of the river was Bramber, from the village of Bramber that stands on it.

Agar Town, district of north London, England.

The district was named after William Agar, who began building what was to become a slum district here in c.1831. The district is now swallowed up by the railway goods yards of St. Pancras and King's Cross stations, although the name survives in Agar Grove, a street that runs along the district's northern boundary, with Agar Place a short street off it.

Akeman Street, Roman road, East Anglia, England.

More than one Roman road in England is so named, and properly the name applies to a road leading to Bath, whose old name was *Acemannes-ceaster* (973). In East Anglia, however, the name appears on modern maps as a Roman road running from Ermine Street at Arrington, Cambridgeshire, through Cambridge and Ely to Denver, Norfolk. This obviously has no connection with Bath and the name was probably devised by an antiquarian as late as the 17th century.

Akroydon, district of Halifax, West Yorkshire, England.

The district was planned as a model village for mill workers in 1849 by Edward Akroyd (1810–87), a local industrialist and Deputy Lieutenant of the West Riding of Yorkshire, and was named after him. Akroyd laid the corner-stone of the church here in 1856 and building began on the estate in 1861.

Albert Village, village, Leicestershire, England.

The village was developed in the 19th century as a coalmining settlement and was named as a compliment to Prince Albert after he had become the consort of Queen Victoria in 1840.

Alde, river, Suffolk, England.

The name is a back formation from the town of Aldeburgh, south of which the river flows. From Orford Ness to its mouth the river is called the Ore. Earliest recorded names of the Alde are: *Ald* 1735, *the River Ald* 1764.

Alderley Edge, town, Cheshire, England.

The town is named after the nearby hill of Alderley Edge, and its site was described in White's *History, Gazetteer and Directory of Cheshire* (1860) as being, up to 1779, 'a dreary common containing nothing but a goodly number of Scotch firs'. Alderley itself is an old name, recorded in the 'Domesday Book' of 1086.

Alexandria, town, Strathclyde, Scotland.

The town arose as a result of the introduction in 1768 of bleaching, printing, and dyeing works here, and it was named after the local Member of Parliament, Alexander Smollett of Bonhill (d. 1799). See also **Renton**.

Allen, river, Dorset, England.

The name is a back formation from Aleyn Bridge (now Canford Bridge) which spans the Stour just south of Wimborne Minster. This town has preserved the earlier name of the Allen, the Wimborne. Aleyn Bridge was in fact named after a person, whose name was perhaps Ealdwine. In the 16th century, however, the name was misunderstood to mean 'bridge over the river Aleyn', hence the river name, whose earliest recorded form is *Alen* 1577.

Aller, river, Devon, England.

The name is a back formation from the small village of Aller, located on it. Earliest recorded forms of the name are: *Aller water c.*1540, *Aller brooke* 1577, *Aller* 1586. The Aller is a tributary of the Teign.

Alre, river, Hampshire, England.

The name is a back formation from (New) Alresford, with the river flowing into the Itchen one mile west of the town. Earliest recorded forms of the name are: *Alresford ryver c.*1540, *Alresforde* 1577, *Arle* 1586. The earlier name of the river was Icene.

Ammanford, town, Dyfed, Wales.

The town was called Cross Inn, after its central inn at the junction of four roads, until *c.*1880, when it was renamed Ammanford, after its location on the river Aman. Its Welsh name is identical: *Rhydaman*, 'ford (of the) Aman'.

Anerley, district of south-east London, England.

The name was that of the first house to be built on this part of Penge Common in *c.*1840. The house belonged to a Scot, William Sanderson, who offered land free to the railway company on the condition that the station should be so called. Anerley Station is mentioned in Kelly's *Directory* of 1859. The name derives from an old Scots word *anerly*, meaning 'only', 'lonely', an appropriate name for the first isolated house here.

Angel, district of east central London, England.

The name is that of an old coaching inn

here dating back to at least 1638 but demolished in 1819. Angel was a common name for an inn: in the mid-18th century there were 23 Angel Alleys and 30 Angel Courts in London. The name was further established by the opening of Angel Underground station in 1901.

Angell Town, district of south-west London, England.

Land here had been held by the Angell family for several generations when in 1853 Benedict J. A. Angell gave the ground on which St. John's Church stood for development. The church, on the corner of Wiltshire Road and Angell Road, had been so dedicated in accordance with the wish of John Angell, of Stockwell Park House (d. 1784).

Anglesey (originally also **Angleseyville**), district of Gosport, Hampshire, England.

The first building erected here was Uxbridge House, the home of the district's founder Robert Cruickshank. The first stone of the house had been laid in 1826 by the Earl of Uxbridge for his father, Henry William Paget, 1st Marquis of Anglesey (1786–1854), whose title gave the name of the district.

Angmering-on-Sea, village and resort, West Sussex, England.

The name was transferred from the nearby village of Angmering, two miles inland from the resort, which itself was founded in c.1913 by a London builder, William Hollis, who planned a 'garden city beside the sea' (*Scribble*, Vol. 1, No. 1, 1916).

Ansdell, district of Lytham St. Anne's, Lancashire, England.

The district was named after the painter Richard Ansdell (1815–85) who had built a large house here called 'Star Hills', now a Methodist Old People's Home.

Anton, river, Hampshire, England.

The name is first recorded in its present form in H. Skrine, *A General Account of all the Rivers of Note in Great Britain* (1801), and seems to have originated as the result of an incorrect identification of a place 'Antona', mentioned by Tacitus, with Andover. (Tacitus is thought to have been referring to the 'Trisantona', an old name of the river Trent in Dorset, now better known as the Piddle.) Andover, which is on the Anton, probably preserves the river's earlier name, recorded as *Andever aqua* 15th century, *Andever water c.*1540, *Andeuer (water)* 1577.

Anzac-on-sea see **Peacehaven**.

Archiestown, village (near Dufftown), Grampian, Scotland.

The village was founded in c.1760 by Sir Archibald Grant of Monymusk (1731–96) who owned land here on the Moor of Ballintomb, with the village name derived from the first name of its founder.

Archway, district of north London, England.

The district takes its name from Archway Road, built in 1813 and named for its impressive viaduct, demolished in 1900. The name was established with the opening of Archway Underground station in 1907.

Ardgoil (Estate), mountainous estate, Strathclyde, Scotland.

The name of the estate was suggested by J. A. Stewart of Glasgow for the Cameron Corbett Estate gifted to Glasgow in 1906 by Lord Rowallan. The name is a compound of *ard*, Gaelic for 'height', and Loch *Goil*, which it borders.

Arfon, administrative district, Gwynedd, Wales.

The name is an old one for the district here, meaning 'opposite Môn', i.e. opposite Anglesey. Compare the name of Caernarfon, in the district, whose name derives from Welsh *Caer-yn-Arfon*, 'fort in Arfon'.

Arkwright Town, village, Derbyshire, England.

The name derives from the family of Sir Richard Arkwright (1732–92), inventor of the spinning frame, who bought the manor of Sutton here in 1824.

Armadale, town, Lothian, Scotland.

The name first appears on a map of 1818, and was transferred here from Armadale in the parish of Farr, Sutherland. This Sutherland Armadale was the name of property inherited here from his mother by William Honeyman, Lord Armadale, and when he bought land in the parish of Bathgate, West Lothian, he brought the name with him for his new property. Armadale was only a small hamlet until the establishment of chemical and paraffin works in 1851.

Arnos Grove, district of north London, England.

The name is recorded as *Arnoldes Grove* 1551, *Arno's Grove c.*1865, and evidently means 'grove or plantation owned by the Arnold family'. Margery Arnold is named in documents dated 1344. The name was established with the opening of Arnos Grove Underground station in 1932.

Arthurstown, village, Wexford, Ireland.

The name derives from its founder in the early part of the 19th century, Arthur, Lord Templemore.

Arun, river and administrative district, West Sussex, England.

The name is a back formation from the town of Arundel, with the old name of the river being the Tarrant (preserved in Tarrant Street, Arundel). Early forms of the name are *Aron* and *Arunus* 1577, but the name doubtless existed some time before this.

Ash Vale, village, Surrey, England.

The village, now an urban development near Aldershot, Hampshire, first appeared on local maps in the 1860s, when two earlier names here, Ash Valley and Ash Common, fell into disuse. All three names ultimately derive from the nearby village of Ash, now also an urban location. Ash Vale first appeared as a settlement in the local directories in 1874.

Auburn, village, Westmeath, Ireland.

The original name of the village, and still the current Irish one, is Lishoy or Lissoy (Irish *Lios uaimhe*, 'fort of the cave'). The poet Oliver Goldsmith (1728–74) lived here, and on the appearance of his 'The Deserted Village' (1770), whose first line is 'Sweet Auburn! loveliest village of the plain', Goldsmith admitted that he had set the scene of the poem in Lissoy. From then on the name Auburn came to be adopted for the village, with several towns in the United States also taking the name, the first of them in 1786 (Auburn, Maine).

Audley End, village, Essex, England.

The name is that of the Jacobean mansion here, Audley End. This was originally a house built by the 1st Earl of Suffolk, Lord Howard de Walden, who inherited the estate of Audley End in 1603. The Abbey of Walden had earlier stood on the estate, and had been given to Sir Thomas Audley (1488–1544), Baron Audley of Walden and Lord Chancellor of England, by Henry VIII after the Dissolution of the Monasteries (1536–9). Early recorded forms of the name are: *Audeley* 1539, *Audleyend* 1555.

Avoca (occasionally **Ovoca**), river and village, Wicklow, Ireland.

The name appears to have been given to a stretch of the river **Avonmore** some time in the 18th century by an antiquarian who identified it with the Oboka on Ptolemy's map. Early forms of the name are recorded as: *Avoca river* 1778, *the river Avoca* 1786, *Ovoca river* 1795. The village takes its name from the river.

Avon, county, England.

The county was created in 1974, from parts of Somerset and Gloucestershire, as a result of the reorganization of local administrative boundaries. It takes its name from the river Avon, which runs through it from east to west. (This is the 'Bristol' or Lower Avon.)

Avonmore, river, Wicklow, Ireland.

The name seems to have arisen in the 17th century and to be an anglicization of an earlier Irish name, *abhainn mhór*, 'great water'. Early recorded forms of the name are: *the Great Water* 1599, *river of Owenmore c.*1660.

Avonmouth, port and suburb of Bristol, Avon, England.

The port was established in the 19th century, with Avonmouth Dock opened in 1877. The name is an old one, recorded in 918 as *Afene muthan*, but this was simply the mouth of the river. Compare **Bournemouth**.

Avonwick, village, Devon, England.

The village was originally called Newhouse, with this being changed to Avonwick in *c.*1878. The village is on the river Avon. Presumably the name was felt to be more appropriate for an established village ('wick') than Newhouse, which simply suggests an isolated dwelling.

B

Babel, village, Clwyd, Wales.

The name derives from the Nonconformist chapel around which the village grew, this being Welsh *pabell*, 'tent', 'tabernacle'. The reference was probably taken to be to *pabell y cyfarfod*, the 'tabernacle of the congregation' (Exodus 29: 42) prepared by Moses for the people to meet God.

Babergh, administrative district, Suffolk, England.

The name is a revival of an old hundred name, said to mean 'Babba's mound'.

Bagenalstown, former name of *Muine Bheag*, town, Carlow, Ireland.

The town was founded in the late 18th century by Walter Bagenal of Dunleckny Manor, with the Bagenal family having settled here in the 16th century. Walter Bagenal had intended the town to be 'of considerable architectural pretensions and to bear the name Versailles' (Killanin & Duignan, 1967). In the 20th century the town reverted to its original Irish name of *Muine Bheag*, meaning 'small thicket'.

Balaclava, village (near Johnstone), Strathclyde, Scotland.

The village was founded in 1856 and named commemoratively after 'the Charge' (Tennyson's 'Charge of the Light Brigade') which was the salient feature of the Battle of Balaklava (1854) in the Crimean War.

Balaclava, village (near Portmahomack), Highland, Scotland.

After 'the Charge' of 1854 (see previous entry) the village of Balnuig ('village on the bay') was renamed.

Balls Green, village, East Sussex, England.

The name derives from Rychard Balle of Pulborough, recorded as a landowner here in 1570.

Ballycastle, town and resort, Antrim, Northern Ireland.

The name, meaning 'town of the castle', derives from the castle built in 1609 by Sir Randal Macdonnell, 1st Earl of Antrim (died 1636), at the order of James I who had commanded him to raise 'faire castels' at reasonable distances on his estates.

Ballyjamesduff, village, Cavan, Ireland.

The village was created in 1831 and named after General Sir James Duff, commander of the Limerick district in the disturbances of 1798.

Banbridge, town, Down, Ireland.

The town is on the river Bann, and came into existence after the building of a stone bridge over the river in 1712, when the Dublin to Belfast road was constructed.

Bandon, town, Cork, Ireland.

The town, on the river Bandon, was founded in 1608 as Bandonbridge by Richard Boyle, 1st Earl of Cork (1566–1643), who had acquired large estates in the county. The Irish name reflects the English original: *Droichead na Bandon*, 'bridge of the Bandon'.

Bankfoot, village (near Dunkeld), Tayside, Scotland.

The village was built in c.1815 by a Mr Wylie and named for its location at the base of an elevated ridge.

Barkingside, district of Redbridge, London, England.

Although 'side' in a place-name can mean 'slope', 'hill', here it seems to mean simply 'beside', thus 'place beside Barking'. The earliest recorded form of the name found is exactly as at present, in 1538. Barkingside was formerly in the parish of Ilford, which now lies between it and Barking to the south. The name was reinforced with the opening of the Great Eastern Railway station in 1903 and the Underground station in 1948.

Barmouth, town and port, Gwynedd, Wales.

The former (and present) Welsh name of the town was Abermaw or Abermo, a contraction of *Abermawddach*, 'mouth of the (river) Mawddach'. The English corruption of this was adopted in 1768 'at a meeting of the masters of the vessels belonging to the port, when, in consideration of the increase in shipping, it was deemed expedient to have an Eng. name inscribed upon the sterns of the vessels' (Lewis, 1849).

Barnes Cray, district of Bexley, London, England.

The name originates from the Barne family who were landowners here in the second half of the 18th century, with Cray the name of the river that runs through the district.

Barons Court, district of west London, England.

The name originated with the building of an estate here by Sir William Palliser at the end of the 19th century. The exact sense is not clear: the name may be a semi-facetious allusion to a baron-court or court-baron, formerly the title of 'the assembly of the freehold tenants of a manor under the presidency of the lord or his steward' (*Shorter Oxford English Dictionary*, 1975), or to 'baron' in the sense of 'commercial magnate'. Most likely, however, the name was devised to match that of **Earls Court**, although there can be no historical connection between the two. The name was reinforced for the district with the opening of Barons Court Underground station in 1905.

Bassetlaw, administrative district, Nottinghamshire, England.

The name was formerly that of a large wapentake in the north of the county, with the present district covering almost the same area. The 'Domesday Book'

form of the name (1086) was *Bernese delaue*, perhaps meaning 'hill of dwellers in burnt place' (i.e. the name might have developed to a modern English form 'Burntslaw').

Batherm, river, Somerset/Devon, England.

The name seems to be a back formation from the town of Bampton, situated on the river. An earlier form of the name Bampton was *Bathampton*, which explains the first four letters of the river name. The Batherm was recorded in 1797 as the *Batham*.

Bathford, village, Avon, England.

The original form of the name was Ford (in the 'Domesday Book' of 1086, *Forde*). The prefix Bath was added some time before 1575, when the name appears (in its present spelling) on a map of Somerset. The addition would have been made to distinguish this place, near Bath, from others of the same name. *Ford* is a common place-name throughout Britain to denote a place on a ford over a stream or river.

Battlebridge see **King's Cross**.

Bay Horse, village, Lancashire, England.

The name derives from the Old Bay Horse inn, south of Lancaster, and was that of a railway station here until it closed in 1960.

Beaufort, town, Gwent, Wales.

The town was founded as an industrial settlement in *c*.1780, when a lease was granted to an ironmaster, Edward Kendall. Its original Welsh name, and its present one, was Cendl, from his name, but this was later changed to the family name of its landowner, the Duke of Beaufort (compare **Dukestown**).

Beckton, district of east London, England.

The district is named after S. A. Beck, governor of the Gas, Light, and Coke Company here in 1869.

Bedford Level, drainage area of the Fens, Cambridgeshire, England.

The name was recorded as *the Great Level (of the Fens)* in 1632. It assumed its new name from Francis, Earl of Bedford, who had undertaken to drain this area of the Fens the previous year.

Bedford Park, district of Chiswick, London, England.

The name is that of a planned estate laid out in 1877, and commemorates the Russells, Dukes of Bedford, who lived here in the 17th century.

Beeswing, village (near Dumfries), Dumfries and Galloway, Scotland.

The name is that of a racehorse depicted on the sign of an inn here, with the village growing up round the inn. The inn itself is said to have been built or bought by the horse's owner, a Mr W. Orde, some time in the 1830s. There are other public houses with the name (for example in Kettering, Northamptonshire), which seems to derive from the same horse, who gained popularity by winning 51 out of 64 races in the eight years 1835–42.

Belgravia, district of south-west London, England.

The name derives from Belgrave Square, in the centre of the district, with the square's name transferred from Belgrave, Cheshire, a property of the Dukes of Westminster, whose family own much of Belgravia. Richard Grosvenor, 1st Earl Grosvenor (1731–1802), purchased Belgrave, Cheshire in 1758, himself becoming Viscount Belgrave in 1784. His son, Robert Grosvenor, 2nd Earl of Grosvenor and 1st Marquis of Westminster (1767–1845), developed part of his Westminster estate in 1842, adding the names of other Cheshire and Flintshire properties here (for example, Eccleston Square, Beeston Place, Balderton Street). The district was largely built by Thomas Cubitt (see **Cubitt Town**), a letter to whom addressed 'Belgravia' was allegedly sent to Hungary before being returned to him.

Thackeray used the name in his *Vanity Fair* (1848): 'Ask the Reverend Mr. Thurifer if Belgravia is not a sounding brass, and Tyburnia a tinkling cymbal.' (Tyburnia, whose name has a similar formation, was used to denote part of Bayswater between Edgware Road and Pembridge Road, with the district extending northwards to Westbourne.)

Bellamour, village, Staffordshire, England.

The name was that of a house built here in *c.*1639 by one Herbert Aston on his marriage. Aston had lived abroad, and named his house *Bellamore*, conventional Italian for 'beautiful love', allegedly because the house 'was finished by the benevolence and assistance of his friends' (Duignan, 1902), but doubtless also as a compliment to his wife. The village grew up round a modern mansion of the same name, recorded in 1834 as Bellamoore Hall, on a site near the original house.

Belle Isle, island, Lake Windermere, Cumbria, England.

The name was first recorded in this form in 1823. The island was originally named The Holme (i.e. 'the island'), then Long Holme. In 1781 it was purchased by one Isabella Curwen who renamed it as Belle Isle, no doubt partly to reflect her own first name.

Belle Vue, district of Wakefield, West Yorkshire, England.

The name derives from that of a house so called, recorded as existing in 1828. The name suggests the commanding position of the house (French 'fine view').

Belmont, district of Sutton, London, England.

Belmont was popular as a street name in London in Victorian times, mainly for its pseudo-Norman associations ('fine hill'). In some cases, as here, it was given to replace an undesirable name. Belmont in Sutton was named Little Hell until the first part of the 19th century. The earlier name may, however, have simply meant 'Little Hill', in which case the new name was a semi-translation as well as an improvement.

Belsize Park, district of Hampstead, London, England.

Belsize itself is an old name of French origin, meaning 'finely situated' (Old French *bel assis*), and first recorded in 1317. The present form of the name relates more directly to Belsize House, the residence of Baron Wotton (Charles Henry Kirkhoven, d. 1683) in the 17th century, with the grounds of the house being the Park of the name. The location of the house and grounds, neither now in existence, is marked by the present Belsize Square and surrounding streets named Belsize (Avenue, Court, Crescent, Grove, Lane, Mews, Place, Terrace). The name was established for the district with the opening of Belsize Park Underground station in 1907.

Berea, village, Dyfed, Wales.

The name is that of a Nonconformist chapel here, itself named after the biblical town in Macedonia where St. Paul preached successfully (Acts 17: 10–13). The association of the name was thus with preaching and conversion.

Bethania, village, Dyfed, Wales.

The name, like that of **Berea**, derives from that of a Nonconformist chapel here, whose own name is a classical form of Bethany, the biblical village where Mary anointed Christ (John 12: 1–3). The name was popularly understood as meaning 'house of song', the reference being to the hymns and songs of praise sung in the chapel. There is another village of the name in Gwynedd.

Bethel, village (near Caernarfon), Gwynedd, Wales.

There are at least three villages of the name in Gwynedd, all deriving from a Calvinistic Methodist chapel so called, with the chapels themselves set up in the early 19th century. The name, of biblical origin, was popularly understood to mean the 'house of God' (Genesis 28: 19) where Jacob rested.

Bethesda, town, Gwynedd, Wales.

The name is that of a Calvinistic Methodist chapel established here in 1820 on a site known as Y Wern Uchaf (Welsh = 'the upper marsh'). The settlement developed over the parish of Y Wern Uchaf and the adjoining parish of Cilfoden (perhaps originally called *Cilcafoden* and meaning 'place sheltered from showers'), so that it was originally called by one or other of these two names before becoming Bethesda. Shortly after the adoption of the chapel name, understood to mean 'house of mercy' as a biblical name, an attempt was made to rename the village as Glan Ogwen ('bank of the Ogwen'), for its location on the river Ogwen. The attempt was unsuccessful, however, and the name Bethesda prevailed. Bethesda was the name of the pool in Jerusalem where the sick came to be treated (John 5: 1–10).

Bethlehem, village, Dyfed, Wales.

Yet one more Nonconformist chapel name, this deriving from the famous biblical town where Christ was born (Matthew 2: 1, etc.). The Welsh village has a seasonal fame for its apt postmark on Christmas cards.

Bettyhill, village (near Armadale), Highland, Scotland.

The village was apparently founded in *c*.1815 by Elizabeth, Countess of Sutherland and Marchioness of Stafford (1765–1839) and takes its name from the pet form of her Christian name. Elizabeth was the only surviving daughter of William, 18th Earl of Sutherland, and a younger relative of Lady Helen Colquhoun who gave her name to **Helensburgh**. Bettyhill was founded to house crofters evicted from Strathnaver during the Highland Clearances.

Beulah, village, Powys, Wales.

The name is that of a Congregational

chapel here, set up some time in the early 19th century. The biblical name was popularly believed to mean 'married' (Isaiah 62: 4).

Bexleyhill, village, West Sussex, England.

The name was recorded in 1736 as Boxall Hill, and the village may well have associations with the Boxall family, whose name is found in the registers of Kirdford from 1586.

Bishopbriggs, suburb of Glasgow, Strathclyde, Scotland.

The name was recorded in 1665 as *Bishop Bridge*, with, however, the second element of the name meaning *rigg(s)*, i.e. 'field(s)', rather than 'bridge'. This would refer to a field or fields here owned by the Bishop of Glasgow. There is no noted bridge in the district that the name could have designated, and the only waterway of significance here, the Forth–Clyde Canal, was constructed in 1790 and thus post-dates the name.

Bishop's Stortford, town, Hertfordshire, England.

The town was originally Stortford (*Storteford* in the 'Domesday Book' of 1086), with the present name first recorded in 1587 as *Bysshops Stortford*. The current name thus seems to be relatively late, although according to the 'Domesday Book' the Bishop of London held the manor here in the 11th century. See also **Stort**.

Black Dog, village, Devon, England.

The name derives from an inn here so called.

Blackpool, town and resort, Lancashire, England.

The original name was simply 'Pool' (*Pul c.*1260, *Le Pull* 1416), with the present form of the name first recorded (as *Blackpoole*) in 1602. The addition to the name, doubtless made to distinguish from other locations nearby so called, apparently refers to the original

dark colour of a pool or stream here, with the colouring caused by peat.

Blaenau Gwent, administrative district, Gwent, Wales.

The name was recorded in 1594 as *Blayne Gwent*, with the first part of the name Welsh *blaenau*, plural of *blaen*, 'source', 'highland', and the second part being an old *cantref* name (see **Gwent**). Blaenau is fairly common as an element in Welsh place-names; compare Blaenau Ffestiniog, Gwynedd, and the coal-mining location of Blaina near **Brynmawr**.

Blairadam, village (near Kinross), Fife, Scotland.

The name was originally that of a house built on the moorland estate of Blair here in *c.*1735 by William Adam (1689–1748), father of the famous four Adam architect brothers. The eldest brother, John Adam, developed and laid out the village of Blairadam, whose original name, however, was Maryburgh.

Blaise Hamlet, district of Bristol, Avon, England.

The small settlement—only nine cottages—arose as a model village built in 1810 to house the pensioners from the nearby Blaise Castle estate.

Blenheim Park, village, Oxfordshire, England.

The Park is that of Blenheim Palace, built over the 17 years 1705–22 on the site of the Royal Manor of Woodstock, conferred by Queen Anne to the 1st Duke of Marlborough to commemorate his victory over the French at Blenheim, 13 August 1704. The English form of the name is a corruption of the German name *Blindheim*, now in West Germany.

Blessington, village, Wicklow, Ireland.

Lands here were granted by Charles II to Michael Boyle, Archbishop of Dublin, in 1667, and formed into the Manor of Blessington. It seems that the earlier name of Ballecomin or Ballecomine was taken to derive from Irish *baile comaoine*, and this was 'translated' into English as 'Blessing Town', from *baile*, 'town' and *comaoin*, 'gift', 'favour bestowed'. (The name actually means 'Comyn's town'.)

Blundellsands, district of Crosby, Merseyside, England.

With the expansion of Great Crosby here as a residential district in the early 19th century, the landowner of Little Crosby, surnamed Blundell, appropriated a long track of sandhills on the coast for building development and named it after himself.

Bognor Regis, town and resort, West Sussex, England.

The main (first) part of the name is very old, and was recorded in 680 as *Bucgan ora* to mean 'Bucge's shore', Bucge being a Saxon woman who owned a landing place here. The town began to develop as a resort in 1785, when a London hatter, Sir Richard Hotham, bought 1600 acres of land, including the nearby village of South Bersted, with the aim of rivalling **Brighton**. He renamed the site *Hothampton*, but the name went out of use after his death in 1790. The royal suffix Regis was given to the town in 1929 to commemorate the convalescence of George V here (actually at Craigwell House in the village of Aldwick, now a district of Bognor). Sir Richard's name survives in Bognor's main park, Hotham Park.

Bonnybridge, village (near Falkirk), Central, Scotland.

The name, meaning 'bridge on the river Bonny', was first recorded in its Latin form, *aquae de Boine*, in 1682. The English form of the name is not found earlier than *c*.1770.

Bonnyrigg, town, Lothian, Scotland.

The name originated as a field name, first recorded as a settlement name, *Bannockrig*, in 1773, probably when a name was needed for a new colliery here. The recorded form of the name shows that the name does not mean 'bonny ridge' but 'bannock ridge', i.e.

refers to a ridge shaped like a bannock (a flat oatmeal cake).

Boothferry, administrative district, Humberside, England.

The name derives from Boothferry Bridge, by the small village of Booth, which today takes the A614 road over the river Ouse. The name of the bridge refers to the time when the only route across the river was by ferry. The earliest recorded form of the name is *Booth's Ferry* 1651, with Booth, via the village name, apparently deriving from a Lincolnshire family name, Booth or Boothby.

Boothtown, district of Halifax, West Yorkshire, England.

The name was originally 'Booth', recorded in 1274 as (*del*) *Bothes* and meaning 'sheds'. The second part of the name was added when the district began to be developed in the late 15th century, with its earliest recorded forms *Boethestown* 1499 and *Boothton* 1509.

Borough Green, village, Kent, England.

The name is first recorded as *Borrowe Grene* in 1575, with this name probably referring either to the manor or the borough of Wrotham.

Boston Spa, village, West Yorkshire, England.

The spa was a mineral spring discovered in 1744 by John Shires, who lived in nearby Thorpe Arch, and the original name of the settlement that began to grow up here in 1753 was Thorpe Arch Spa, recorded in 1771 as *Thorp Spaw*. Shortly after, however, the name Boston began to take over, with the settlement recorded as *Bostongate* in 1799 and *Boston* in 1822. The present form of the name seems to have been established with the coming of the Penny Post in 1840, with the suffix Spa both descriptive and designed to distinguish the place from Boston, Lincolnshire. The name Boston appears to be an old one, perhaps originally derived from a personal name such as Bosa. It is hardly likely to derive 'from the Latin "bos", an ox, with the Anglo Saxon ending "ton", a township' (Beatrice M. Scott, *Boston Spa*, 1976), and it is not historically or etymologically connected with Boston, Lincolnshire.

Boundary, village, Derbyshire, England.

The name is recorded in 1857 as *Bondary or Burton Road*, with the place being formerly an extra-parochial liberty on the Derbyshire–Leicestershire border ('boundary').

Bournemouth, town and resort, Dorset, England.

The name means 'mouth of the stream', the latter word being *burna* in Old English, related to modern 'burn' and 'bourn'. In the Christchurch Cartulary (collection of charters) dated 1407 there is a reference to *la Bournemouthe*, but this simply denotes the sandhills at the mouth of the stream, and the name was used to record that a whale ('magnus piscis, anglice a whale') was washed up on the shore here ('iuxta litus maris prope la Bournemouthe'). The region later became notorious as a haunt of smugglers. The modern town stems from a villa built in 1812 for his family and himself by Captain Lewis Tregonwell, with the only other existing building being a wayside inn, the Tapps Arms, built in 1809. In 1836 Sir George Jervis laid out his marine village round Tregonwell's house, and the modern name became established from this year. The stream, which now runs through the Pleasure Gardens, is still called the Bourne.

Bourne Rivulet, stream, Hampshire, England.

The stream joins the river Test near Hurstbourne Priors, and before 1577, when it was recorded as *Bourne*, was known as the Hurstbourne.

Bournville, district of Birmingham, West Midlands, England.

The district arose as a model estate for workers at George Cadbury's chocolate factory here, and was founded by him in 1879. The name was originally intended to have been Bournbrook, after a mansion here called Bournbrook Hall (in turn named after the river Bourne or Bournbrook here), and an early print announcing the forthcoming building of the factory refers to 'Cadbury's Cocoa and Chocolate Manufactory, Bournbrook'. Before work started on the factory, however, the name Bournville was chosen 'because it had a French sound, and French chocolate was then looked upon as the best' (Iolo A. Williams, *The Firm of Cadbury: 1831–1931*, 1931).

Bowrington see Maesteg.

Box, river, Suffolk, England.

The name is a back formation from Boxford, a village which stands on it, its own name meaning 'ford where box grows'. The original name of the river, a tributary of the Stour, was 'Amalburna', perhaps deriving from a personal name, with *-burna* meaning 'stream'.

Box Hill, hill, Surrey, England.

The first recording we have of the name is for 1629, with the origin either a farm name or a field name. It is known that a Thomas Atteboxe lived at Boxhill Farm in 1263, and William de la Boxe lived there in 1268. The name means simply 'hill where box grows' (as it still does here). It seems strange, however, that no earlier record of the name exists.

Boxmoor, district of Hemel Hempstead, Hertfordshire, England.

The earliest recorded forms of the name are *Boxmoore* 1638, *Boxemore* 1650. The name shows that the box tree was once common here, although it is rare in the district now.

Brain, river, Essex, England.

The name is a fairly recent back formation from the town of Braintree, near where it rises. The river seems to have had a number of different earlier names, among them *aqua de Wyham* ('water of

Witham') 1254, *ripa de Nottele* ('stream bank of Notley') 1385, and *Pod's Brook* 1777, the latter probably being derived from a family name. In its modern form the name is first recorded in 1848.

Branksome, district of Poole, Dorset, England.

The name seems to derive from a house here, Branksome Tower, built in 1855 by Charles William Packe of Loughborough, Leicestershire, with the aim of developing an estate. The house name may in turn be taken from 'Branksome Tower', the setting of Walter Scott's *Lay of the Last Minstrel* (1805), with this being perhaps inspired by Branxholm Castle, near Hawick, Scotland. The house, as Branksome Towers, became a hotel and subsequently was converted into private apartments.

Breckland, administrative district, Norfolk, England.

The name, meaning 'broken land', was first used in the 19th century when land here was still being 'broken in' for cultivation. For many years the district was a barren region of heathland, but since 1919 the Forestry Commission have been implementing a vast treeplanting programme here.

Brent, borough of north-west London, England.

The name has been transferred from the river Brent, which flows through it and links the former boroughs here of Wembley and Willesden. Brentford, a district of Hounslow, London (formerly in Middlesex) is also on the river, but not Brentwood, Essex, whose name means 'burnt wood'. The borough of Brent was constituted in 1965. See also **Brentham**.

Brentham, district of west London, England.

The name was adopted for a residential estate developed in *c.*1910 in the northern part of the parish of Ealing, with its name apparently intended to mean

'district by the river Brent'. (Compare previous entry.)

Bridgend, town, Mid Glamorgan, Wales.

The name, recorded in 1535 as *Byrge End*, is an English translation of the Welsh name of the place: *Pen-y-bont (ar Ogwr)*, 'end of the bridge over the (river) Ogwr'. A stone bridge was built here across the Ogwr (English Ogmore) in *c.*1435.

Bridgeton, district of Glasgow, Strathclyde, Scotland.

The name indicates the proximity of the district to a bridge over the river Clyde. Land was purchased here in 1705 by John Walkinshaw with the aim of building a village. His venture met with no success, however, so the Corporation repurchased the land from him and sold it to John Orr, a Glasgow merchant, in 1731. Orr can thus be regarded as the proper founder of the settlement. When Walkinshaw first purchased the land here it was known as *Barrowfield*.

Bridgewater Canal, canal, Greater Manchester/Cheshire, England.

The name preserves the title of the Dukes of Bridgewater. The 1st Duke projected the canal and the 3rd Duke, Francis Egerton (1736–1803), was responsible for the actual construction over the period 1759–65. The canal links the Leeds and Liverpool Canal at Leigh, Greater Manchester, with the Trent and Mersey Canal at Preston Brook, Cheshire. See also **Egerton**.

Brierfield, town, Lancashire, England.

The town arose as a textile community next to **Nelson** in the 19th century. Its name seems to be arbitrary, although it could have been chosen to blend with the adjacent district of Briercliffe (an old name).

Briestfield, village, West Yorkshire, England.

The original name of the village was Briestwistle, so recorded on the

Ordnance Survey map of 1840. Earlier forms of this are recorded as *Brerethuisel* c.1150, *Brerethwisel* 1243, *Brestwill* 1546, *Briestwizle* 1777, all meaning 'briar fork', i.e. indicating land in a fork of the river that is overgrown with briars. Some time in the 19th century, when the village grew, the name was wrongly understood as 'Briest-well', with the 'well' replaced by the apparently more appropriate 'field'.

Brighton, town and resort, East Sussex, England.

The original name of the site here was recorded in the 'Domesday Book' of 1086 as *Bristelmestune*, this being a form of Old English *Beorhthelmes tūn*, 'Beorhthelm's farmstead'. Later forms of the name came to be *Brighthelmeston* 1493 and *Brightelmston* 1816, with the present, shorter version of the name established only in the 19th century (although said to have been used in deeds in the time of Charles I). Lewis (1840) begins his account of the town: 'BRIGHTHELMSTONE . . . now, by contraction, generally Brighton'. Development of the settlement as a seaside resort began in the late 18th century, and this, continuing rapidly in the early part of the 19th century, doubtless encouraged a more concise form of the name, helped by its fortuitous association with 'bright'.

Brit, river, Dorset, England.

The river name is probably a back formation from the town of Bridport, located on it. Bridport itself was earlier known as Britport, and derives its name from that of *Bredy*, in turn a borrowing from the name of the river Bride, south-east of the Brit. Although the Brit was recorded in 1577 as the *Bride* there in fact appears to be no geographical link between the names, since the two rivers were as distinct then, a mile apart from each other, as they are today. The earlier name of the Brit appears to have been the 'Wooth'.

Britannia, village, Lancashire, England.

The name presumably derives from an inn here. It dates from the late 19th century, since this is the highest point of the railway line from Rochdale which opened in 1881 and promoted development in this region.

Broadford, village (Isle of Skye), Highland, Scotland.

The name is an English translation of the Gaelic *an t-Ath Leathan*, 'the broad ford', with the ford being apparently that over the Broadford river or possibly that over the small Allt a' Mhuillin half a mile to the east. The English form of the name appears in the second *Statistical Account of Scotland* of 1840 but not the first, dated c.1790–1800, and there seem to be no earlier records of the name.

Broadland, administrative district, Norfolk, England.

The name was devised for the new district in 1974 from the (Norfolk) Broads, located here.

Broad Oak, village, East Sussex, England.

The name was recorded in 1567 as *Broadoke formerly Motts*, with the earlier name deriving from the Mott family, known to have lived here in the 16th century. The modern name seems to mean what it says, and refer to a large oak-tree here.

Broadstairs, town and resort, Kent, England.

The earliest recorded form of the name seems to be *Brodesteyr Lynch* 1434, this referring to a broad flight of steps on a ledge (*Lynch*, modern dialect *linch*) in the cliff-face cut a few years previously to lead down to the sea. Later forms of the name are recorded as *Brodestyr* 1479 and *Broadstayer* 1565.

Brookeborough, village, Fermanagh, Northern Ireland.

The name is that of the Brooke family whose seat is here at Colebrooke. The first Brooke of Colebrooke was Sir Henry Brooke of Donegal, knighted by

Elizabeth I in the 17th century and given the grant of the manor house of Colebrooke together with a considerable estate in Fermanagh. Among his descendants who have lived here have been Alan Francis Brooke, 1s Viscount Alanbrooke (1883–1963) and the former Prime Minister of Northern Ireland, Sir Basil Brooke, 1st Viscount Brookeborough (1888–1973).

Broughton Poggs, village, Oxfordshire, England.

The name was originally 'Broughton' (*Brotone* in the 'Domesday Book' of 1086). In 1401 the village was recorded as *Broughton Maulditz* for John Maudut who had held the manor here in 1285, and later the name became *Broughton Pouges* (so recorded in 1526) for Sir Robert Pugeys, who had held land in the nearby village of Broadwell in the 13th century. The latter's surname (the Poggs in the modern name) may be the same as the Poges in Stoke Poges, Buckinghamshire.

Broxburn, town, Lothian, Scotland.

The earliest available record of the name is apparently *Broxburne* 1638. This means 'badger's stream' and replaced an earlier name Easter Strathbrock, meaning 'eastern half of (the barony of) Strathbrock' (the latter name meaning 'badger's valley').

Broxtowe, administrative district, Nottinghamshire, England.

The name is that of an old hundred here, recorded in the 'Domesday Book' of 1086 as *Brochelestou*, 'Brocwulf's place'. In current use, the name is that of a district of Nottingham.

Brynmawr, town, Gwent, Wales.

The name, first recorded in 1832 as *Bryn-mawr*, means 'big hill', and was used for the industrial town that grew rapidly here in the early 19th century. An earlier name of the site was *Gwaunhelygen*, 'moorland of the willow tree', but 'when it became an important seat of the iron and coal trades, the old name

was changed for the new and more dignified one of Bryn-mawr' (Morgan, 1887).

Bucklers Hard, village, Hampshire, England.

The name derives from the family of Richard Buckler, recorded as living here in 1664, with 'Hard' meaning 'firm landing place', as The Hard in Portsmouth (Bucklers Hard has a quay on the river Beaulieu). On a plan of 1727 the location is named as *Montaguetown*, after John Montagu, 2nd Duke of Montagu (?1688–1749), who had drawn up a prospectus for developing the site in 1724. On a map of 1759 the name appears as *Montague Town vulgar Bucklesbury* (sic), but by 1789 had settled to its present form.

Bucks Green, village, West Sussex, England.

The name is that of the family of Richard Buck, a landowner here in 1725.

Budleigh Salterton, town and resort, Devon, England.

The earliest recorded form of the name is *Saltre* 1210, this referring to the 'salterns' or salt pans which were at the mouth of the river Otter here. Various forms of the name were subsequently recorded, among them *Salterne in the manor of Buddeleghe* 1405, *Saltern Haven* c.1550, and *Salterton* (without prefix or suffix) 1667, until the name settled to its present form, first recorded in 1765.

Bull Bay, bay and resort, Gwynedd, Wales.

The name may be a translation of the Welsh name *Pwll y Tarw*, 'pool of the bull', with a false association between Welsh *pwll* and English 'bull'. The place became established as an alternative resort to nearby Porth Llechog in the late 19th century, and the English name is first recorded in 1878.

Burdiehouse, district of Edinburgh, Lothian, Scotland.

The name is said to be a corruption of

'Bordeaux House', this being the name given to the place by French servants of Mary, Queen of Scots (1542–87), when they were quartered here while the court was at nearby Craigmillar Castle. Such an explanation may, however, be a semi-historical fiction.

Bure, river, Norfolk, England.

The name seems to be a back formation from either or both of the names of two villages on it: Briston (formerly known as Burston) and Burgh next Aylsham. The river name is first recorded in 1577.

MAKE

Burgess Hill, town, East Sussex, England.

The town developed after the opening of the Brighton railway in 1841. Earlier the name had been recorded in 1597 as *Burgess Hill al. Hachers*, this perhaps being a settlement name derived from the family of John Burgeys, known to have lived here in the 14th century.

Burncourt, village, Tipperary, Ireland.

The village was originally Clogheen (Irish *An Cloichin*, 'the little stone'), but became Burncourt after the building of Burncourt Castle here in 1641 by Sir Richard Everard of Ballyboy, Clogheen, presumably to avoid confusion with the latter Clogheen, five miles south-east of it. The Irish name of Burncourt is *An Chúirt Dóite*, 'the burnt court'.

Burnhaven, village and port (near Peterhead), Grampian, Scotland.

The village was built c.1840 by George Mudie near the mouth of the burn of Invernettie. Its name thus means 'port on the burn'. Compare the name of **Sandhaven**.

Burntisland, town, Fife, Scotland.

The name seems to have been first recorded in 1530, as *Bruntisland*, with this possibly meaning 'burnt island' and

referring to the burning of fishermen's huts on an island here east of the present harbour. But such an event is not documented, and the name may mean simply 'burnt land', i.e. land that has been cleared by burning.

Burnt Oak, district of Edgware, London, England.

The name originates directly from a field here, recorded in 1754 as being called Burnt Oak Close. This was near a notable oak-tree, perhaps one that had been struck by lightning. In popular tradition, the Romans are said to have had a site near here where they lit fires near a boundary mark. The name became promoted as that of a residential district when the Underground station of Burnt Oak opened in 1924.

Burtonport, village, Donegal, Ireland.

The village takes its name from William Burton, 4th Marquis Conyngham, who founded it shortly after 1785 as a countermove to the Duke of Rutland's port on **Rutland Island** nearby. Its Irish name is *Ailt an Chorráin*, 'ravine of the curve'.

Bute Town, village, Mid Glamorgan, Wales.

The name derives from that of John Crichton-Stuart, 2nd Marquis of Bute (d. 1848), who developed a number of industrial enterprises in Glamorgan, among them the docks at **Butetown**, Cardiff.

Butetown, district of Cardiff, South Glamorgan, Wales.

The name, as for **Bute Town**, is that of the 2nd Marquis of Bute, who began construction of extensive docks here in 1830, with Bute West Dock opened in 1839 and Bute East Dock in 1854. Also named after the Marquis in Cardiff are Bute Street and Bute Road railway station.

C

Caersalem Newydd, former village, West Glamorgan, Wales.

The name is that of an early 19th-century Baptist chapel, meaning 'New Jerusalem'. The former Welsh name of the village, now a district of Swansea, is *Tirdeunaw*, 'land (rented for) eighteen (pence)'. The chapel name is no longer current.

Cainscross, district of Stroud, Gloucestershire, England.

The name was recorded as *Cain's Cross* in 1776, and seems to derive from the surname Cain, common in Bristol in the 18th century. It is possible, however, that the name may not be as recent as it appears from this dating.

Cairnryan, town and port, Dumfries and Galloway, Scotland.

The name was changed from Macherie or Macharyskeeg (said to be Gaelic *machar a' sgitheig*, 'links with the hawthorn') to Cairnryan in *c.*1830 as the result of a recommendation by the Post Office. The new name presumably derives from nearby Cairn Point, also known as Cairn Ryan Point, which shelters it. The town is on Loch Ryan.

Caledon, village, Tyrone, Northern Ireland.

The site, previously named Kennard (Irish *Cionn Ard*, 'high head'), was developed as an English-style model village by the 1st Earl of Caledon in 1816. Lord Caledon changed its name as an extension of his home near here, Caledon House, built in 1779.

Caledonian Canal, canal, Highland, Scotland.

The canal runs right across Scotland from the North Sea (Moray Firth) in the north-east to the Atlantic (Loch Linnhe) in the south-west, passing through the highland lochs Ness, Oich, and Lochy and the mouth of Loch Eil. The canal was begun in 1805, opened as partially completed in 1822, and in full use in 1847. Its name commemorates the latinized name of Scotland, Caledonia, which particularly relates to the Highlands although used today in certain contexts to denote the whole of Scotland.

California, village (near Falkirk), Central, Scotland.

The name seems to derive from a farm or house so called. If a farm name, it could have originated as a 'match' for the nearby farm of Mexico, recorded on an 1817 map of Stirlingshire. A local explanation is that a traveller named his cottage 'California', and this was adopted for the mining village that arose here. On the other hand it is known that a number of English farms and hamlets were named California at the time of the Californian gold rush in 1849, and in some cases the name was given facetiously to a poor settlement or district, as were names like 'Paradise' and 'Mount Pleasant'.

Cam, river, Essex and Hertfordshire/Cambridgeshire, England.

The river has two sources: one in Essex, where it is called the Granta, the other in Hertfordshire, where it is the Rhee. The two rivers join at Grantchester, Cambridgeshire, to form the Cam, with the river then flowing through Cambridge to join the Ouse south of Ely. The name is a back formation from Cambridge, with its earlier forms recorded as *Chamus* 1571, *Camus* 1586 and *Cam* itself in 1610. The earlier name of the river was *Cante* 1372, this deriving from the pre-Norman name of Cambridge recorded in 1120, *Cantebruge*. The alternative modern name for the Cam is the Granta (as in Essex), and this reflects both the early form of Cambridge and the name of Grantchester.

Cam, river, Somerset, England.

The river rises near Yarlington and flows past Cadbury Castle into the Yeo at Yeovilton. The villages of West and Queen Camel are on the river, whose name is a back formation from their common 'Camel'. The river's former name was probably 'Gifl', related to Yeovil and Yeovilton.

Camberley, town, Surrey, England.

Development of the town began some time after 1809 with the aim of attracting retired military men from the Royal Military Academy, which had transferred to Sandhurst near here from Farnham, Surrey (senior department) and Great Marlow, Buckinghamshire (junior department) from 1812. The new district was originally called *Cambridge Town* in 1862 as a tribute to the newly-appointed Commander-in-Chief of the British Army, George William Frederick Charles, 2nd Duke of Cambridge (1819–1904), but in 1877, on the establishment of a railway station here, the name was changed to Camberley. This was a name invented by a Dr E. Atkinson with the aim of suggesting both the previous name and other local names ending in '-ley' such as Frimley, Surrey, and Eversley and Yatesley, Hampshire. The new name was also more to the liking of the Post Office, who had found some confusion between Cambridge Town and the city of Cambridge. There may also have been some wrong association with **Cambridge Town**, Essex (see next entry), or even **Camden Town** (see also).

Cambridge Town, district of Southend-on-Sea, Essex, England.

The district seems to have been named after the family of John Cambridge, recorded as living here in Elizabethan times (16th century).

Camden Town, district of north-west London, England.

The district was laid out on the property of Sir Charles Pratt, Earl of Camden (1714–94), in c.1791. Sir Charles took his title from Camden Place, Kent (in turn named after William Camden, the 16th-century antiquarian), and coincidentally came into possession of Kentish Town, Middlesex (now Greater London) through his marriage in 1749 to Elizabeth, daughter of Nicholas Jeffreys. Earl Camden had his seat at Bayham Abbey, East Sussex, and this name, together with others mentioned here, still features in Camden Town streets, among them Bayham Street, Jeffreys Street, Pratt Street, and Camden Street itself.

Campbelltown, village (near Nairn), Highland, Scotland.

The former name of the place, and still today the preferred Post Office name of the village, was *Ardersier*. Lands here were acquired from the bishops of Ross in 1574 by the Campbells of Cawdor, and in 1623 they obtained a charter to erect a burgh of barony called Campbelltown, with the name coming directly from John D. Campbell of Calder. The name still has some local usage, however, in spite of the possible confusion with **Campbeltown**, Strathclyde (see next entry).

Campbeltown, town and port, Strathclyde, Scotland.

The Register of the Great Seal records that on 15 October 1667 a grant was made to Archibald, Earl of Argyle, 'erecting the said town of Lochead into a free burgh of barony, to be called the burgh of Campbeltown'. Lochead, or Lochhead, translates the Gaelic name *Ceannloch*, 'head of the loch', the loch now being Campbeltown Loch.

Canning Town, district of east London, England.

The name is mentioned in White's *History of Essex* (1848) to refer to an area that expanded to include another new settlement called first *Plaistow New Town*, then *Hallsville*. The latter name derives from that of Richard Hall, managing director of the Eastern Counties Railway under construction here. The final origin of the name has yet to be proved. For an industrial settlement, it would seem logical to derive the name from that of Sir Samuel Canning, who was associated with the India Rubber, Gutta Percha and Telegraph Works Company whose original managing director was Colonel Silver (see **Silvertown**). However, the name could also have been taken from an engineer, George Canning, who was connected with the development of railways and docks here, or could even be commemorative, for the Prime Minister, George Canning (1770–1827), although this seems less likely.

Canons Park, district of Edgware, London, England.

The name, recorded as *Canons* in the early 16th century, originally applied to six acres of land here granted to the prior and canons of St. Bartholomew's, Smithfield, in 1331. On this site James Brydges, 1st Duke of Chandos (1673–1744), built a large mansion house named 'Canons', demolished in 1747, and the grounds of this were the Park. The name was established for the residential district with the opening of Canons Park Underground station in 1932.

Canons Town, village, Cornwall, England.

The name comes from the title of Canon John Rogers (1778–1856), who owned estates and mines here and elsewhere in Cornwall.

Capel Isaac, village, Dyfed, Wales.

In 1650, the Revd Stephen Hughes, vicar of the nearby village of Meidrim, left the Church of England and with his parishioners founded a Congregationalist chapel community. When persecuted, they at first took refuge in a cave, then built a chapel in 1672 on the land of one Isaac Thomas—hence the name, as local history records it.

Caradon, administrative district, Cornwall, England.

The name was transferred from a conspicuous natural feature here, Caradon Hill on Bodmin Moor, with Caradon being an old name meaning 'tor hill'. The name is also preserved in Caradon Town, a small village four miles northwest of Callington.

Carmel, village, Dyfed, Wales.

The name, here as elsewhere in Wales, derives from that of a Nonconformist chapel and is of biblical origin. In the Bible (I Kings 18: 19) Carmel is the name of the vine-covered mountain where Elijah gave offerings. As such, it was popularly understood to mean 'God's vineyard', a suitably fruitful and propitious name for a religious settlement.

Carrick, administrative district, Cornwall, England.

The name is an old one, taken from Carrick Roads in the estuary of the river Fal, with *carrag* the Cornish for 'rock'.

Carrington, village, Lincolnshire, England.

The village arose as a township created from the draining of Wildmore Fen and East and West Fens here in 1812, together with **Eastville**, **Frithville**, **Langriville**, **Midville**, **Thornton-le-Fen**, and **Westville**. The name is that of the principal landowner here at the time, Robert Smith, Lord Carrington (1752–1838), with his title apparently deriving from the already existing name of Carrington here, recorded in 1067 as *Coringatun*. Lord Carrington also gave his name to **Carrington**, Nottinghamshire (see below).

Carrington, village (near Dalkeith), Lothian, Scotland.

The name derives from that of William Ramsay, 2nd Baron Ramsay of Dalhousie and 1st Earl of Dalhousie (d. 1674), who obtained lands here in 1613 and was created Earl of Dalhousie and Lord Ramsay of Carrington in 1633 on the occasion of the coronation of Charles I in Scotland. The property was purchased from him subsequently by

Sir Archibald Primrose (1616–79), created Lord Carrington in 1661, whose successor, Archibald Primrose, 1st Earl of Rosebery (1661–1723) was created Viscount Primrose in 1703 and in turn gave his name of *Primrose* to the village. The name Primrose is still in local use, although it is not officially recognized by the Post Office.

Carrington, district of Nottingham, Nottinghamshire, England.

The name comes from that of the banker Robert Smith (1752–1838), created 1st Baron Carrington in 1796, who owned six acres of property here at the junction of Mansfield and Hucknall Roads. See also **Carrington**, Lincolnshire (above).

Carstairs Junction, village (near Carstairs), Strathclyde, Scotland.

The village is one mile from Carstairs and arose at an important railway junction where the lines divide to Edinburgh and Glasgow. The railway reached here in 1845 and the settlement was originally intended for its workers. The railway station is now named Carstairs.

Carterton, village, Oxfordshire, England.

The village was founded in 1901 by a William Carter with the aim of establishing a smallholding colony. This did not flourish, however, and the present prosperity of the village is due almost entirely to the nearby air base of Brize Norton.

Castle Bellingham, village, Louth, Ireland.

The village is named after Henry Bellingham of Castle Bellingham (burnt 1689 by the forces of James II), who had displaced the Gernon family here in the time of Cromwell earlier in the 17th century. The village was earlier known as *Garlandstown*, after the Gernons.

Castleblayney, town, Monaghan, Ireland.

The town is named after Sir Edward Blayney who built a castle here and was governor of the county of Monaghan in the reign of James I (i.e. in the early 17th century).

Castlecaulfeild, village, Tyrone, Northern Ireland.

The name derives from that of Sir Toby Caulfeild, who in 1610 was granted lands on the Ballydonnell estate by James I. In 1614 he began to build a mansion here in the Elizabethan style which came to be called Castle Caulfeild. The house was burnt down in 1641 by Patrick Donnelly and today remains in ruins. As 1st Baron Charlemont, Sir Toby Caulfeild founded **Charlemont**. Some sources prefer the spelling Caulfield for both the place-name and surname.

Castle Dawson, village, Londonderry, Northern Ireland.

The name is that of the proprietors, the Dawson family. On the plantation of Ulster, eight townlands of Mayola were granted by James I to Sir Thomas Philips, who in 1633 sold them to Thomas Dawson. The village seems to have adopted its present form and name in about 1710, when the proprietor was Joshua Dawson, chief secretary for Ireland. An alternative name for the village is *Dawson's Bridge*. Its Irish name is *An Seanmhullach*, 'the old hill-top'.

Castle Douglas, town, Dumfries and Galloway, Scotland.

The original name of the settlement, as a small hamlet, was Causewayend. In 1765, however, when marl was discovered in nearby Loch Carlingwark, the village grew and was renamed Carlingwark. In 1792 it became a burgh of barony and was further renamed after Sir William Douglas of Gelston, a merchant who had made his fortune in the trade with Virginia and who had bought the village in 1789. Sir William was the founder of **Newton Stewart**. The Castle of the name was that of the ancient castle of Threave, the seat of the Douglas family.

Castlegregory, village, Kerry, Ireland.

The name derives from a castle built here in the 16th century by one Gregory Hoare. It was destroyed under Cromwell and no trace remains today.

Castle Howard, village, North Yorkshire, England.

The name is that of a mansion built here in the 1730s for the Howard family to replace Henderskelfe Castle, burnt down in 1693. The house was designed by Vanbrugh at the request of Charles Howard, 3rd Earl of Carlisle (1674–1738). The name *Henderskelfe* is recorded as having survived in local use down to the 20th century.

Castlemartyr, village, Cork, Ireland.

The name was originally Ballymartyr, from the Irish *Baile na Martra*, 'town of the relics'. The castle here was captured and recaptured several times by English and Irish forces, ultimately passing to Roger Boyle, Lord Broghil (1621–79), later Earl of Orrery, to whom Charles II granted a charter in 1675 in which the castle, town, and lands of Ballymartyr should be a free borough under the designation of 'Borough and Town of Castlemartyr'. The Irish name, however, remains unchanged.

Castle Point, administrative district, Essex, England.

When the urban districts of Benfleet and Canvey Island were about to be reorganized as a single administrative unit of local government in 1974, there was felt to be no obvious name for the new district. A public contest was therefore arranged, and the outcome was the name Castle Point, deriving from two prominent features: Hadleigh *Castle*, today a ruined Norman fortress, and Canvey *Point*, a 'Site of Special Scientific Interest' (for the wildlife on its mud flats and marshland), on Canvey Island.

Castlerock, town and resort, Derry, Northern Ireland.

The name comes from two isolated rocks on the seashore here which resemble a castle. The town developed with the coming of the railway and has grown as a resort since 1949.

Castletown, village, Dorset, England.

The village is named after nearby Portland Castle, built by Henry VIII in the first half of the 16th century to defend the harbour. The name may have been consciously influenced by that of Castleton, also in Dorset, which was named after Sherborne Castle nearby, with its name recorded as *Castelton* in 1333 and *Casteltown* in 1535.

Castletownshend, village, Cork, Ireland.

The name derives from a fort built here in *c*.1650 by the English settler Colonel Richard Townshend. The castle is now in ruins.

Cattewater, stretch of river Plym estuary, Devon, England.

The name was recorded as *Cat Water* in 1576 and *Catwater* in 1577. It probably derives from the 'cat' that was here, this being a type of fortification common in the 16th century. The riverside area here, now a district of Plymouth, was known as Catdown.

Ceredigion, administrative district, Dyfed, Wales.

This is the old name of the county of Cardigan, now part of the district. It means 'territory of Ceredig', one of the sons of Cunedda, a 5th-century Welsh ruler. The Welsh name of the town Cardigan is *Aberteifi*, 'mouth of the (river) Teifi'.

Chalk Farm, district of Camden, London, England.

The name is first recorded in its present form in 1819, and is apparently a corruption of an earlier name 'Chalcot', recorded as *Chaldecote* 1253, *Caldecote* *c*.1400, *Chalcot* 1593, and *Chalk* 1746, and meaning 'cold cottages'. 'Chalcot' survives in Chalcot Road and Crescent here. There is no evidence that there was a farm here. The name became established for the district in 1907 with the opening of Chalk Farm Underground station.

Charlemont, village, Armagh, Northern Ireland.

The name comes from the fort, Charlemont, erected here in 1602 by Sir Toby Caulfeild (see **Castlecaulfeild**) under the command of Charles Blount, 8th Lord Mountjoy (1563–1606) in the English campaign against the Irish forces of Hugh O'Neill, Earl of Tyrone. The fort's name derives from Lord Mountjoy's Christian name and title. The Irish name of the village is *Achadh an Dá Chora*, 'field of two weirs'.

Charlestown, village and port, Cornwall, England.

The original name of the settlement was Porthmear ('great bay', for its location on St. Austell Bay). In 1790 it was recorded as having only nine inhabitants, and either this same year or the next Charles Rashleigh (d. 1825), a wealthy local industrialist, founded a pier and harbour here to exploit the china clay works in the neighbourhood. Shortly afterwards the village was renamed after him.

Charlestown, village, Derbyshire, England.

The name was first recorded in 1843 and may derive from that of Henry Charles Howard (1791–1856) who had become the 13th Duke of Norfolk here the previous year and who was Lord of the Manor of Glossop. This may have influenced the name of the nearby village of Charlesworth, which one would expect to have a modern name something like 'Chavelsworth', judging by its earlier forms (*Cheuenesuurde* 1086, *Chauelisworth* 1286, *Chavelesworth* 1290).

Charlestown, village and port (near Dunfermline), Fife, Scotland.

The village was founded in *c.*1765 by Charles Bruce, 5th Earl of Elgin (1732–1771), to house the workers in the

collieries and limeworks on his estate here, and was named after him.

Charlestown (of Aberlour), town, Grampian, Scotland.

The town was founded by Charles Grant of Wester Elchies in *c.*1812 as a model village. The settlement here before this was called Skirdustan ('Drostan's slice', after a local saint), and today the town is frequently known simply as Aberlour, its preferred official Post Office name.

Charlestown, village (near Ballater), Grampian, Scotland.

The present village was largely created by Sir Cunliffe Brooks of Glentanar, and dates from the 1880s. The original village, however, was founded by Charles Gordon, 1st Earl of Aboyne (d. 1681), who in 1670 obtained a charter authorizing him to erect a burgh of barony near Aboyne Castle. Today the village is usually known as Aboyne, after the latter, or at most Charlestown (or Charleston) of Aboyne, and its official Post Office name is also Aboyne. (For a similar name status, see the previous entry.)

Charleville see **Ráthluirc.**

Charlotteville, district of Guildford, Surrey, England.

The district was laid out in 1892 on behalf of a local doctor, Thomas Sells, who named it after his wife Charlotte. He also named a number of roads here after medical men, including Jenner, Harvey, Bright, and Addison.

Charminster, district of Bournemouth, Dorset, England.

The name was probably not that of a locality originally, but of a property, very likely a farm. It first came into use for the district in the early 19th century, and could have been a farm or other property name transferred from the village of Charminster, also in Dorset and under 30 miles away.

Charterville (Allotments), village, Oxfordshire, England.

The village was originally a land colony set up here in 1847 by the Chartists under Fergus O'Connor. Compare **O'Connorville**.

Chelmer, river, Essex, England.

The name is a back formation from Chelmsford, through which it flows. It was first so recorded in 1576, and owes its spelling to the early form of the name Chelmsford—*Chelmeresford* (derived from a personal name with the suffix 'ford').

Chelt, river, Gloucestershire, England.

The name is a back formation from Cheltenham, through which it flows. It was first recorded in this form in *c*.1540, with later spellings *Chilus* 1586, and *Chilt* 1712. In 1577 it was recorded as *Chiltenham water*, with the *i* also found in early forms of the name of Cheltenham (as *Chilteham* 1159).

Cherry Tree, village, Lancashire, England.

The village is probably named after an inn. An inn named The Cherry Tree at Livesey, south of Blackburn, was recorded near here in *c*.1850.

Chesil, village, Dorset, England.

The village, today largely absorbed by Fortuneswell, is named after **Chesil Beach**. Its various forms have been recorded as *Chesill* 1608, *Chessell* 1783, *Chissell* or *Chiswell* 1795, and an alternative *Cheselton* 1575, *village of Chisleton* 1650, *Chisell Tonne* 1710. Ekwall (1960) gives the only form as Chiselton, although contemporary sources do not record this version of the name as in use in the 20th century. Chesil is at the east end of **Chesil Beach**, on the Isle of Portland.

Chesil Beach (also **Chesil Bank**), shingle bank, Dorset, England.

The name was first recorded in *The Itinerary of John Leland in or about the years 1535–43*, as *the Chisil* or *Chisille bank*. In 1710 it appears on a map as *The Beach of Pebbles*, and in J. Hutchins, *The History and Antiquities of the County of Dorset* (1774) it is referred to as *The Beach or Chesil, called also Steepstone Beach*. The name derives from Old English *cisel*, 'shingle'. See also **Chesil** (previous entry).

Chess, river, Buckinghamshire/Hertfordshire, England.

The name of the river is a back formation from Chesham, near which it rises.

Chiswick Ayot, island, river Thames, London, England.

The name of the island was recorded in 1650 as *Ye Twigg Eight*, with the second word presumably being the ordinary word 'twig'. In 1819 the name was stated as *Chiswick Ait*, with this spelling in use in the 20th century. *Ait* or *Eyot* are both old words for 'islet'.

Christmas Common, village, Oxfordshire, England.

The name was recorded in 1617 as *Christmas Coppice*, and in the early 18th century as *a village called Christmas*, as well as *Christmas Green*. The origin of the name may lie in prominent holly bushes here. The *Oxford English Dictionary* gives 'Christmas-tree' as a dialect term for holly.

Christmas Pie, village, Surrey, England.

The most likely source of the name is that of a family named Christmas who lived here. One Thomas Christmas is known to have been living here in 1575, and a John Christmas in 1619. A farm here is recorded as being called *Christmas Pie Farm* in 1823. As is to be expected, various popular explanations of the name exist, including accounts of a standpipe resembling a huge pie built here for housewives drawing water from the brook in the early 18th century, and a Mr Christmas who was a local baker famed for his pies offered in a huge stone dish measuring five feet in circumference.

Chryston, village (near Muirhead), Strathclyde, Scotland.

The earliest recorded form of the name is *Crystoune* 1605, with the form *Carystoune* given in 1705. The first part of the name may be that of a person, although it is hard to see what this could be. Johnston (1934) says the name means 'Christ's village', but it is really unexplained.

Churchbridge, village, Staffordshire, England.

The earliest recorded form of the name is *a pasture called Chirchebrigge* 1538. Its origin is thus in a field name, for land by a bridge that belonged to a Lichfield guild. The bridge, carrying Watling Street, is one that the guild may have built or rebuilt. There has never been a church here.

Churchtown, village, Lancashire, England.

The village, near Garstang, contains the church of St. Helen, the old church of Garstang. The name was recorded first in 1786 as *Church Town*.

Churchtown, district of Southport, Lancashire, England.

This is the modern name of North Meols, referring to the church of St. Cuthbert that was built here on the site of an earlier church. The name was first recorded in about 1725 as *Church Town*.

Cinderhill, district of Nottingham, Nottinghamshire, England.

The name was first recorded, as *Cinder Hill*, in 1775. It is said to derive from lime kilns here that formerly stood near the Collier's Arms inn. These were used for burning lime.

Cissbury Ring, Iron Age hill fort, West Sussex, England.

The name was first recorded in *c.*1588 as *Sieberie hille*, and appears on a map of 1610 as *Sissabury*. Before this, the fort was known simply as Bury. Its more modern name appears to be the invention of a 16th-century antiquarian, who

saw a connection between the ancient earthworks and Cissa, the reputed first king of the Saxons in the 6th century. He lived much later than the construction of the fort, however, which is believed to date back to some time between 400 and 250 BC.

City Dulas, village, Gwynedd, Wales.

The name first appears in a letter dated 21 December 1755 from William Morris (d. 1763), poet and customs officer at Holyhead, Anglesey, to one of his brothers. Doubtless the name was simply a jocular one for the small hamlet near the brothers' Anglesey home. The hamlet stands on Dulas Bay.

Clapham Common, district of south London, England.

The name of the common was recorded in 1472 as the two areas of *Estheth* and *Westheth*. In 1718, however, the name appears as *Washingham Comon al. East Heath or West Heath . . . of late . . . called Clapham Common*. Clapham is itself an old name, recorded in the 'Domesday Book' of 1086. The name became established for the district with the opening of Clapham Common Underground station in 1900.

Clay Cross, town, Derbyshire, England.

The name derives from a family named Clay who lived here, for example John Clay in 1518. The nearby village of Clay Lane, already known as Clay Cross in the 19th century, officially merged with the larger settlement as Clay Cross in 1935.

Clementstown, village, Cavan, Ireland.

Lewis (1837) records that the village was named after its proprietor, a Colonel Clements.

Clifden, town, Galway, Ireland.

The town was named after Clifden Castle, built here in 1815 by John d'Arcy of Killtullargh when there was only one other house. The house name in turn derives from Clifden Bay, at the head of the northern arm of which (Ardbear

Bay) d'Arcy's residence is situated. The name seems to be a corruption of Irish *An Clochán*, 'the stepping stones' (across the river here) or perhaps 'the stone dwellings' located nearby.

Cliftonville, district of Margate, Kent, England.

The name seems to have originated in the Cliftonville Hotel, opened in 1868 in the new district being built east of Margate, with its own name perhaps suggested by one of the new streets here, Clifton Street. The district was planned as a select residential neighbourhood, unlike the main town of Margate with its 'trippery' associations, and doubtless the name Cliftonville was welcomed for its suitable 'class'. Cliftonville in its early days was known by other names, as is reflected in a paragraph by a local historian, Charles James Feret, in his weekly series 'Bygone Thanet' in the Margate newspaper *Keble's Gazette* dated 22 April 1916: 'It is, perhaps, not generally known that the great Sir Robert Peel was once a Margate landowner. He possessed a considerable amount of land at New Town, now dubbed Cliftonville . . . as far as West Northdown Corner. For a short time the district was locally termed Peel Town.' It is possible that the name was influenced by that of Clifton, Bristol, which had earlier developed as a fashionable residential district, and the suffix *-ville* may have been prompted by names of fashionable French watering places across the English Channel, such as Trouville, Deauville, and Granville. The Margate Cliftonville, too, came later than the Cliftonville at Brighton, and this may have been an additional suggestive factor for the name. In another of his articles, Feret records that Westbrook, a district of west Margate, was at one time known as Westonville under the influence of the 'new-fangled' Cliftonville.

Clwyd, county, Wales.

The name was used for the new administrative county designated in 1974 and comprising the former counties of Flint and Denbigh but excluding the Conway Valley east of the river (which was transferred to the new county of **Gwynedd**). The name was borrowed from the river Clwyd, which flows entirely in the new county, with the river's own name an old one meaning 'hurdle', 'wicket' (and related to the last word in the Irish name of Dublin, *Baile Átha Cliath*, 'town of the hurdle ford').

Clydebank, town, Strathclyde, Scotland.

The town, with its name of obvious origin ('bank of the river Clyde'), sprang from a shipyard opened up here in 1871 by two brothers from Govan, James and George Thomson. The town was a burgh of barony from 1886.

Coalisland, town, Tyrone, Northern Ireland.

The town originated in the formation of the Tyrone Canal, begun in 1744 to allow transportation of the coal mined locally to the river Blackwater. The town's Irish name has the same meaning: *Oileán an Ghuail*, 'island of coal'.

Coalville, town, Leicestershire, England.

The town, in a coal-mining district, was originally just a few scattered cottages known as Long Lane. William Stenson, who founded Whitwick Colliery near here in 1824, had a house built which he called Coalville House. The mining settlement grew up round it, promoted by the Leicester and Swannington railway built here in 1832, and by 1841 had officially adopted the name Coalville in place of the earlier Long Lane.

Coatbridge, town, Strathclyde, Scotland.

The earliest record of the name is *Coittis* in 1584, with later forms of the name found as *Coatburn* 1617 and *Cotts* 1676. The settlement developed in the 19th century as a mining town, and it seems that the bridge referred to in the name was not built until c.1800. The 'coats' are as in **Saltcoats**, i.e. 'cots' or 'cottages'.

Cober, river, Cornwall, England.

The river runs through Helston to the sea at Looe Pool. Its alternative name is the Looe or Loe. The original name is recorded in 1284 as *Coffar* and in 1576 as *Cohor*. In this latter year the name *Loo* is recorded for the river. In 1610, however, the form *Cober* is found. This could perhaps have been an artificial revival of the old name, with a misreading of the *h* of *Cohor* as a *b*.

Cóbh, town and port, Cork, Ireland.

The town developed as a port in the 17th century, with its name being an adaptation of the English 'cove' (as the name is pronounced today) and recorded in this spelling in 1659. From 1849 to 1922 it was renamed **Queenstown**.

Cockfosters, district of north London, England.

The name is first recorded in 1524, and may derive from a personal name or from a house on the edge of Enfield Chase here so called. If the latter, this could have been the home of the chief or 'cock' forester, with these two last words providing the name. The Underground station of Cockfosters, opened in 1933, reinforced the name for the residential district.

Colindale, district of north-west London, England.

The name comes from a family called Collin, on record here in 1574, with the earliest form of the name found in 1550 as *Collyndene* and meaning 'Collin's valley'. Colindale Underground station was opened in 1924 to establish the name more firmly for the residential district. At some stage the original 'dene' became 'dale'.

Colinsburgh, village (near Elie), Fife, Scotland.

The village was built in c.1705 and named after its founder, Colin Lindsay, 3rd Earl of Balcarres (?1654–1722). The earl built the village at the gates of his home, Balcarres House, for his disbanded soldiers after they had fought for the Stuart cause.

Colliers Wood, district of Merton, London, England.

The name means 'charcoal-burners' wood', with the place being either their source of material for making charcoal or their property. The name may well be earlier than the form *The Colliers Close* found in 1576. There is no longer a wood here. Colliers Wood Underground station opened in 1926 and the name became firmly established for the district.

Connah's Quay, town and port, Clwyd, Wales.

The town owes its origin to a new channel that was cut in the Dee estuary in 1737, with a stone pier subsequently built for vessels sailing to or from Chester. The name of the settlement was originally *New Quay*, so recorded on maps of 1771 and 1795. The name Connah's Quay appeared some time after this, with Connah said to be an Irish merchant who had business interests on Deeside. He has not been positively identified, but there are other transferred Irish names in the region to support the origin. Referring to such names here as Cork Row and Dublin Row, a writer in the *Liverpool Daily Post* of 24 May 1949 comments, 'They can be traced to the middle of the 18th cent. when an Irish Colliery Company employing Irish labour worked the mines in the neighbourhood . . .' (quoted by Davies, 1959).

Cooksbridge, village, East Sussex, England.

The lands here are recorded as belonging to the family of Thomas Coke of Hamsey in 1543, with the name first found, as *Cooke's Bridge*, in 1590.

Cookstown, town, Tyrone, Northern Ireland.

The town is named after its English

founder, Alan Cook, who laid out the straight High Street here, over a mile in length, in 1609. The town proper, however, began to arise much later, from c.1750. The Irish name is *An Chorr Chríochach*, 'the boundary hill'.

Coolestown, former name of Edenderry, town, Offaly, Ireland.

The name was in use for a time in the 16th century, and derives from the family of Cooley, granted a castle here in 1562. In 1599 the castle was defended by Sir George Cooley against insurgents in the Earl of Tyrone's rebellion. The name Edenderry, in use for the place before and since, is an Irish one meaning 'hill-brow of the oak grove'.

Cooteshill, town, Cavan, Ireland.

The name derives from that of the Cootes, English settlers, the first of whom was Sir Charles Coote who acquired lands here in the 17th century.

Copeland, administrative district, Cumbria, England.

The name is an old one meaning 'bought land', and first recorded in c.1125 as *Couplanda*. The new 1974 district, however, was probably named more directly after Copeland Forest here.

Coryton, industrial village, Essex, England.

The name derives from the oil refining and storage plant opened on the site in 1922 by Messrs Cory Brothers & Co., whose chairman was Sir Clifford Cory (d. 1941), second son of John Cory of **Glyn-Cory**. In 1946 Cory Brothers' Oil Division moved to Barry, South Glamorgan, and a new refinery was developed on the site by the Mobil Oil Company in 1950–3 (opened 1954). The location had previously been known for a time as *Kynochtown*, after Messrs Kynoch's munition works here, purchased by Cory Brothers when they first developed the site. Coryton is adjacent to **Thameshaven**, and immediately to the west of **Shellhaven**. It is a mere

coincidence that the nearest town is that of Corringham, two miles west of Coryton.

Coryton, suburb of Cardiff, South Glamorgan, Wales.

The origin of the name lies in that of James Herbert Cory, who built a house called Coryton here in c.1900. The Cardiff Railway Company established a passenger service here in c.1910 and named the halt Coryton, after the house. Cory planned a garden suburb here in c.1911 and advertised it widely, but it never materialized. James Cory was the son of John Cory, a Cardiff shipowner originally from Padstow, Cornwall. John Cory was not the Cardiff shipowner and coal owner of the same name who came from Bideford, Devon (see **Glyn-Cory**).

Cottenham Park, district of south-west London, England.

The name is that of the estate and residence of Charles Christopher Pepys, 1st Earl of Cottenham (1781–1851), Lord Chancellor, with the estate being built about 15 years after Cottenham's death.

Covesea, village (near Lossiemouth), Grampian, Scotland.

With a simply descriptive name ('cove by the sea'), the village was planned by Sir William Gordon Cumming (see **Cummingstown**) in c.1810.

Cowes, town and port, Isle of Wight, England.

The name seems to derive from a sandbank off the coast here, or two sandbanks, called 'The Cow'. This name was then apparently transferred to two forts on either side of the mouth of the river Medina. The name was first recorded in a mention of *Estcowe* and *Westcowe* made in a document of 1413. A century later, there is a record of *the Cowe, betwixt the Isle of Wight and England* (1512). There is a local legend that Cowes Castle, built in 1540 for local defence by Henry VIII, was named for its guns, which when fired sounded like the lowing of cows.

Coxside, district of Plymouth, Devon, England.

The name was first recorded as *Cocke syde* in 1591, and is possibly associated with the family of Richard Cokke of Plymouth, known to have been living here in 1468. 'Side' means 'end', 'quarter of the town'.

Craigavon, town, Antrim, Northern Ireland.

Craigavon was designated as a new town in 1965, designed to link the boroughs of Lurgan and Portadown, with construction beginning in 1966. It was named after the first Prime Minister of Northern Ireland, James Craig, Viscount Craigavon (1871–1940).

Crane, river, Dorset/Hampshire, England.

The river rises two miles north west of Cranborne, its old name, with Crane thus being a back formation.

Crane, river, London, England.

The river rises at Harrow as the Yeading Brook and runs into the Thames at Isleworth. On its 15-mile course it passes Cranford, now a district of Hounslow, and its modern name is a back formation of this. The former name of the river was the Bourne, so recorded (as *Borne*) in 1375.

Craven, administrative district, North Yorkshire, England.

The name is an old one for the district round the sources of the rivers Aire and Wharfe, first recorded in the 'Domesday Book' of 1086 as *Crave* and possibly meaning 'garlic'.

Craven Arms, town, Shropshire, England.

The origins of the town lie in the Craven Arms, an inn set up here in the early 19th century as a rival to a nearby coaching inn, the New Inn. The inn, first referred to in 1808 in the *Cambrian Travellers' Guide and Pocket Companion*, was so named after the Earls of Craven, who held the manor of Stokesay near here from *c.*1620. When the Craven Arms was built, the line of the road from Stokesay Bridge was altered, and the new road junction formed here was named after the inn. The junction was important enough, when the railway came here in 1851, for the station to be named after it (originally as Craven Arms and Stokesay), rather than after the more highly populated centre of Wistanstow. The present town developed from the railway and station as a railway junction.

Creetown, village (near Newton Stewart), Dumfries and Galloway, Scotland.

The original name of the village was *Ferrytown of Cree*, for its location on the estuary of the river Cree, with a ferry route across here. This was changed to Creetown in 1785 by a local laird, McCulloch of Barholm.

Crewton, district of Derby, Derbyshire, England.

The district was so named in 1895 after Sir Vauncey Crewe, a large landowner locally. For some time previously it had apparently been known as Newton.

Cross Fell, mountain, Pennines, Cumbria, England.

The original name of the mountain was 'Fiendsfell', recorded as *Fendesfeld* in 1340 and *Fendesfell* in 1479, this possibly referring to the 'fiendish' (i.e. evil) wind that came down from it. The name Cross Fell, first recorded in 1608, may have been an attempt to give a Christian association to a place whose name conjured up the devil to superstitious minds.

Cross Hands, village, Dyfed, Wales.

The name was that of a colliery here, in turn probably deriving its name from an inn.

Cross-in-hand, village, East Sussex, England.

The name is first recorded in 1547 as (via) cruce manus i.e. 'the way (leading) by the cross of the hand'. According to local legend, the locality was a meeting place for Crusaders on the way to Rye for embarkation to the Holy Land. As an inn sign, the cross is interpreted as a quartered standard.

Cross Inn see **Ammanford**.

Crosskeys, village, Gwent, Wales.

The name is almost certainly that of an inn here, with the crossed keys on the inn sign representing the insignia of the papacy.

Cross Town, district of Knutsford, Cheshire, England.

The name was recorded in 1598 as Crosse of Knottesford, the reference apparently being to an ancient stone cross that stood here. This could have been the market cross of the old town of Knutsford.

Crouch, river, Essex, England.

The river is first so named on a map of 1576. The name may be a back formation from some place on it containing 'Crouch', which would originally have meant 'cross' (Old English crūc), or else be an antiquarian's name based on the small village of Creeksea, located on it. On the other hand the lower reach of the river may have been called 'The Creek', with the modern name deriving from this. The old name of the river may have been either 'Bradewater' or 'Burnham Water'.

Crouch End, district of north London, England.

The name seems to mean 'district by a cross', this perhaps being a wayside crucifix here in the Middle Ages. The first recording of the name is Crouchend in 1465.

Crownhill, district of Plymouth, Devon, England.

The name was invented, perhaps arbitrarily, in c.1880 to replace an earlier name 'Nackershole', so recorded in 1765. This was presumably felt to have unpleasant associations.

Crowthorne, town, Berkshire, England.

The earliest recorded form of the name is on a map of 1607 (in the present spelling). Here it designated an isolated tree at a junction of the roads from Bracknell and Wokingham. The settlement arose here after the establishment of Wellington College in 1856 and Broadmoor Asylum in 1863.

Crystal Palace, district of south-east London, England.

The name began as that of a large building originally erected in Hyde Park for the Great Exhibition of 1851 and re-erected here in 1854. The building, destroyed by fire in 1936, received its name as a popular nickname.

Cubitt Town, district of east London, England.

The district was laid out in c.1843 by the builder and London lord mayor William Cubitt (1791–1863) and is named after him. William Cubitt had taken over the building enterprise of his brother, Thomas Cubitt (1788–1855), famous for his extensive work in **Belgravia** in the 1820s. Cubitt Town is on the **Isle of Dogs**.

Cuminestown, village (near Turriff), Grampian, Scotland.

The village was planned in c.1760 by Joseph Cumine of Auchry, an associate of Sir Archibald Grant (see **Archiestown**). The new model village was first advertised in the Aberdeen Journal on 7 December 1761.

Cummingstown, village (near Burghead), Grampian, Scotland.

The village was built for local fishermen in c.1810 by Sir William Gordon Cumming, owner of estates here. Its name was recorded in 1811 as Port Cumming, for its location on the coast. See also **Covesea**.

Cwmbrân, town, Gwent, Wales.
The name, recorded in 1707, means 'valley of the river Brân', and the present development arose as a result of the new town designated here in 1949, at the junction of Nant Brân ('raven brook') and Afon Lwyd ('grey river').

D

Dacorum, administrative district, Hertfordshire, England.

The name is that of an old hundred here, originally somewhat larger than the present district. The first record of the name is in the 'Domesday Book' of 1086, as *Danais*. Subsequent forms of the name are recorded as *Daneshundred* 1161 and *Daneys* 1255, with *Dacorum* first found in documents of 1196. This is a Latin form meaning 'of the Danes', and apparently designated a hundred that was on the English side of the Danelaw boundary, that is, a hundred in an Anglo-Saxon region having a Danish overlord.

Dawson's Bridge see **Castle Dawson**.

De Beauvoir Town, district of Hackney, east London, England.

The district centres on Balmes House, which prior to 1650 was in the possession of a Guernseyman, Richard de Beauvoir. In the 1830s the house was inherited by a curate named Benyon, a relative of the Tyssens, lords of the manor of Hackney. He let the former gardens and paddocks for building, and an estate was planned out by a local builder named Rhodes. The grandiose plan, however, was only partially realized.

Deben, river, Suffolk, England.

The name of the river is a back formation from the village of Debenham, located on it. The name is recorded as *Deue* in 1577 and *Deben* in 1735.

Delyn, administrative district, Clwyd, Wales.

The name was artificially blended from the names of two rivers in the district, the Dee and the Alyn. The latter is popularly known as the Alun, but this spelling of the name also occurs in that of the adjacent administrative district, Alyn and Deeside (also named after these two rivers). Fortuitously, *delyn* is the mutated form of the Welsh word for 'harp', *telyn*, the instrument being specially associated with Wales.

Dennystoun, district of Dumbarton, Strathclyde, Scotland.

The district was founded in 1853 and named after the shipbuilder, William Denny. The *Cutty Sark*, built by Denny, was launched here in 1869.

Derry, city and county, Northern Ireland.

The name is both ancient and modern, from Gaelic *doire*, 'oak grove'. The town was granted its first charter in 1604 and in 1613 the city was given to the City of London as part of the district to be colonized by English settlers. From this latter year its name became *Londonderry*, to mark the association between the two cities. In recent years, and especially with the growth of the Irish nationalist movement, the name has shown a marked tendency to revert to its original form, which is now acceptable to the Post Office. A similar usage applies to the county of Derry, which also added the name of the English capital in 1613.

Derwentside, administrative district, Durham, England.

The name derives from the river Derwent, which flows through the district from north to south, as it does through the county of Durham.

Devonport, district of Plymouth, Devon, England.

The original name of the district, which arose round the dockyard established here in 1689 by William III, was *Plymouth Dock*, or simply *Dock*. It was renamed Devonport when the docks were enlarged in 1824, and became a separate town in 1837. In 1914, however, Devonport and the district of

Stonehouse amalgamated with Plymouth to form the city of **Plymouth**.

Dinefwr, administrative district, Dyfed, Wales.

The name is an old one, and is that of the historic castle at Llandeilo, first mentioned in 876, when Rhodri the Great, a descendant of Cunedda (see **Ceredigion**), divided his kingdom among his three sons in order to preserve the unity of Wales against the Danes. According to tradition, one son was to hold the north, or **Gwynedd**, one the south, or Deheubarth, and one the centre of Wales, or **Powys**, which Cunedda had himself established in the 5th century. The name, alternatively spelt in its English form as Dynevor (although not for the administrative district), means 'fort of the yew tree'.

Dollis Hill, district of north-west London, England.

The name was first recorded in 1593 as *Daleson Hill*, but this may be a corrupt form, especially in view of later spellings: *Dalleys Hill* 1612, *Dallis* 1710, *Dollys* 1754, *Dolleys Hill* 1819. The precise origin of the name is uncertain; perhaps some family named Dawley or Dolley held a manor here, or possibly the name was that of a house. Dollis Hill Underground station opened in 1909 to give the name further status as that of the residential district here.

Dormanstown, village, Cleveland, England.

The place was planned as a company town in 1918 for the firm of Dorman Long, bridge constructors and steel manufacturers, but did not develop fully. The company's headquarters are at Middlesbrough, eight miles away.

Dorn, river, Oxfordshire, England.

The river name is a back formation from Dornford, a rural area north of Woodstock through which the river runs. An earlier name of Dornford may have been 'Melkford', in which case the river was perhaps called the 'Melk', for its milky

colour. The name Dornford probably means 'hidden ford'.

Douglastown, village (near Forfar), Tayside, Scotland.

The village was founded in c.1790 by William Douglas of Brigton. Douglas owned an extensive cornmill here and allowed his buildings to be used for trials of a new machine for spinning flax.

Dovecot, district of Liverpool, Merseyside, England.

The name was that of a house here in Pilch Lane named Dovecot House (recorded as *Dovecoat House* in 1710). The house was demolished in the 18th century.

Downham, district of Lewisham, London, England.

The district was laid out after World War I by the London County Council as an artisan settlement, similar to those at Dagenham and East Acton. The district was named after Lord Downham, chairman of the London County Council in 1919.

Drake's Island, island, Plymouth Sound, Devon, England.

The island is named after the famous Devon navigator Sir Francis Drake (?1540–96), who as a small boy had taken refuge here from the Catholics in 1548 with his father and other Protestants, and who had anchored the *Golden Hind* near here in 1580 on his return to Plymouth. The earlier name of the island had been 'St. Nicholas Island' (*isle of St. Nicholas* 1396, *Sent Nicholas Ilond* 1573) for the chapel of St. Nicholas on it, demolished in 1548. The name was changed to Drake's Island in c.1590. Drake is said to have declared that 'he who holds the island, holds the town'.

Draperstown, village, Derry, Northern Ireland.

The original name of the village, still in use locally, was The Cross (of Ballynascreen), Irish *Baile na Croise*, 'town of the cross'. This referred to an ancient church site here, the shrine of Columcille, otherwise St. Columba. In 1818 the name was changed to Draperstown to mark the commercial developments in the village made by the London Drapers' Company.

Dresden, district of Longton, Stoke on Trent, Staffordshire, England.

An area of approximately 30 acres of land was purchased here in *c.*1850 from Sir Thomas Boughey by the Longton Freehold Land Society. Since most members of the Society were engaged in the manufacture of china, the name Dresden was chosen for the new suburb, after the famous porcelain made near Dresden, Germany, from 1710. The name also matched that of nearby **Etruria**, as well as having the appropriate historical and cultural associations.

Droichead Nua, town, Kildare, Ireland.

The town is also known in English as *Newbridge*, translating its Irish name. It grew up from 1816 and took its name from a bridge over the river Liffey here.

Drybridge, village (near Buckie), Grampian, Scotland.

According to Killanin & Duignan (1967), the village was so named because its first bridge was built over a railway. The railway which ran through Drybridge was the Keith to Buckie branch of the Highland Railway, opened in 1884. The name Drybridge occurs in the census of 1851, however, and the village would therefore seem to be named after a road bridge here. This could have been a bridge, now demolished, which crossed the road here from Buckie to Parkhill. The bridge would have been 'dry' as distinct from a bridge over a river.

Dufftown, town, Grampian, Scotland.

The town was founded in 1817 by James Duff, 4th Earl of Fife (1776–1857) and was named after him. For a similar name, see **Macduff**.

Dukestown, village, Gwent, Wales.

The village is now an industrial locality on the edge of the South Wales coalfield, and takes its name from the mine, Duke's Pit, owned here in the first half of the 19th century by the Duke of Beaufort.

Dunkirk, village, Kent, England.

The name of the village was recorded in 1790 as *Dunkirk alias the ville of the Hundred of Westgate*. This was a commemorative transferred name from Dunkirk (Dunkerque), France, which for some years in the 17th century was an English possession. The name exists elsewhere in England, for example in Cheshire and Staffordshire.

Dutch River, lowest reach of river Don, Humberside, England.

This section of the river Don was made navigable in the 17th century by the Dutch-English engineer Sir Cornelius Vermuyden (?1595–?1683) and his Dutch settlers.

Dwyfor, administrative district, Gwynedd, Wales.

The name is that of the river that flows in the district, probably meaning 'great water'.

Dyfed, county, Wales.

The ancient name for this south-west part of Wales was adopted for the new county formed in 1974. The land of Dyfed, embracing the former counties of Carmarthenshire and Pembrokeshire, derived its name from the Demetae, a tribe inhabiting this part of Wales during the Roman occupation of Britain. The name was recorded by Ptolemy in the 2nd century AD as *Demetai*.

E

Eaglesfield, village (near Ecclefechan), Dumfries and Galloway, Scotland.

The village arose some time either at the end of the 18th century or beginning of the 19th, and is said to have been named after the Annandale laird who built it. Johnston (1934) says that the village is supposed to be called after 'a Mrs. Smith's Christian name', although it is hard to see what this could be.

Earlestown, district of Newton-le-Willows, Merseyside, England.

The district developed shortly after 1826 around railway wagonworks, and stands on the Liverpool to Manchester railway line. It is named after Sir Hardman Earle, director of the Liverpool and Manchester Railway Company at the time.

Earls Court, district of south-west London, England.

The name means 'earl's manor house'. After the Norman Conquest, a manor on this site was granted to the de Vere family, with the head of the family in the 12th century, Aubrey de Vere (d. 1194), created 1st Earl of Oxford in 1124. The Earls of Oxford were lords of the manor here until the 16th century, when the settlement of Earls Court grew up round it. The earliest record of the name is in 1593 as *Earles Court*. The house was finally demolished in 1886. The name became fully established for the district with the opening of Earls Court Underground station here in 1871 (reopened further to the west in 1878 after a fire). The site of the former manor house is today just east of the Underground station in the area bounded by Barkston Gardens in the north and Bramham Gardens in the south.

Earlsfield, district of south-west London, England.

The name implies 'land held by an earl', and traditionally this is said to have been either one of the Earls of Surrey (a Fitzalan or a Howard) or else a member of the Spencer family, an Earl Spencer. There is no evidence, however, that the land was held by any of these families, so the name may therefore derive simply from a family named Earl or Earle. One such family is recorded as having lived here in 1606. The railway station of Earlsfield, on the Waterloo to Wimbledon line, came from Earlsfield Road nearby, with this in turn named after Earlsfield House, a residence near Spencer Park. Compare **Earlswood**.

Earlswood, district of Reigate, Surrey, England.

The name was first recorded in 1447 as *Erleswode*, with later forms being *a comon called Erleswode* 1550 and *Earlswood Common* 1823. Down to the 19th century the area was a piece of waste land attached to Reigate. It was held by the first Earls of Surrey—hence the name.

East Anton, village, Hampshire, England.

The village was originally 'Easton', probably meaning 'east farmstead' (in this case, one east of Charlton). In 1582, however, the name is recorded as *Eston towne*, and in 1611 *Estentowne*, with this Middle English 'towne' added to produce the modern form of the name, which is additionally influenced in its spelling by the river **Anton**.

East End, area of east London, England.

The name is recorded by the *Oxford English Dictionary* no earlier than 1883. It must have been in use long before this, however, although originally without its later associations with poverty. Perhaps it arose as an area name by contrast with the fashionable **West End**.

East Guldeford, village, East Sussex, England.

In 1505 an entry was made in the *Register*

of Richard Fitzjames (d. 1522), bishop of London, that in this same year 'the church of New Guldeford, within the *marisco* [marsh] commonly called Guldeford Innyng, now reclaimed from the sea and made dry land by Richard Guldeford, Kt., having been newly built at his expense' was consecrated as the parish church by the bishop. The Guldeford family came from Guildford, Surrey, and gave their name to the place where they made their home. The village began to emerge in 1480, when Sir Richard Guldeford is recorded as having rented 1500 acres of the Romney marshes from the Abbey of Robertsbridge for a payment of twelve pence a year. The name itself is first found in 1508 as *Newguldford*, becoming *Est Guldeford* in 1517. The village, which is 'East' of Guildford, Surrey, is today still pronounced like this town, and is sometimes even spelt 'Guilford'.

Eastleigh, town, Hampshire, England.

The name is an old one, recorded in the 'Domesday Book' of 1086 (as *Estleie*), meaning 'east wood'. There was no town or even village here until some years after the railway reached Southampton in 1840, with the station here being called Bishopstoke. Eastleigh was still the name of an isolated farm in the locality when a village was built some ten years later to house the railway employees.

East Lothian, administrative district, Lothian, Scotland.

The original name of the district was the county of Haddingtonshire, recorded from the 12th century. In due course, however, Haddingtonshire, the official county name, became popularly known as East Lothian, just as Edinburghshire became **Midlothian** and Linlithgowshire **West Lothian**. These three names, together with Edinburgh City, were adopted in 1975 for the four new administrative districts that comprised the region of Lothian, itself an old name for the whole area between the Firth of Forth and the river Tweed.

Eastville, village, Lincolnshire, England.

The name originated as that of a township formed here in 1812 with six others (**Carrington**, **Frithville**, **Langriville**, **Midville**, **Thornton-le-Fen**, and **Westville**) when the Fenlands were drained. Eastville was reclaimed from the East Fen.

Ebbw Vale, town, Gwent, Wales.

The name means 'valley of the river Ebwy'. Industrial development began here in 1786, and when ironworks were built here in the 19th century the original name of the place was Pen-y-cae ('top of the field'), after a farm on the site. This was soon changed, however, to the half-Welsh, half-English name of Ebbw Vale, after the river that rises north of the town. The current Welsh name of the town is Glynebwy, with the same meaning.

Ebenezer, village (near Caernarfon), Gwynedd, Wales.

The better-known name of the village, and so marked on most modern maps, is Deiniolen (apparently a shortened form of *Llanddeiniolen*, 'church of Deiniolen', traditionally said to be a son of Deiniol, founder of Bangor). Ebenezer is a chapel name originating some time in the early 19th century, and as a biblical name was popularly understood to mean 'stone of help'.

Eden, river, Surrey/Kent, England.

The river name is a back formation of Edenbridge, Kent, through which it runs on its way east into the Medway. The name is first recorded, in this spelling, in 1577. An earlier name of the river has been recorded as *Haggicorte Ryver* (1559), from the name of Hedgecourt (Pond), Surrey, and a later name of *Felbridge Water* (1749), from Felbridge, Surrey, has also been noted.

Edenderry see **Cooleston**.

Edgeworthstown, village, Longford, Ireland.

The village is named after the English

family of Edgeworth, who settled here in c.1582 and came to make their home here at Edgeworthstown House. This was largely the work of Richard Lovell Edgeworth (1744–1817), father of the novelist Maria Edgeworth (1767–1849), who herself lived at the house for some years. The village is also known as Mostrim, an anglicized form of the Irish name, *Meathas Troim*, 'frontier of the elder tree'.

Eel Pie Island, island, river Thames, London, England.

The original name of the island seems to have been *The Parish Ayte* (1608), i.e. 'the islet of the parish'. Its present name suggests that the island was used by picnickers, who consumed eel pies there.

Egerton, village, Greater Manchester, England.

The name probably derives from the Egerton family who held property here. Egerton was the family name of the earls and dukes of Bridgewater (see **Bridgewater Canal**) and also of the earls of Ellesmere and their descendants.

Eglinton, village, Derry, Northern Ireland.

The original name of the village was Muff (Irish *An Mhá*, 'the plain'), but this was changed in 1858, probably to avoid confusion with the nearby larger Muff in Donegal, four miles to the west over Lough Foyle. The new name of the village was Eglinton, after the Lord Lieutenant of Ireland at the time, Archibald William Montgomerie (1812–61), 13th Earl of Eglinton. See also **Winton**.
MAKE

Egremont, district of Wallasey, Merseyside, England.

The original name of the settlement here was Wellington. The present district was founded by a Captain J. Askew, a land investor, who in 1823 built a house here for himself and called it 'Egremont' after his birthplace in Cumberland.

Ellesmere Port, town, Cheshire, England.

The town grew up at the point where the Ellesmere Canal joined the estuary of the river Mersey, with the canal itself named after the Shropshire town of Ellesmere, from which it ran to the Mersey as an arm of the Shropshire Union Canal. The plan to cut the canal was made at Ellesmere in 1791, and the new port is recorded as having been referred to as Ellesmere Port as early as 1796. The preferred name, however, was the local name of Whitby Wharf or Whitby Locks, and the railway station here was named Whitby Locks when it opened in 1863. For a similar name, see **Stourport**.

Elliotstown see **New Tredegar**.

Ellistown, village, Leicestershire, England.

The coal-mining village was named after a colliery owned by Joseph Joel Ellis here on the newly acquired and newly named Ellistown estate. The inscription on the silver spade with which Ellis' wife cut the first turf on the site read, 'The first sod turned on the Ellistown new colliery estate, by Mrs. J. J. Ellis, July 2, 1873' (*The Colliery Guardian*, 11 July 1873). The colliery opened in 1876.

Elmbridge, administrative district, Surrey, England.

The name is that of a hundred here in Saxon times, meaning 'Emel bridge', with *Emel* a former name of the river **Mole** which flows through the district. The bridge referred to may have been over the Mole between Esher and Hersham, where the Albany Bridge is today. The borough of Elmbridge, whose territory almost coincides with that of the old hundred, was formed in 1972.

Ems, river, Hampshire, England.

The river name is a back formation of that of Emsworth, through which it flows on its way to Chichester Harbour.

The name was first recorded in 1577 as *Emill*, this spelling deriving from the early forms of Emsworth (*Emelesworth* in 1286).

Enham Alamein, village, Hampshire, England.

A centre for disabled servicemen had been set up in the village, then called Knight's Enham, after World War I. In 1945, at the end of World War II, the Egyptians opened a fund to extend the special facilities offered by the village, in gratitude for the British victory over the Germans at El Alamein in 1942, and the name was changed to Enham Alamein, in commemoration of this victory.

Erewash, administrative district, Derbyshire, England.

The name is that of the river Erewash and the Erewash Canal, which runs besides it. The river forms the eastern boundary between Derbyshire and Nottinghamshire here.

Etruria, district of Stoke-on-Trent, Staffordshire, England.

The district grew up round a pottery works established by Josiah Wedgwood on the Ridge House Estate in 1769, with Wedgwood building a house here called Etruria Hall. The settlement was intended to accommodate the workers at his pottery, and the name was chosen in allusion to Etrurian, i.e. Etruscan, pottery. The precise motivation for the name may have not been so honest as it appears. *Cassell* (1893) states that the name was due to the 'erroneous notion that the vases in Sir William Hamilton's collection, which Wedgwood copied, had been found in Etruria' (the reference is to the collection of Greek vases made by Hamilton in the 18th century), and a more recent writer expresses the view that the name may have been chosen 'to encourage people to think they had really ancient pieces' (Bill Morland, *Portrait of the Potteries*, 1978). Original Etrurian (or Etruscan) pottery was represented by the elegant vases, friezes and life-size sculptures found in Italy in the 8th century BC.

Evanton, village (near Dingwall), Highland, Scotland.

The village was founded in *c.*1810 by Evan Fraser of Balconie to replace the older village on the west side of the river Allt Graat.

Evenlode, river, Gloucestershire/Oxfordshire, England.

The name is a back formation of the village of Evenlode, Gloucestershire, past which the river flows on its way to the Thames. Early forms of the name are recorded as *Euenlode* 1577, *Enload* 1612. The former name of the river was the 'Bladon', preserved in the names of two villages on it: Bledington, Gloucestershire, and Bladon, Oxfordshire.

Eyrecourt, village, Galway, Ireland.

The name is that of the Eyre family, who had an estate here in the 17th century. Their seats were Eyre Castle and Eyreville, both in the locality.

F

Fairfield, district of Droylesden, Greater Manchester, England.

The district arose as a model village established by the Moravians here in 1783. The name appears to be an arbitrarily favourable one, although possibly it originated as the name of an already existing house. Compare the next entry.

Fairfield, suburb of Warrington, Cheshire, England.

The name of the district was taken from Fairfield House, built here in the mid-18th century and itself named for its location amid fields.

Fairhaven, district of Lytham St. Anne's, Lancashire, England.

The residential district arose in the early 20th century with a generally agreeable name for an area of this popular resort on the estuary of the river Ribble.

Fairlands, district of Guildford, Surrey, England.

The district arose as a new housing estate after World War II, with its semi-arbitrary name inspired by former farmland here.

Fairmile, village, Surrey, England.

The name is first recorded in 1749 as *Fair Mile*, with this perhaps referring to a dry straight stretch of the Portsmouth road here (now the A3). Compare the Devon village of Fairmile, similarly located on the main road (now the A30) to Exeter.

Fair Oak, suburb of Eastleigh, Hampshire, England.

The name is first recorded in 1596 as *Fereoke in decenn' de Stok'* (i.e. 'Fair Oak in the tithing of Stoke'). The reference must have been to a handsome oak-tree here.

Fairseat, village, Kent, England.

The name is recorded in 1782 as *Fairseat* or *Farsee Seat*, and must refer to the fine view from this point. The village is on the North Downs.

Fauldhouse, village (near Whitburn), Lothian, Scotland.

The name means 'house on fallow land', and was first recorded as *Fawlhous* in 1523. From the 16th century the first element of the name became confused with Scots *fauld*, 'fold'.

Fife-Keith, district of Keith, Grampian, Scotland.

The district was originally laid out as a planned village in 1817 by James Duff, 4th Earl of Fife (1776–1857), who also founded **Newmill**.

Finnieston, district of Glasgow, Strathclyde, Scotland.

The district was named in 1768 after the Revd John Finnie, who was the tutor of the proprietor here, Matthew Orr. (In Scots law *tutor* is the term for the guardian of the person and estate of a boy under fourteen or a girl under twelve.)

Finsbury Park, district of north London, England.

The name dates from 1857 and originally referred to an open area on the site of the former Hornsey Wood here. This had been officially set aside for the use of the inhabitants of the old parliamentary borough of Finsbury, which once extended to here. Finsbury Park opened in 1869, and the Underground station so named first operated in 1904, thus establishing the district. Today the Park itself is in the borough of **Haringey**.

Finstown, village (Mainland), Orkney, Scotland.

According to local legend, the name derives from David Phin, an Irish drummer from Limerick who came here in 1811 with the 19th Royal Veteran Battalion and built an inn, round which the village grew up.

Fitzwilliam, village, West Yorkshire, England.

The mining village derives its name from one of the sons of Charles William Wentworth Fitzwilliam, 3rd Earl Fitzwilliam (1786–1857), who owned collieries at Elsecar and Parkgate in 1833. The son was landowner here in 1876 when the Hemsworth Colliery was opened, and in 1890 the colliery company changed its name to the Fitzwilliam Hemsworth Colliery Company. The village of Fitzwilliam itself, 'formed for the accommodation of the miners working at Hemsworth colliery' (*Kelly's West Riding Directory*, 1912), seems to have arisen some time soon after 1900.

Five Ashes, village, East Sussex, England.

The name of the village was recorded in 1512 in its present form, and Glover (1975) reports that the village green still has five ash trees on it.

Fivemiletown, village, Tyrone, Northern Ireland.

The village was founded in 1619 by Sir William Stewart, to whom James I had granted lands called Ballynacoole ('town of the recess', i.e. a remote settlement). The name is popularly believed to indicate the town's equidistant location five miles from Clabby, Clogher, and Colebrooke (with some latitude for the 'five'). For some time Fivemiletown was known as *Mount Stewart*, after its founder.

Five Oaks, village, West Sussex, England.

The name is so recorded on a map of 1740, and probably refers to a notable group of oak-trees here. Compare the name of **Five Ashes**.

Fleetwood, town and port, Lancashire, England.

The name was given in 1836 to the northern part of the estate here of the town's founder, Sir Peter Hesketh Fleetwood (1801–66), who 'perceiving the facilities afforded by the river [Wyre], for the construction of a capacious harbour and docks, and the great advantages the locality derived from its proximity to the manufacturing districts, projected the erection of a town, the plan of which was drawn by Decimus Burton, Esq.' (Lewis, 1849). Sir Peter's home was at Rossall Hall, now Rossall School (founded 1844).

Fleur-de-Lis, village, Gwent, Wales.

The village takes its name from that of a brewery at the lower end of the valley here. The village's Welsh name is *Trelyn*, interpreted as 'place by a lake' and according to Morgan (1887) is a name given 'as a mark of respect to the Welsh idiosyncracies of Lady Llanover'. Lady Llanover was born Augusta Waddington, the daughter of Benjamin Waddington of Llanover. In 1823 she married Sir Benjamin Hall (1802–67), who was created Baron Llanover in 1859. Both husband and wife were assiduous promoters of the Welsh language.

Flushing, village, Cornwall, England.

Local legend maintains that the village was founded some time in the mid-17th century by Dutch families, who named it after their famous port. Lewis (1849), however, states that the village 'owes its origin and prosperity to Robert Cotton Trefusis, Esq., who, in the early part of the last [i.e. 18th] century, constructed quays, erected numerous buildings, and endeavoured, though without success, to establish a station for the government packets'. There are in fact two villages named Flushing in Cornwall, within a few miles of each other. The one under consideration here, and the larger of the two, is located on the north bank of the estuary of the river Penryn, north of Falmouth, to which it is connected by ferry. The other, smaller Flushing is south of this, on the south side of Gillan Harbour east of Helston.

Forest Gate, district of east London, England.

The name seems to date back to the 18th century, and to refer to a gate leading into Epping Forest here. The gate was in Woodgrange Road, and served mainly to prevent cattle from straying from the forest onto the main road.

Forest Heath, administrative district, Suffolk.

The name refers to the predominant area of forest-covered heathland here. Compare the name of **Breckland**, which adjoins it to the north.

Forest Hill, district of south-east London, England.

The district, which is partly in Lewisham, is first recorded in 1797 and takes its name from a wood here known as Forest Wood (so recorded as early as 1520 and as late as 1801). This was part of the great forest of Northwood (see **Norwood**).

Forest Row, village, East Sussex, England.

The name is first recorded as *Forstrowe* in 1467, although the modern parish of Forest Row was formed from East Grinstead in 1894. The name probably refers to a former row of houses or cottages in Ashdown Forest here.

Fort Augustus, village (south end of Loch Ness), Highland, Scotland.

The original fort here was the one built to check the Highlanders after the 1715 rising. The fort was enlarged by General George Wade in 1730, and subsequently took its name from the military commander William Augustus, Duke of Cumberland (1721–65), who formed a camp here after the suppression of the Jacobite rising of 1745 ('the '45') and who defeated the Young Pretender, Charles Edward Stuart ('Bonnie Prince Charlie') at the Battle of Culloden the following year. The Gaelic name of the village is *Cil Chumein*, 'church of Cummen (or Cumin)' (a saint who was an abbot of Iona in the 7th century). See also **Fort George**.

Fort George, military depot (near Nairn), Highland, Scotland.

The fort was built here by the architect Robert Adam in the fifteen years following 1748 to replace the earlier fort built by General Wade in 1726 on Castle Hill in Inverness. This earlier castle, also named Fort George (after King George II, then the reigning monarch), had been blown up by the Jacobites in 1746. See also **Fort Augustus**.

Fortuneswell, village, Dorset, England.

The name is first recorded in 1608, as *Fortune Well*, when the place was simply a cattle fold with a well or spring. Doubtless the name denoted a 'lucky' well, or one in which fortunes could be told.

Fort William, town, Highland, Scotland.

The fort here had its origins in the earth-and-wattle defence built by General George Monck, commander-in-chief in Scotland, in 1655. When this was rebuilt in stone as a garrison in 1690, it was named Fort William in honour of the reigning monarch, William III, by the Scottish general, Hugh Mackay. Earlier names of the fort had been *Gordonsburgh*, after the Duke of Gordon, on whose property it had originally been built, and *Maryburgh*, after Queen Mary, wife of William III.

Four Elms, village, Kent, England.

The name appears as that of a field called *Four Elms Green* on the one-inch Ordnance Survey map of 1840, and doubtless this had been so known for several years previously. The locality had begun to develop as a village by the end of the 19th century.

Four Marks, village, Hampshire, England.

The name, recorded as *Fowrem'kes* in 1548, refers to the boundaries of four parishes that met here: those of Medstead, Ropley, Chawton, and Faringdon.

Four Mile Bridge, village, Gwynedd, Wales.

The village is on Holy Island, off Anglesey, and the distance of four miles is that from Holyhead. The bridge here, first mentioned by this name in the early 19th century, had been the only one linking Holy Island to Anglesey before the building of the Stanley Embankment at **Valley**, just north of this point. The Welsh name of the village is *Pontrhypont*, 'bridge of the ford-bridge'. Presumably the first *pont* ('bridge') was added to the original name, so that the whole means 'Bridgeford Bridge'.

Fraserburgh, town and port, Grampian, Scotland.

The original name of the town was Faithlie, recorded as having been raised to a free burgh of barony in a charter dated 2 November 1546. In 1592 the town is documented as *burgum et portum de Fraser* ('town and port of Fraser'), and is first recorded in its present form in 1601. The new name was that of Sir Alexander Fraser of Phillorth (?1537–1623), who had built a new harbour here and founded what was virtually a new town. The Frasers had long had connections in the district, however, and Sir William Fraser is recorded as having bought land here in 1504. The nickname of Fraserburgh, used over a wide area of north-east Scotland, is 'The Broch', referring to the *broch* or castle (today a lighthouse) built at the end of the 16th century and forming the pivot around which the new town arose.

Freemantle, former district of Boscombe, Bournemouth, Dorset, England.

The name was in use for some thirty years for that part of Boscombe (itself today a seaside district of **Bournemouth**) that lay between Wolverton Road and Pokesdown railway station (still open). A sub post office here was so named from *c.*1890 to 1917 when its name was changed to Boscombe East.

According to David S. Young in *The Story of Bournemouth* (1957) the name was possibly transferred here from the old manor and estate of Freemantle between Kingsclere and Basingstoke, both in Hampshire, and it is significant that two streets in Boscombe are named after two villages in that area, Hannington and Wolverton. On the other hand, there is a Freemantle in Southampton (the next coastal city to Bournemouth), where it is the name of a district west of the city centre, and the transfer could have been made from here. Young mentions that the name is perpetuated in Freemantle Hall, Somerset Road, Boscombe, and the district name is still listed in Kelly's Directory as late as 1939.

Freshfield, district of Formby, Merseyside, England.

The district was originally a village on a site called Church Mere. This was buried under sand for approximately a hundred years from the mid-18th century, after which the land was said to have been cultivated by a Mr Fresh who laid top-soil over the sand. When this was used for further building, the new village was named after him.

Friday Street, village, Surrey, England.

The name is found on a map of 1765, and could derive from a family here called Friday. However, there are a number of places called Friday Street, which name was given to a plot of barren land or a poor settlement because of the unlucky associations of Friday (the day of the Crucifixion). It is thus likely that this particular Friday Street originated in such a way.

Frimley Green, village, Surrey, England.

The village is one mile south of Frimley, and when developed in the mid-18th century was originally called South End, Frimley. To avoid ambiguity and to indicate the separate identity of the place, however, the Post Office changed this name to Frimley Green in *c.*1868.

Friockheim, village (near Arbroath), Tayside, Scotland.

The original name of the village was 'Friock', recorded in 1613 as *Freok* and 1663 as *Friock*. This is almost certainly from the Gaelic *fraoch*, 'heather'. The name changed to its present form in 1824, as described by a handbill in the Angus Folk Museum at Glamis:

'FRIOCKHEIM
The Spinning Mill and Village of Friock, of which Mr. GARDYNE of Middleton is the Superior, and Mr. JOHN ANDSON, Proprietor holding in Feu, hitherto called "*Friock Feus*", from this date henceforward is to be named "FRIOCKHEIM", and of which change of designation, this, on the parts of Mr. Gardyne and Mr. Andson, is notice unto all whom it may concern.

FRIOCKHEIM, 22nd May, 1824.'

The suffix *heim* is the German word for 'home', 'abode', this serving as a commemorative element to John Andson, who had long lived in Germany. The name is currently pronounced 'Frickum' or 'Frickim'.

Frithville, village, Lincolnshire, England.

The village arose together with six others (**Carrington**, **Eastville**, **Langriville**, **Midville**, **Thornton-le-Fen**, and **Westville**) as a township created by act of parliament in 1812, when an extensive area of Wildmore Fen and the East and West Fens was drained. 'Frith' means 'woodland' (Old English *fyrhthe*), but there was certainly no wood here when the drainage was carried out. The name seems to have been given to refer to the remnants of a submerged forest found here when the new drains were being dug, with -*ville* added to match the names of the other townships (and to mean 'township' itself, in the fashion of the 19th century).

Frognal, district of north-west London, England.

The name is first recorded in 1795, as *Frognall*. Its origin is uncertain. It may have come from a family so named who lived here: Thomas and Alexander Frogenhall are known to have held the manor here in 1542, and their family may have originally come from Frognall in Kent. Many streets here bear the name, notably Frognal Close, Court, Gardens, Lane, Rise, and Way, as well as the road of Frognal itself, which runs from just east of Finchley Road & Frognal railway station (on the Richmond to Broad Street line) to a point north-west of Hampstead Underground station.

Fulneck, suburb of Bradford, West Yorkshire, England.

The present district arose as a model village established here by a Moravian community in 1744. The village was originally called Lamb's Hill, then Grace Hall, then finally Fulneck, after what Goodall (1913) describes as one of the 'principal seats of the community', in other words Fulneck in Silesia, the Moravians' original home. But also an estate here is recorded as being named *Fall Neck*, meaning 'neck of land by a clearing', in 1592, and conceivably the Silesian place-name assimilated to this. The resemblance between the two names is so remarkable as to make one suspicious of this explanation, however.

Furnace, village (near Machynlleth), Dyfed, Wales.

The site was occupied by silver-smelting furnaces in the 17th century. In 1755 an iron ore blast furnace was established here by Jonathan Kendall, of Staffordshire, and the village grew up round it. The furnace closed, however, in *c*.1813, with a consequent decline in the size of the village.

Furnace, village (near Inveraray), Strathclyde, Scotland.

The village was named after the local iron-smelting works in 1754. Today, however, it is best known for the granite quarries here, established in 1841.

Furner's Green, village, East Sussex, England.

The village, and originally the 'green', are named after Thomas Furnar, recorded as living here in 1618.

Fylde, administrative district, Lancashire, England.

The name was adopted from an existing district name, The Fylde ('the plain'). It also exists in the name of Poulton-le-Fylde, now in the administrative district (and so named to distinguish it from Poulton in Merseyside, now a district of Wallasey).

G

Gade, river, Hertfordshire, England.

The river rises near Little Gaddesden, and flows past Great Gaddesden and Gadebridge into the Colne east of Rickmansworth. Its name is a back formation from Gaddesden, which in the 'Domesday Book' of 1086 was *Gatesdene*. The present name of the river is first recorded as *Gadus* in 1577, in *The Description of Britaine*, by the antiquarian and topographer William Harrison, and it is possible that he may have invented the name. Before this, the river was recorded in the 15th century as *aqua de Gateshede*, and as *Gatesden water* c.1540.

Gardenstown, village (near Macduff), Grampian, Scotland.

The village was founded in 1720 by a local laird, Alexander Garden of Troup (1685–1756), from whom it takes its name. The agreeable associations of the name are thus fortuitous.

Garlieston, village (near Wigtown), Dumfries and Galloway, Scotland.

The village was founded in c.1760 by the 7th Earl of Galloway, when Lord Garlies.

Gasstown, village (near Dumfries), Dumfries and Galloway, Scotland.

The village was founded in c.1810 by one Joseph Gass.

Gatehouse of Fleet, town, Dumfries and Galloway, Scotland.

On a map of 1759 the site appears as just a single house on a road. This was the 'gate house', with 'gate' meaning 'road', as it often does in place-names of Scotland and the north of England (for example Harrogate, North Yorkshire). The present town was founded in c.1790 and stands on the mouth of the river named the Water of Fleet.

Gavinton, village (near Duns), Borders, Scotland.

The village was so named in c.1760 by its proprietor, David Gavin, 'who, finding the ancient village of Langton an impediment to the extensive improvements he was making on his estate, induced the inhabitants [. . .] to abandon their old residences, and build themselves houses on the site of the present village' (Lewis, 1846).

Gedling, administrative district, Nottinghamshire, England.

As with **Broxtowe**, the name is that of an old hundred here, recorded in the 'Domesday Book' of 1086 as *Ghellinge*, perhaps meaning 'Gedel's people'. The name (also as with Broxtowe) is in current use as that of a district, here in Carlton, east of Nottingham.

Georgeham, village, Devon, England.

The village was originally just 'Ham' (*Hama* in the 'Domesday Book' of 1086), with the earliest recorded mention of St. George, to whom the church was dedicated, found in 1471, when the name was noted as *Ham Sancti Georgi*. The name was first found in its present form in 1535. 'Ham' is still the important element of the name, which is stressed on its second syllable even today.

Georgeton, village, Gwent, Wales.

The building of the village began in 1856, and it is named after some local prominent man called George, perhaps one of George Homfray, William George, or Watkin George, all of whom lived in the neighbourhood.

Gerrards Cross, town, Buckinghamshire, England.

The earliest record of the name seems to be *Gerards Cross* in 1692. The origin may well lie in a family here named Gerrard, although this has not been conclusively established.

Gipsy Hill, district of south-east London, England.

The name refers to the gypsies who frequented the district in the 18th and early 19th centuries. Local legend maintains that there was a popular gypsy who gave her name to the district. This was one Margaret Finch, a famous fortune teller, who died there in 1760 allegedly aged 109.

Glanford, administrative district, Humberside, England.

The name is the old name of the town of Brigg, recorded as *Glanford* in 1183 and as *Glannford Brigg* in 1235.

Glan Ogwen see **Bethesda**.

Glenrothes, town, Fife, Scotland.

Glenrothes is a new town, apparently first referred to by this name in the 'Draft New Town (Glenrothes) Designation Order, 1948', published by the Secretary of State for Scotland. The name seems to be a combination of the *glen* or valley of the river Leven, which runs past the northern area of the town on its way east from Loch Leven into the sea near Leven, and the old connections of the region with the Earls of *Rothes*, especially at Leslie, just west of the town. The latter part of the name also has a modern link, since the Fife Coal Company began construction of the Rothes Colliery here in 1946, and the new town was primarily designed to provide housing for the miners. The colliery failed through flooding, however, and closed.

Globe Town, district of east London, England.

The district is named after Globe Road, which today runs south from Bethnal Green to Mile End Road. The road's own name probably comes from an inn here named the Globe, and dates from *c.*1700. Before this, the road was called Theven Lane, i.e. 'thieves' lane', and the change of name may have been deliberate.

Glyn-Cory, village, South Glamorgan, Wales.

The settlement was laid out as a garden village in 1907 by the philanthropist, coal-owner, and ship-owner John Cory (1828–1910), who chose part of his estate at Peterston, west of Cardiff, for the site. The name, meaning 'Cory valley', 'Cory glen', reflects the situation of the village in the valley of the river Ely. John Cory must not be confused with the Cory of **Coryton**, South Glamorgan.

Glyndŵr, administrative district, Clwyd, Wales.

The name is that of the 14th-century Welsh rebel better known to Englishmen as Owen Glendower, who was lord of Glyndŵr and Sycharth. The district name, now revived, is thus that of the territory held by Owain ap Gruffydd (?1359–?1416), and is a contraction of *Glyndyfrdwy*, 'valley of the (river) Dyfrdwy'. This valley lies west of Llangollen on the river Dee, with Dyfrdwy being the Welsh form of this English rivername.

Gog Magog Hills, hills near Cambridge, Cambridgeshire, England.

The name is first recorded in 1576, as *Gogmagoghill*, and derives from a large figure of Gogmagog, a legendary giant chieftain in western England, cut in the chalk here. The antiquarian William Camden, writing in 1586, says that university students gave the name (*studiosi vocant*). Today there is no trace of the figure, from either the ground or the air. The local nickname for the hills, especially among university students and golf-players, is 'The Gogs'.

Golders Green, district of north-west London, England.

The name seems to derive from that of a family here named Goder or Godyer, with one local legend telling of a farmer named Godyer who sold his property in the locality and left. No such person, however, has been recorded in the early history of the parish, although there could possibly be some association with John le Godere or John Godyer, both known to have lived in Hendon in the

14th century. The present form of the name is first recorded, as *Golders Greene*, in 1612. The green was once a field in Middlesex, and the modern built-up district developed only after the coming of the railway. Golders Green Underground station opened in 1907.

Gordonsburgh see **Fort William**.

Gordon's Mills, village (near Invergordon), Highland, Scotland.

The village arose round a snuff factory in *c.*1796 and seems to have been named after a local landowner, Henrietta Gordon of Newhall.

Gordonstoun, estate (near Lossiemouth), Grampian, Scotland.

The original name of the estate was Bog of Plewlands. It was renamed in 1638 when acquired by Sir Robert Gordon (1580–1656), who was the son of the 12th Earl of Sutherland and the first Scottish baronet (from 1625). The estate subsequently passed to the Gordon-Cunningham family, with the present mansion house, replacing the old fortress here, dating from 1775–6 and currently (from 1934) a school.

Gordonstown, village (near Banff), Grampian, Scotland.

The village was founded in 1770 by a laird named Gordon from Badenscoth.

Goresbridge, village, Kilkenny, Ireland.

The first part of the name is that of the family of the original proprietor, Colonel John Gore, with the bridge being that over the river Barrow. The Irish name of the village is *Droichead Nua*, 'new bridge'.

Gospel Oak, district of north-west London, England.

The name refers to the old custom of beating the bounds, observed annually on Ascension Day in many parishes. In the course of the ceremony, and the procession round the bounds of the parish, a halt would be made under an oak-tree for the gospel to be read. The tree for this particular place was on the

boundary of the parishes of Hampstead and St. Pancras, and is mentioned in documents of 1761 and 1819. It has since been cut down, however, and the name is now that of the residential district that grew up here in the 19th century. There are other places of the name in different parts of the country, with a Gospel Oak near Wednesbury, West Midlands, for example, standing at the boundary of three parishes.

Gowerton, town, West Glamorgan, Wales.

The community was originally called Gower Road, for its location on the main road leading to the English-speaking Gower Peninsula. In the last quarter of the 19th century, however, the village had grown to a size that seemed to demand a more appropriate name. The procedure of changing the name is described by Morgan (1887): 'At a vestry meeting of the ratepayers of the parish of Loughor, held October 15th, 1885, it was unanimously passed—"that the name of this village be changed from Gower-road to Gowerton". A few gentlemen were appointed to communicate with the railway and postal authorities with the view of making the necessary arrangements for the new name to be adopted January 1st, 1886.' The Welsh form of the name, with the same meaning, is *Tre-gŵyr*.

Gracehill, village, Antrim, Northern Ireland.

The village was founded as a Moravian settlement in 1746 by the Revd John Cennick (1718–55). Its name was chosen for its religious associations (compare the early similar name of **Fulneck**). The Irish name is *Baile Uí Chinnéide*, anglicized as Ballykennedy, 'Kennedy's town'.

Grahamston, district of Falkirk, Central, Scotland.

The district arose on Graham's Muir, so recorded in 1774 and said to be named after Sir John de Graham, slain here in 1298.

Grangemouth, town and port, Central, Scotland.

The town was founded in 1777 by Sir Lawrence Dundas in connection with the construction of the Forth and Clyde Canal here (begun 1768, opened 1790), and was named for its location at the mouth of the Grange Burn, itself named after the grange of nearby Newbattle Abbey. The canal closed to navigation in 1963.

Grange-over-Sands, town and resort, Cumbria, England.

The original name of the place was Grange (so recorded in 1491), this referring to a farm, later Grange Farm, that belonged to Cartmel Priory. A village subsequently grew up here, in turn developing into a seaside resort, and acquired the distinctive suffix since it lay at the end of a route across the sands of Morecambe Bay. It was thus a 'farm above the sands' of this bay.

Grantown-on-Spey, town and resort, Highland, Scotland.

The town arose as a model village planned in 1765 by James Grant (1738–1811) on a site a mile from his home, Castle Grant. Grant, later Sir James Grant, was the 7th Baronet of Grant, chief of the Clan Grant, and Member of Parliament for Elgin and Forres and for Banff. A contemporary 'advertisement' announcing the proposed town states that 'the place for the proposed Town is called Feavoit', although Dorward (1979) says the site was formerly Freuchie, from *fraochach*, 'heathery place'. (In this respect, compare the name of **Friockheim**.) The town founded by Grant in 1765, however, was not built at Freuchie, for this was the name of a site (in full Castletown of Freuchie) half a mile south-west of Castle Grant which had been chosen earlier, in 1694, for a new town here. This original 'Grantown' ('now and in all time to be called the Town and Burgh of Grant', according to a charter granted in this earlier year by William III and Queen Mary) never flourished, and thus led to the decision made in the 1760s to build the new town on a slightly different site.

Grantshouse, village (near Eyemouth), Borders, Scotland.

The village took the name of a station here built in the 19th century by the North Britain Railway Company, with the station in turn being named after the nearby Tammy Grant's Inn. Tammy Grant was said to be a famous Highlander at the end of the 18th century.

Gravesham, administrative district, Kent, England.

The district adopted the 'Domesday Book' version of the name of Gravesend in 1086, *Gravesham*.

Great Gable, mountain in Lake District, Cumbria, England.

The name is a translation of the mountain's 14th-century name, *Mykelgavel* (from Old Norse *mikill*, 'great' and *gafl*, 'gable'). This denoted the sharp-sided triangular outline of the mountain. The present name is first recorded in 1783.

Great Grimsby, town and port, Humberside, England.

With the rapid growth of the fishing port in the 20th century, and its operation in conjunction with nearby Immingham, the 'Great' prefix to the name had come to be dropped, and although appearing in 19th-century gazetteers and specialist works such as Ekwall (1960), the town had come to be known and referred to simply as 'Grimsby', with the *Encyclopaedia Britannica* (1976) even rating 'Great Grimsby' as the former name. Since the port had now achieved international fame, therefore, and with every justification for naming it 'Great' in both size and importance, the name 'Great Grimsby' was formally adopted for the town in a resolution passed by the Borough Council on 1 July 1979. Historically and geographically, the place is 'Great' by comparison with Little Grimsby, a small village 15 miles south of it. Little Grimsby is in Lincolnshire, as Great Grimsby was until the local government boundary changes of 1974.

Greatstone-on-Sea, town and resort, Kent, England.

The resort, which lies south of **Little-stone-on-Sea**, developed after World War II, and takes its name from the rocky headland here called Great Stone that formerly lay on the south side of Romney Sand, now drained.

Greenacres, district of Oldham, Greater Manchester, England.

The district developed after an act of 1807 permitted the common land here called Greenacres Moor to be enclosed.

Green Island, island, Poole Harbour, Dorset, England.

The oldest name of the island was 'the island at the estuary of the Frome' (934). Later, after a chapel here, it was called *St. Helen's Island*, with this name first recorded in 1310 (as *Insula Scē Elene*). Later still, when the chapel no longer existed, the name became Green Island, first so documented in 1773.

Griffithstown, suburb of Pontypool, Gwent, Wales.

Morgan (1887) states that the former village was named 'after a Mr Griffiths, who now resides in the place'. This was Henry Griffiths, the first stationmaster at Pontypool Road, who founded a new settlement here in c.1856 and named it after himself. It became an ecclesiastical parish formed from Llanfrechfa Higher and Panteg and included the industrial village of **Sebastopol** before itself becoming a southern suburb of **Pontypool**.

Groomsport, village and port, Down, Northern Ireland.

The name is a simplified anglicization of the original Irish name, *Port an ghiolla ghruama*, said to mean 'port of the gloomy individual', recorded in 1880 as *Gilgroomes port*.

Guildtown, village (near Perth), Tayside, Scotland.

The village was founded in 1818 on lands of the Guildry of Perth, a 'guildry' being a corporation of a royal burgh in Scotland.

Gunsborough, village, Kerry, Ireland.

The village was named for its former proprietor, a man named Gun.

Gwash, river, Leicestershire/Lincolnshire, England.

The original name of the river seems to have been 'Wash', and its early names have been recorded as *le Whasse c.*1230, *Wasse* 1275, *Was de Welond* 1276. The last of these relates to the river Welland, into which it flows near Stamford, Lincolnshire, with the Welland in turn flowing into the North Sea at The Wash. Perhaps by association with this, or even with the verb 'to wash', the name acquired its next form with letter *h*, recorded in *c.*1540 as *Wasch* and *Washe*. The spelling with initial G is first recorded in 1586, and is a quasi-Welsh version of the name probably invented by the antiquarian William Camden.

Gwent, county, Wales.

The name is a revival for the new 1974 county of the ancient territory here named Gwent, said to mean 'favoured place' or 'market place', from Latin *vendere*, 'to sell'. The new county roughly corresponds to the former county of Monmouthshire.

Gwynedd, county, Wales.

As with **Gwent**, the name is that of an old territory. The ancient Gwynedd included Anglesey, the mountains of Snowdonia, the Lleyn peninsula, and the Conway valley, and seems to represent the name of Cunedda, the 5th-century leader who held a kingdom here.

H

Hale End, district of east London, England.

The first part of the name is the oldest, deriving from Old English *halh* or *healh*, 'corner', 'angle', 'nook', with 'end' denoting the end of the parish, in this case the parish of Walthamstow. The whole name can thus be translated approximately as 'corner of land at the end of the parish'. The name is first recorded, as *The Hale*, in 1517, and in 1636 appears exactly as at present. An alternative name recorded in 1640 was *Woodend*, this referring to Epping Forest.

Halfway, village, Dyfed, Wales.

The village takes its name from an inn here that was halfway between Trecastle and Llandovery. The name is additionally appropriate since the village is almost exactly on the border between Dyfed and Powys, so is 'halfway' in this sense as well.

Halfway Reach, stretch of river Thames, London, England.

The stretch so called is below London between Dagenham to the north and Erith Marshes to the south. The name is first recorded in 1746, and derived from an inn, the Halfway House at Dagenham. Travellers journeying from Gravesend to London Bridge by tilt-boat (a large rowing-boat with a *tilt* or awning) would frequently stop at the inn for a midway meal.

Hallsville see **Canning Town**.

Halse Town, village, Cornwall, England.

The village takes its name from a local businessman and Member of Parliament active in tin-mining, James Halse (d. 1838).

Hamilton, town, Strathclyde, Scotland.

Before 1445, the place was a village named Cadzow. This was created a royal burgh in 1548 under its new name of Hamilton, said to have been brought to Scotland by an English family named Hamilton who came from the (now lost) village of Hamilton in Leicestershire. The name could, however, have originated locally, but could not have come from the dukes of Hamilton, at Hamilton House near by, since they took their title from the name of the town.

Hamoaze, section of estuary of river Tamar, Devon/Cornwall, England.

The name applies to the section of the Tamar estuary that lies between Saltash and Plymouth Sound. It was first recorded in 1588, as *ryver of Hamose*, with this name apparently referring to just a small creek which ran up to Ham Manor in Weston Peverell. The name thus originally meant 'Ham ooze'.

Hampden Park, district of Eastbourne, East Sussex, England.

The district was developed in the second half of the 19th century as part of the Ratton estate, and named after Lord Hampden, who owned Ratton Manor then.

Handcross, village, West Sussex, England.

The name is first recorded, in the modern spelling, in 1617. This seems to originate from a signpost here, perhaps one that showed a main route in the forest dividing fanwise into five, like the fingers of a hand.

Harborough, administrative district, Leicestershire, England.

The name is a revival of the old name of Market Harborough, recorded in 1177 as *Hauerberga* and in 1237 as *Haverberge*. The town was first called by its present name in 1312, as *Mercat Heburgh*.

Harewood, village, West Yorkshire, England.

The village arose as a model estate built

in *c*.1760 beside Harewood House by Edward Lascelles, 1st Earl of Harewood.

Harringay, district of north London, England.

The district is in the London borough of Haringey, created in 1963 and restoring the old name of the locality. The spelling 'Harringay' was devised for a house built here in the 1790s and was used for local government in the 19th century. The first recording of the name is in 1201, as *Haringeie*. See also **Hornsey**.

Hart, administrative district, Hampshire, England.

The name derives from the river Hart which flows north through the district. It was chosen after public consultation as the name of the new district council when the former Fleet urban district council and Hartley Wintney rural district council were combined to form the Hart district council in 1974. The name also reflects that of Hartley Wintney itself.

Hartley's Village, district of Liverpool, Merseyside, England.

The district arose in 1888 as a settlement of workers' cottages built by William Hartley for workers at his jam factory here.

Hassocks, village, West Sussex, England.

The village is a modern settlement developed since the railway line to Brighton opened in 1841. The name was originally that of a field, so called for its rough tussocks of grass. The name occurs elsewhere as a field name, for example near Marsden in West Yorkshire.

Haverstock Hill, district of north-west London, England.

The name is first so recorded in 1741. Its precise origin is uncertain. There may have been a family called Haverstock living here at some time: such a family could have come from Stock, Essex, whose name was recorded in 1627 as *Haverstocke*. The surname is not a common one, and there is only one person of the name listed in the London Postal Area telephone directory of 1981.

Haywards Heath, town, West Sussex, England.

As implied, the name was originally that of a heath, recorded in 1544 as *Haywards Hoth* and in 1607 as *Hayworths Hethe*, with the first part of the name found as early as 1261, as *Heyworth*. The name thus means 'heath of the hedged enclosure'. A railway was laid across the heath in 1841, and the town began to grow up round it soon after. Local legend tells of a highwayman called Hayward who used to rob travellers on the heath.

Hebron, village, Gwynedd, Wales.

The name is that of a Congregationalist chapel built here in the early 19th century. The popular biblical interpretation of the name was 'society', 'fellowship', and the origin lies in the city of Hebron mentioned in Numbers 13: 22, Joshua 14: 15, Judges 1: 20, and elsewhere in the Bible.

Heddon, river, Devon, England.

The river flows into the Bristol Channel at Heddon's Mouth, and probably takes its name as a back formation from this cave, which in turn probably contains the name of the Heddon family found in North Devon in the 17th and 18th centuries.

Helen's Bay, village and resort, Down, Northern Ireland.

The residential resort takes its name from the bay on which it is located at the mouth of Belfast Lough. The bay itself was named after the poet Helen Selina Sheridan, Countess of Dufferin (and later Countess of Gifford) (1807–67), wife of Commander Price Blackwood, 4th Baron Dufferin and Clandeboye, whose residence was at Clandeboye here. Also named after her here is Helen's Tower, built in memory of her to house a famous library by her son, Frederick Temple Hamilton-Temple Blackwood, 1st Marquis of Dufferin and Ava (1826–1902). The latter building has famous literary associations, and the circumstances of its erection are inscribed in the tower in a verse by Tennyson:

> 'Helen's Tower, here I stand,
> Dominant over sea and land.
> Son's love built me and I hold
> Mother's love in letter'd gold.
> Love is in and out of time,
> I am mortal stone and lime.'

Verses by Browning and Kipling are also inscribed on tablets in the tower. Helen herself was the granddaughter of Richard Brinsley Sheridan.

Helensburgh, town, Strathclyde, Scotland.

The land known as Mulig (or Malig or Milrigs) was first advertised for feuing in 1776 by Sir James Colquhoun of Luss, and when first laid out as a residential district continued to be known as Mulig or as the New Town. Within a few months, however, Sir James renamed the new settlement after his wife, Lady Helen Sutherland, the daughter of William Sutherland, Lord Strathnaver.

Helvellyn, mountain in Lake District, Cumbria, England.

The name is first recorded in 1577, as *Helvillon*, although in 1600 William Camden gives the name as *Lauuellin*. Both Taylor (1896) and Johnston (1914) derive the name from two Celtic roots, to mean 'yellow rock', but the forms we have of the name are too late for it to be interpreted with any degree of certainty.

Henderskelfe see **Castle Howard**.

Herne Bay, town and resort, Kent, England.

The resort was founded in 1830 and was named after the bay, which in turn took its name from a location here called 'Herne'. This is an old name meaning 'corner', recorded as *Hyrnan* c.1100,

Hirne 1264, *Herne* 1298. It survives today as a district of Herne Bay town. Compare **Herne Hill** (below).

Herne Hill, district of south-east London, England.

The name seems to have originated as that of a field, recorded near here in c.1490 as *Le Herne*, meaning 'corner', 'nook' (as for **Herne Bay**). In its modern form it is not found on any map before 1798. The name thus does not apparently mean 'heron hill', as popularly supposed, and it is not connected with the village of Hernhill in Kent, whose name (recorded in 1247 as *Harenhull*) probably means 'grey hill'.

Heronsgate, village, Hertfordshire, England.

The name is first recorded in 1599 as *Heryngarste* (sic), with later versions appearing as *Herringat* 1656 and *Herring Gate* 1890, the latter on the one-inch Ordnance Survey map. Because of these earlier forms, the name almost certainly does not mean 'herons' gate', as might be thought, and its sense must remain obscure until further evidence is available. The village was also formerly known as **O'Connorville**.

Hertsmere, administrative district, Hertfordshire, England.

The name was devised artificially as a combination of *Herts*, for the name of the county, and *mere*, an old word meaning 'boundary', in this case the boundary between Hertsmere itself and the Greater London area. Hertsmere became a borough in 1977.

Highcliffe, town and resort, Dorset, England.

The locality appears to have been called 'New Town' as early as the late 16th century, with the name *Black Cliffe* recorded here in 1610 and *High Clift* (sic) first in 1759. The present name derives from a Gothic-style mansion here, formerly the home of the Marchioness of Waterford. On some maps and in tourist publications the name often appears as Highcliffe-on-Sea, presumably to match neighbouring Barton-on-Sea and Milford-on-Sea. The resort is now virtually a suburb of Christchurch.

High Peak, administrative district, Derbyshire, England.

The district contains the Peak District, with its Peak or High Peak being an area of hills with Kinder Scout as the highest. The name is that of a former hundred here centred on Buxton, and is contrasted with the 'Low Peak' hundred to the south-east, centred on Wirksworth.

Hightown, village, Merseyside, England.

The name is first recorded in 1702 as *High Town*. This seems to mean what it says: the village is on higher ground to the south of Formby, which is the 'Low Town' (although apparently never named as such). Alternatively it could have denoted a village that was 'higher' or more important than another.

Hillsborough, town, Down, Northern Ireland.

The name comes from the descendants of Sir Moyses Hill, an English army officer who obtained lands here in c.1608 to which he added further properties in 1611. His son Peter Hill began to build the village in c.1630. In 1662, Colonel Sir Arthur Hill (?1601–63), Peter's uncle and heir, obtained a charter for a new town here to be called Hillsborough, himself building a fort called Hillsborough Fort. The former name of the locality was apparently Cromlyn, a fairly common name in Ireland (also as Crumlin), meaning 'crooked glen'. See also **Hilltown**.

Hillsborough, district of Sheffield, South Yorkshire, England.

The original name of the locality was 'Hill', recorded first in the 13th century as *Hulle*, then in 1538 as *Hylls*. This basic name was expanded in some form from then on, appearing as *The Hills* 1654, *Hill Top* 1817, and *Hill Foot* (sic) 1841. The present addition of *borough* seems to have been made some time in the second half of the 19th century, presumably to reflect the development of the place as a residential district.

Hilltown, village, Down, Northern Ireland.

The name evolved at some time in the 17th century from the Hill family who gave their name to **Hillsborough** (above).

Hindhead, town, Surrey, England.

The name is first recorded in 1571, as *Hyndehed*, this being the name of the high ground to the south of the Devil's Punch Bowl and rising to its peak of Gibbet Hill. Later versions of the name, which probably means 'hind hill', appear as *Hynde head lane* 1606, and *Hindhead Hill* 1861. The town developed as a residential locality only in the early 20th century: in *Cassell* (1896) the entry for *Hindhead* speaks only of a 'hill ridge and common' two miles from Haslemere. The precise sense of 'hind' is not certain, although according to Thomas Wright's *Hindhead* (1907), 'Some say the name was given to the place by Queen Anne's huntsman, because the contour of the hill reminded him of the head of a hind'. But this is the familiar local legend, and the true meaning is more likely to be 'hill where hinds are found'. (Queen Anne, moreover, reigned in the early 18th century, and the name predates this by more than 130 years.)

Hogs Back, chalk ridge, Surrey, England.

The original name of the ridge running west from Guildford (today along the A31) was 'Guildown', recorded as *Geldedon* 1195, *Gildowne* 1485 and *Gill Down* 1744, which seems to suggest 'Guildford Down'. The descriptive name Hogs Back is first recorded in 1823, and presumably began as a local nickname for the long, straight outline of the ridge seen from below as a hog's back.

Holland Arms, village, Gwynedd, Wales.

The village, better known by its Welsh name of *Pentre Berw* ('water-cress village'), derives its name from an inn here, itself named after the Holland family of nearby Plas Berw. The name is first recorded in *c*.1830.

Holland Park, district of west London, England.

The district is named after Holland House, which from 1621 became the home of the Earls of Holland. The first Earl of Holland was Sir Henry Rich (1590–1649), created Earl of Holland (in Lincolnshire) in 1624. He married the daughter of Sir Walter Cope (d. 1614), Isabel, who inherited the house originally built by her father in 1607 and then called Cope's Castle. The first reference to the name is recorded as *The Earle of Hollands House* in 1658. The present name was established for the district with the opening of Holland Park Underground station in 1900.

Holly Village, district of Highgate, London, England.

The place arose as a model village (just a few cottages and a gateway) built for her servants in 1865 by Baroness Angela Georgina Burdett-Coutts (1814–1906), who named it after her own house, Holly Lodge.

Honor Oak, district of south-east London, England.

The name was originally that of a wooded hill here, and was first recorded in 1609 as *the Oke of Honor*, with later versions of the name being *Oak of Arnon Wood c.*1745 and *Oak of Honour Wood* 1763. The first of these refers to an individual oak which served as a boundary mark (compare **Gospel Oak**). The 'honour' seems to have been accorded the oak on the occasion of a visit of Queen Elizabeth I to it in the first few years of the 17th century. What exactly she did when here is not clear: one account says she dined in the shade of the tree, another says that she 'went hither a-maying' on May Day, 1602. The tree no longer exists.

Hopeman, village and resort (near Lossiemouth), Grampian, Scotland.

The village was founded in 1805 by a local landowner, William Young of Inverugie, who is said to have given it the name, Haudmont, of an estate here. This came to be assimilated to the present English version. Presumably the estate name derives from French *haut mont*, 'high hill'.

Hopkinstown, district of Pontypridd, Mid Glamorgan, Wales.

The district seems to have been named after one or other of two men called Thomas Hopkin. The first of these, who died in 1791, was a partner in the Blaenavon ironworks and also in mineral extraction locally. The second sank the No. 3 Rhondda Seam in a coal mine here in 1859. The Welsh name of the district, *Trehopcyn*, has the same meaning as the English.

Horeb, village, Dyfed, Wales.

The name derives from a Nonconformist chapel here erected some time in the first half of the 19th century, with its biblical name taken to mean 'desert'. It is that of the mountain in Sinai where both Moses and Elijah stayed for forty days, referred to in Exodus 3: 1 and elsewhere in the Bible. There are several villages and other localities named Horeb in Wales, including three in Dyfed. The background for each of them is as stated here.

Hornsey, district of north London, England.

The name developed as a variant of Haringey, recorded successively as *Haryngey* 1488, *Harnesey* 1524, and *Hornsey* 1564. Haringey itself is an old name: see **Harringay**, the spelling adopted for the district within the old borough of Hornsey in the 19th century.

Hothampton see **Bognor Regis**.

Hoylake, town and resort, Merseyside, England.

The seaside resort grew up round a

hotel, the Royal Hotel, built here for bathers in 1792. The earliest recorded name of this hamlet is *Highlake* in 1766, this being a corrupt form of a roadstead off the coast here recorded as *Hyle Lake* in 1687, with the first part of the name deriving from Old English *hygel*, 'hillock'. The roadstead is now silted up, and the 'lake' of the hamlet name, and the present district name, seems to refer to a tidal lake inshore of the sandbank that was the 'hillock'. The resort name continued to develop as *High Lake* 1794 and finally *Hoylake* in 1806. By 1882 the settlement had grown to such an extent that it came to include Little Meols and Great Meols, both former villages here.

Hugh Town, town, Scilly Isles, Cornwall, England.

The name derives from a hill above the town on which Star Castle was built in 1593. This was recorded as *Hew Hill* that year, with *Hew* probably a form of Old English *hōh*, 'ridge', 'hill', as in Plymouth *Hoe*.

Hullshire, former county, Humberside, England.

The name is recorded as *Comitatus Hull* 1505, *the countie of Kyngeston upon Hulle* 1546, *Hull Shyer* 1546, *Hullshire* 1828. The county was constituted by Henry VI in 1440 and included the parishes of Kingston-upon-Hull, Hessle, **Kirk Ella**, and North Ferriby. It ceased to exist in 1835.

Hundred End, village, Lancashire, England.

The settlement grew up round a former railway station on the Southport to Preston line, so named after its location on the north-west boundary of the old hundred of West Derby.

Hunter's Quay, village and resort (near Dunoon), Strathclyde, Scotland.

The resort takes its name from the Hunter family of Hafton House, northwest of the village. A yacht club was founded here in 1856, and the original club-house was a gift from the Hunter family in 1872. The yacht club, now the Royal Clyde Yacht Club, was the first in Scotland.

Huntly, town, Grampian, Scotland.

The town was laid out as a planned village in 1769 by Alexander Gordon, 4th Duke of Gordon and Earl of Huntly (1743–1827), whose second title derives from the lost Berwickshire village of Huntly south of here. When the Berwickshire Gordons settled here in Aberdeenshire in 1376, they thus brought the name of Huntly with them. Earlier names for the two hamlets here before the establishment of Huntly town were Strathbogie (or Raws o'Strathbogie) and Torriesoul. In 1545 Queen Mary had granted a charter to the then Earl of Huntly promoting Torriesoul into a free burgh of barony.

Hutchesontown, district of Glasgow, Strathclyde, Scotland.

The name derives from Hutcheson's Hospital here, founded in 1639–41 by two brothers, George Hutcheson (?1580–1639) and Thomas Hutcheson (1589–1641). The Hospital purchased land here in 1647, and a residential settlement began to grow round it in 1794.

Hyndburn, administrative district, Lancashire, England.

When the borough came into existence in 1974 it was felt that none of the existing town names could satisfactorily represent the new authority, therefore the name of the small river Hyndburn which runs through the district was chosen for it. The Hyndburn is a tributary of the Ribble.

Hyndland, district of Glasgow, Strathclyde, Scotland.

The name was first recorded in 1538 as *Fermeland callit the Hynde land*, i.e. 'farmland called the Hinterland'. The district lies back from the river Clyde.

Hyson Green, district of Nottingham, Nottinghamshire, England.

The district was so called in c.1825, and earlier may have been 'High Sands Green'. The first house on the estate here was built in 1802.

I

Inverclyde, administrative district, Strathclyde, Scotland.

The name means simply 'mouth of the river Clyde', whose estuary forms the northern and western border of the district set up in 1975. The name is based on other *Inver-* names, common in Scotland, including that of the village of Inverkip in the district.

Invergordon, town and port, Highland, Scotland.

The original name of the village was *Inverbreckie*. Some time in the 18th century the castle and estate were purchased by a local landowner variously identified as either Sir William Gordon of Embo, Sir Alexander Gordon, or Sir John Gordon. The latter is said to have built the town as a planned village some time after 1759.

Ironbridge, town, Shropshire, England.

The town, administratively in **Telford**, is named after its bridge, designed and cast by Abraham Derby II in 1778 as the first cold cast iron bridge in the world. Derby's foundry was at nearby Coalbrookdale.

Ironville, village, Derbyshire, England.

The village seems to have arisen in *c.*1850 round the iron works built by the Butterley Iron Company, with the name recorded first in 1837. *Cassell* (1896) notes that at the end of the 19th century the place had become a small market town with over 3000 inhabitants.

Irvinestown, town, Fermanagh, Northern Ireland.

The original name of the settlement was *Lowtherstown*. In *c.*1860, however, this was changed to Irvinestown for the associations with the Irvine family of Castle Irvine (now Necarne Castle).

Isis, alternative name for the river Thames above the junction with the Thame (Oxfordshire), England.

The name seems to have been artificially devised from an early name of the Thames, the *Tamise* (the present French name for the river), apparently from a combination of *Thame*, a headstream of the Thames, and a non-existent 'Ise'. The present spelling, first recorded in 1577 (with earlier *Isa* in 1347), may derive from the medieval Latin form *Tamesis*, which came to be popularly associated with the goddess Isis. The name is particularly associated with the Thames as it flows through Oxford.

Islandbridge, suburb of Dublin, Ireland.

The name derives from a former wooden bridge over the river Liffey here. This was replaced by a stone bridge in 1791, named Sarah Bridge after Sarah Anne Fane, wife of John Fane, 10th Earl of Westmorland (1759–1841). Sarah, Countess of Westmorland, died in 1793. This bridge has now been replaced by the South Circular Road.

Isle of Dogs, district of east London, England.

The earliest record of the name is as *Isle of Doges ferm*, in 1593. Before this, the district was known as Stepney Marsh. The name has not been finally explained. Traditionally, it referred to dead dogs that had been borne down the river Thames and deposited on the district's west bank. Alternatively, it may have been a site of the royal kennels when the court was at Greenwich. An unlikely explanation is that the name is a corruption of 'Isle of Ducks', if only because an 'island' like this would more likely be named after an unusual feature rather than a commonplace one. There is another Isle of Dogs in Loch Laggan, Scotland, also said to have been used as a kennelling-place (in this case by the ancient Scottish kings when they were hunting in Lochaber). Both stories may amount to no more than local legend, but the coincidence is noteworthy. Ultimately, however, the name would appear to be derogatory, rather than complimentary.

Islwyn, administrative district, Gwent, Wales.

The name is that of the mountain here so called (*Mynydd Islwyn*, 'underbush mountain'). It also commemorates the name of a local bard, the romantic poet Islwyn (pseudonym of William Thomas (1832–78), born near the mountain and named after it).

J

Jacobswell, village, Surrey, England.

The name is of uncertain origin. It was first recorded in 1838 as *Jacob's Well Meadow*, this presumably being a field name.

Jamestown, village, Leitrim, Ireland.

The village was founded in 1622 by Sir Charles Coote (d. 1642), military commander in Ireland, in order to control the crossing here across the river Shannon. Coote named it after James I who had incorporated the village this same year.

Jemimaville, village (near Cromarty), Highland, Scotland.

Slightingly described and dismissed by Johnston (1934) as 'a modern type of name happily confined chiefly to across the Atlantic', the village was in fact named by Sir George Munro, 4th Laird of Poyntzfield, after his wife Jemima Charlotte Graham. They married in 1822 and the name was in use by 1836.

Jenkins' Green, village, East Sussex, England.

The name is so recorded in 1720, and derives from the family of Thomas Jenkin of Hailsham, who held land here in 1712.

John o' Groats, village (near Duncansby), Highland, Scotland.

The village, famous as the northernmost point of the mainland of Great Britain, derives its name from the house of a Dutchman, John de Groat or John de Groot, who is said to have settled here with his two brothers in the late 15th century with a royal letter of protection. John de Groat was apparently appointed as baillie to the earls of Caithness here. The house no longer exists.

Johnstone, town, Strathclyde, Scotland.

The town was founded in 1782 by George Houston, laird of Johnstone, on the site of a hamlet called Brig o' Johnstone.

Johnstown, village, Dyfed, Wales.

According to Morgan (1887), the village was named after a 'Mr John Jones of Ystrad'. He was presumably a landowner here, or the initiator of a commercial concern. The village is just west of Carmarthen.

Joppa, district of Edinburgh, Lothian, Scotland.

The district was so named in c.1780, after Joppa in Palestine. The name doubtless originated as that of a farm here, with its own name derived from the biblical town of Joppa (otherwise Jaffa, and today a suburb of Tel Aviv, Israel), this having favourable associations. Joppa is now a resort and virtually a suburb of the larger district of **Portobello**.

Jordans, village, Buckinghamshire, England.

The name is first recorded in 1766, as *Jurdens*. This may be an abbreviated form of 'Jourdemayns', from the name of the family Jourdemayn, found here in 1301.

Juniper Green, district of Edinburgh, Lothian, Scotland.

The name seems to derive from the juniper bushes that formerly grew here, and is first recorded in 1812. The village (now district) of Juniper Green arose on Currie Muir, from which it derives its current local name of *Curriemuirend*, first recorded in 1707.

K

Kemp, river, Shropshire, England.

The river name is a back formation from Kempton, a small village on it. The name was first recorded in 1851 as *Kemp Brook*. The river is a tributary of the Clun.

Kemp Town, district of Brighton, East Sussex, England.

The district is named after Thomas Read Kemp (?1781–1844), Member of Parliament for Lewes (retired 1816), who had a passion for building and who laid out the district in the ten years commencing *c*.1820.

Kendal, town, Cumbria, England.

The town was originally 'Kirkby' ('church village'), recorded in the 'Domesday Book' of 1086 as *Cherchebi*. The name soon came to acquire the affix 'Kendal', however, to distinguish it from Kirkby Lonsdale and Kirkby Stephen, and is first so recorded in this form in 1090, as *Cherkaby Kendale*, with *Kirkeby in Kendale* found in *c*.1240 and some form of 'Kirkby Kendal' in use down to the 18th century. (The affix means 'Kent dale', from the name of the river on which Kendal stands.) At the same time, 'Kendal' alone was coming into use as the name of the borough by the 15th century, and eventually predominated as the sole name of the town.

Kenmare, town, Kerry, Ireland.

The town was founded by the political economist and adventurer Sir William Petty (1623–87) in 1670, on land assigned him by the English government. The previous name of the place seems to have been 'Nedeen', from the Irish name *Neidín*, 'little nest', still current for the town. According to *AA Ireland* (1962) the present name of the town 'was taken from the nobleman of that name at the close of the 18th century', although it seems much more likely, as evidenced by Joyce (1875), that Kenmare is an Irish name in origin, meaning 'head of the sea', and that the Earls of Kenmare took their title from their seat here. The Irish name thus refers to the highest point reached by the tide in the river Roughty, on whose estuary Kenmare stands. Doubtless both names, Nedeen and Kenmare, had long existed side by side for the locality or for different areas of it.

Kennet, administrative district, Wiltshire, England.

The name is that of the river Kennet, which rises in the district, and also that of the Kennet and Avon Canal, which crosses the whole district from east to west.

Kerrier, administrative district, Cornwall, England.

The name is that of an old hundred here, recorded in 1201 as *Kerier*. This is said to mean 'area of rounds' and to refer to fortified Iron Age homesteads found in Cornwall, notably by the river Helford.

Kidmore End, village, Oxfordshire, England.

The village was originally just Kidmore. In 1853 it was formed into an ecclesiastical parish and in 1902 was renamed Kidmore End, with the affix presumably chosen to refer to the bounds of the parish.

King's County, former county, Ireland.

The former Leinster territory of Offaly, held by the O'Connors, was shired as King's County in 1556 by Queen Mary (reigned 1553–8) and named after her husband, Philip II of Spain. In 1920 the county reverted to its Irish name, properly *Uí Failghe*, 'people of Failghe'. See also **Philipstown** and compare **Queen's County**.

Kingscourt, village, Cavan, Ireland.

The village was founded towards the end of the 18th century by a local landowner, Mervyn Pratt, with the completion of the village carried out by Pratt's brother, the Revd Joseph Pratt. The name does not seem to have been given by either Pratt, but to have been that of a house here, known in Irish as *Dún an Rí*, 'the king's fort'.

King's Cross, district of north London, England.

The original name of the district was 'Broadford', first recorded in 1207 as *Bradeford*. Some time in the 14th century or before, this name acquired the suffix 'bridge', and was recorded successively as *Bradefordebrigge c.*1387, *Bradfordbrege* 1492, and *Bradfordbrige in the parish of St. Pancras* 1532. This name in turn gave way to 'Battlebridge', apparently as a corrupt variant, and is first so recorded, as *Battyl brydge*, in 1559. The name Battlebridge survived well into the 19th century here, and occurs in the works of a number of contemporary writers, including *Oliver Twist* (1837–8). Later, however, this name came to be replaced by the present name of King's Cross, from a statue of *King* George IV that stood from 1833 to 1845 at the *cross*roads formed by the junction of Gray's Inn Road, Euston Road, and Pentonville Road. The name became firmly established for the district when the Great Northern Railway (later the London and North Eastern Railway) chose it for their terminus, built here in 1852. The former name survives in that of Battle Bridge Road, a street behind King's Cross Station. Local legend maintains that the 'battle' of Battlebridge was one between Boudicca (Boadicea) and the Romans here in *c.* AD 59. King's Cross Underground station opened in 1863, further perpetuating the name, although the present station (King's Cross St. Pancras) is a short distance west of the original. King's Cross railway station is now, with Liverpool Street, a terminus of the Eastern Region of British Rail.

Kingsgate, suburb of Margate, Kent, England.

The name originated in a 'gate' or gap in the cliffs here where on 30 June 1683 King Charles II and his brother the Duke of York landed on their way from London to Dover. The earlier name of the cliff-gap seems to have been St. Bartholomew's Gate.

Kingsland, district of Holyhead, Gwynedd, Wales.

The name is popularly believed to have originated from a visit paid by King George IV to Holyhead in 1821. Local evidence seems to suggest, however, that the name predates this, and that it refers to lands once held here by the Crown. Kingsland is a fairly common place-name in Britain and usually has this origin. On the other hand it is certain that **Kingstown** in Ireland was named after George IV in 1821 when he left for England (landing at Milford Haven), and it was from Holyhead that he had departed for Ireland on this very visit.

King's Lynn, town and port, Norfolk, England.

The name of the town was originally just 'Lynn', so recorded (as *Lun*) in the 'Domesday Book' of 1086. The name then became 'Bishop's Lynn' or 'Lynn Episcopi' for the town's connection with the see of Norwich. When this connection was severed by Henry VIII's charter of 1537, the name was changed to 'King's Lynn' or 'Lynn Regis' in his honour. Locally the town is still usually known as Lynn.

Kingston-upon-Spey, village and port (near Elgin), Grampian, Scotland.

The village was founded in 1784 by two Yorkshiremen from the firm of Messrs Dodsworth and Osbourne, timber merchants and shipbuilders, whose premises were in Kingston-upon-Hull, and the two men named the new settlement after their native town. Timber for the houses of the village and for the ships to be built in the new shipyard here were purchased by the firm from the Duke of Gordon's forest of Glenmore. Several sailing ships were built in the yards here in the 18th and early 19th centuries, but the place subsequently declined to its present status as a small village near the mouth of the river Spey. It is possible that the name may have been additionally suggested by that of **Grantown-on-Spey**, some distance inland on the same river Spey. In many gazetteers and on many maps today the village often appears as Kingston, without its original suffix.

Kingstown, former name of Dun Laoghaire, town and port, Dublin, Ireland.

The town was so named in 1821 in commemoration of the departure of George IV for England after a state visit to Dublin. The town's earlier name was Dunleary, restored in 1920 in its more correct Irish form as *Dún Laoghaire*, 'fort of Laoghaire'. Laoghaire has not been identified with any certainty: according to Joyce (1875) he may have been a king of Ireland in the 5th century.

Kingswells, village (near Aberdeen), Grampian, Scotland.

According to the Register of the Great Seal of Scotland, the land known as 'Kingswells' was granted to one John Mar in 1553, having been bought as an estate of virgin land by one John Arthur two years previously: *JOANNI MAR terras de Kyngiswallis, tunc per Joh. Arthur et ejus subtenentes occupat* ('to John Mar the lands of Kingswells, then held by John Arthur and his subtenants'). It is not clear from this first recorded form of the name, however, what its precise origin is, and which 'king', if any, had a connection with some wells or walls here.

Kingswilliamstown, former name of Ballydesmond, town, Cork, Ireland.

The original name of the town, as stated, was 'Ballydesmond', this being the anglicized form of the more correct Irish name *Baile Deasmhumhna*, 'town of Desmond'. The old name was changed when the town was improved in c.1832, with its new name presumably given in honour of William IV (reigned 1830–7). The Irish name was resumed in 1951.

Kirk Ella, suburb of Hull, Humberside, England.

The original name of the settlement was simply 'Ella', recorded in the 'Domesday Book' of 1086 as *Aluengi* and in 1215 as *Auuele* ('Aelf's clearing' or 'Aelfa's clearing'). The prefix 'Kirk' was added in the 15th century, or even earlier, to distinguish the place from West Ella. Early forms of this new name are recorded as *Kyrkella* 1447 and *Kirkella* 1594. The prefix refers to the church, which the village is known to have had since the time of the 'Domesday Book' at the latest. See also **Hullshire**.

Knotty Ash, district of Liverpool, Merseyside, England.

The name of the district, originally a village, derives from a distinctive gnarled ash tree that grew here at the top of Thomas Lane. The village seems to have been called simply Ash in c.1700.

Kym, river, Northamptonshire/Cambridgeshire, England.

The river name is a back formation from the town of Kimbolton, that stands on it. The former name of the Kym was the 'Hail', preserved in the village of Hail Weston, Cambridgeshire, also on it.

Kynochtown see **Coryton** (Essex).

L

Ladykirk, village (near Coldstream), Borders, Scotland.

The former name of the village was *Upsetlington*. The name was changed for the church built here in 1500 by James IV as a token of gratitude after he had nearly lost his life by drowning in the river Tweed, on which the village stands, when trying to ford it in a flood the previous year. The church, dedicated to the Virgin Mary, was one of the last to be built in Scotland before the Reformation.

Lake District, district of Cumbria, England.

The name is a touristic one, first recorded in 1829 as *Lakeland*, in its present form in 1835, and as *Lake Country* in 1842. The name is something of a misnomer, since although it indicates the lakes for which the region is famous (the chief ones are Windermere, Coniston Water, Ullswater, Derwentwater, Thirlmere, Bassenthwaite Lake, Wastwater, Buttermere, and Ennerdale Water), it does not denote the mountains such as Scafell, **Great Gable** and **Helvellyn** for which the region is equally well known. The name today is also associated with the literary figures who have visited the district or lived in it in the past, notably the Lake Poets (Wordsworth, the Coleridges, and Southey). The only extent to which the name has become official is that in 1951 the district was designated the Lake District National Park.

Landport, district of Portsmouth, Hampshire, England.

The name is a 19th-century one, deriving from the former Landport Gate that was on the landward side of the wall of the old town of Portsmouth. (The second half of the name indicates 'port' meaning 'gate', and does not relate to the 'port' or harbour after which Portsmouth is named.)

Lanesborough, town, Longford, Ireland.

The name derives from that of Sir George Lane, 1st Viscount Lanesborough, whose lands of Ballyleagh and elsewhere were erected into the manor of Lanesborough by a charter of Charles II in 1677. The Irish name of the town is the 'Ballyleagh' mentioned above: *Béal Átha Liag*, 'ford-mouth of the standing stones'.

Langbaurgh, administrative district, Cleveland, England.

The name is that of Langbaurgh Ridge in the district. On this ridge, running from east to west along a basaltic dike, the former Wapentake Courts of Langbaurgh were held. The village of Langbaurgh, on the south border of the district with North Yorkshire, also preserves the old name, which means 'long mound' (referring to the ridge).

Langley Vale, village, Surrey, England.

The village has grown up since *c.*1900, when it was known as Langley Bottom and was simply a valley in the Epsom Downs. Presumably the name was felt to be 'inferior', so was changed.

Langriville, village, Lincolnshire, England.

The village was created a township in 1812 by act of parliament and arose as the result of an extensive draining operation over some 14,000 acres in Wildmore Fen and the East and West Fens here. The place took its name from an existing village just to the south across the river Witham. This was Langrick, an old name dating back to 1243 (as *Langrak*, apparently meaning 'long reach'). Langriville was thus originally *Langrick-ville*, and the name is so spelt in Lewis (1849). The shorter form doubtless arose through the pronunciation of the name, with the middle *ck* omitted. Other townships in the area

created at the same time as Langriville
were **Carrington, Eastville, Frithville,
Midville, Thornton-le-Fen**, and **Westville**.

Lark, river, Suffolk/Cambridgeshire,
England.

The river name appears to be a back
formation from the Suffolk village of
Lackford, located on it. The spelling of
the name (instead of the expected
'Lack') may perhaps be due to associations with the bird or even 'larks' or
sports at the ford of Lackford. ('Lark' in
this sense is a dialect word that predates
the 1813 evidence of the word in the
Oxford English Dictionary.) The name is
first recorded in 1735. Before this, the
river was known as the *Pryckewil-
lowewayter*, so recorded in 1549, with
this name denoting the 'water' or river
of the nearby village of Prickwillow. It
seems to be no mere coincidence that
south of Bury St. Edmunds the Lark is
joined by its tributary the **Linnet**.

Laurencekirk, town, Grampian, Scotland.

The town was founded by Francis
Garden, Lord Gardenstone (1721–93) in
c.1770, after he had bought lands here in
1762. The name was given for the
church, dedicated to St. Laurence of
Canterbury, and at first the new settlement was called Kirkton of St.
Laurence. Previous to this, the location
was known as Conveth, which may be a
form of Conway and derive from Gaelic
coinmheadh, 'free quartering'. Lord Gardenstone was the second son of Alexander Garden of Troup, who founded
Gardenstown.

Laurieston, village (near Kirkcudbright),
Dumfries and Galloway, Scotland.

The village was known as Clauchan-
pluck to the late 18th century, when its
name was changed by William Kennedy
Laurie, who bought the lands on which
it stood.

Laurieston, village (near Falkirk), Central, Scotland.

The original location here was known as
Langton, 'long village' or 'long homestead'. This name was changed in 1756
to *New Merchiston*, after Francis Napier,
5th Baron Napier of Merchiston, on
whose lands a new village was laid out.
Finally, in 1774 the name was changed
again to *Laurencetown*, later Laurieston,
after its subsequent proprietor and
promoter, Sir Lawrence Dundas of
Kerse. See also **Port Dundas**.

Leedstown, village, Cornwall, England.
The village takes its name from one of
the Dukes of Leeds, most likely Francis
Osborne, 5th Duke of Leeds (1751–99),
whose family inherited the Godolphin
estates here in 1785.

Lee-on-the-Solent, town and resort,
Hampshire, England.

The original name of the settlement here
was simply Lee, this being first recorded
in 1242 as *la Lye* and meaning 'woodland'. The place was exploited as a
resort in 1888 by Sir John Robinson, a
local property developer, and the lengthy touristic suffix was added shortly
after. (Local residents like to insist on
the definite article, which is regarded as
an essential component of the four-
element name.)

Len, river, Kent, England.
The river name is a back formation from
the village near which it rises, Lenham.
The name is first recorded in 1607 as
Leno (in the Latin ablative form).

Lennoxtown, town, Strathclyde, Scotland.

The original name of the village here
was the Clachan of Campsie, 'clachan'
being a Scots word for a small village
(from Gaelic *clach*, 'stone'). The new
village of Lennoxtown, or Newtown of
Campsie as at first called, arose with the
introduction of calico printing in 1785-6
and took its name from the Lennox
family here, long associated with the
district. The earls and dukes of Lennox
in turn took their name from the ancient
Scottish territory of Lennox, with this

perhaps deriving from Gaelic *leamha-nach*, 'place abounding in elms'. At the old parish church of Lennoxtown, abandoned in 1828, is a graveyard with the Lennox family vault.

Leverburgh, village and port (Harris), Western Isles, Scotland.

The original name of the village was *Obbe*, from the Gaelic word for 'bay', and when in 1918 the islands of Lewis and Harris were bought by William Hesketh Lever, 1st Viscount Leverhulme (1851–1925), with the aim of transforming the village into a major fishing port, the name was proposed by the villagers themselves when Lord Leverhulme expressed his dislike of the name Obbe. Most of Leverhulme's development was completed when his scheme failed in 1923 and the village declined from then on. Lord Leverhulme's development of **Port Sunlight** was more successful.

Lewistown, village, Mid Glamorgan, Wales.

The name commemorates that of the coal magnate and pit owner Sir William Thomas Lewis, 1st Baron Merthyr of Senghenydd (1837–1914), who was head of the Lewis-Merthyr colliery combine that sank the pit here in 1914. It closed in 1924. The village arose on the estate of Sir William, who lived at Bontnewydd House.

Libanus, village, Powys, Wales.

The name is that of a Congregationalist chapel here, built some time in the first half of the 19th century. Libanus is a form of the biblical name of Lebanon, usually understood to mean 'white mountain' and in certain references in the Bible taken to stand for the Church itself, as for example in Isaiah 33: 9.

Limpley Stoke, village, Wiltshire, England.

The village was originally known as 'Hanging Stoke', with this name first recorded in 1263 (as *Hangymdestok*). The reference was to the position of the village below a steep hill. The present name is first noted, as *Lymply Stoke*, in 1585, with the changed first element of uncertain origin. The *Victoria County History of Wiltshire* states that in 1578 Queen Elizabeth I granted to John Mersche and John Turpin 'a ruined chapel called "Our Lady of Limpley's Chapel"' and that the name thus seems to have derived in some way from the dedication of the chapel. Johnston (1914) links the name with Limpenhoe in Norfolk and Limpsfield in Surrey, both of which may derive from a personal name (not necessarily the same person). Perhaps the origin will become clearer when the identity or location of the chapel dedication can be established. It may not even be in England: there is, for example, a French village of Limpiville just across the English Channel, in the *département* of Seine-Maritime.

Linnet, river, Suffolk, England.

The river is a tributary of the **Lark**, which it joins just south-east of Bury St. Edmunds. The name is first recorded in 1834, before this apparently being simply called *The Brook* (1791). It is possible that the name was chosen as an agreeable match for the larger river, helped by alliteration, since both the lark and the linnet are songbirds.

Lisburn, town, Antrim, Northern Ireland.

The original name of the town was Lisnagarvey or Lisnegarvey, from Irish *Lios na gCearrbhach*, 'fort of the gamblers'. Some time in the 17th century the name was changed to Lisburn, for reasons that have not yet been conclusively established. The new second element of the name has been taken to mean either 'spring' (O'Connell, 1979) or English 'burn' referring to a fire that destroyed the town: 'To commemorate the burning of the town in 1641, the inhabitants changed its ancient name, Lisnegarvy, into Lisburn' (J. O'Laverty, *Historical Account of the Diocese of Down and Connor*, 1880). The most detailed consideration of the changed name occurs in W. P. Carmody, *Lisburn Cathedral and its Past Rectors* (1926) and is worth quoting in full:

It is often stated that the old name of this place was Lisnagarvey, but it came to be called Lisburn after the burning of the town. The note on this subject by Dr. Cupples is—'A prevailing conjecture is, that this designation (Lisnagarvey) was abolished after the burning of the town by an accidental fire in 1707, and the present one framed in allusion to, and in commemoration of the calamitous event. But this is an error, for it appears by the registry of baptism, marriages and funerals, that the modern name began and the ancient one ceased, so early as January, 1662, the reason of which cannot now be ascertained.' The word Lisburn is found for the first time in a baptismal entry January 11th, 1662; and Lisnagarvey is so called in a burial entry 13th February, 1662, and is not found again. It may be argued that Lisnagarvey was changed to Lisburn because the town was burned by the Rebels in 1641. This seems to be most improbable; after twenty years the burning would be a memory, and the loyal people of the town would not be disposed to give it a name that would be forever reminiscent of its destruction by rebels. The reason must be sought elsewhere. In the absence of any other I will hazard the following conjecture—to me it is conclusive, others may not think so. It is well to be reminded that this is not the only place named Lisburn. In a very learned book 'The Place Names of Decies,' by the Rev. P. Power, there is mention of a place in the south of County Tipperary called 'The Lisburn'—of which the author says: 'Meaning unknown.' Now, in the 1641 depositions it is stated that the rebels entered the town 'at a place called Louzy Burne'; this is the deposition of an English soldier, and English soldiers have still difficulty in pronouncing Irish names. I take it, then, that 'Louzy Burne' is Lisburn. Just as we find Lisnagarvey called by an English writer of that period 'Linsley Garvin,' if I am correct in this, it would seem that there was a fort called Lisburn from an early period just as there was a fort called Lisnagarvey. And I believe, also, the site of that fort called Lisburn is still to be seen at the top of Hill Street on the east side; there are the remains of an important and well-fortified primitive town, with strong fortifications guarding any approach from the river and the surrounding country: in a garden close by can still be seen part of the quern or grinding stone used in early days; and around it on the west side of the original stone pavement may be traced down to the river [Lagan]. Also, this is just the course that anyone entering Lisburn from the south-west would come from. I take it, then, that Lisburn and Lisnagarvey existed together; that the name Lisnagarvey became at first more frequent in use for Sir Fulke Conway [later Viscount Conway, the English settler to whom James I granted the town in 1609] had built his castle [in 1627] close by it; but it had to compete with Lisburn, which in reality was the more important place in pre-plantation days, and finally Lisburn, being shorter and more easily pronounced by the English settlers, became the familiar name and Lisnagarvey gradually dropped out.'

Carmody's theory of 'name dominance' is a valid one, and at least his facts seem to rule out fairly conclusively the reference to a fire. Pending further evidence, the final interpretation of the name must be left unresolved.

Littlestone-on-Sea, town and resort, Kent, England.

The settlement here first developed in 1886 as a seaside resort extension of New Romney, although it did not come to be fully exploited until after World War II. In spite of its name, which derives from the former rocky headland here called the Little Stone, the place is thus older and bigger as a residential centre than its neighbouring resort of **Greatstone-on-Sea**. This is largely due to its proximity to the town of New Romney, of which it is now virtually a suburb.

Littleton, village, Tipperary, Ireland.

Lewis (1837) states that the village is 'of modern date, having been chiefly erected by the late Rev. Thomas Grady'. The Irish name means the same as the English, *An Baile Beag*, 'the little town'.

Littleworth, village, South Yorkshire, England.

The original name of the village was 'Shittleworth', recorded in the 'Domesday Book' of 1086 as *Scitelesuuorde*, as *Sitlewrth* in the 12th century, and as *Schutlesworth* in 1210. The present name is first recorded in 1724, as *Littleworth yard*, with the change in the first part of the name made some time before this, presumably because of the indelicate associations of the original name, which in fact means simply 'barred enclosure' (from Old English *scyttels*, 'bar', 'bolt', to which modern English 'shut' and 'shoot the bolt' are related). For names apparently changed on similar grounds, compare **Middlestown**, **Netherton**, and **Overton**.

Llandrindod Wells, town and spa, Powys, Wales.

Originally the name was *Llanddwy*, 'church of God' first recorded (as *Lando*) in 1291. By 1536 the name had been modified to *Llandynddod*, 'church of the Trinity', after the medieval church built to replace the original one. In 1749 development began of the wells and springs discovered round the town at the end of the 17th century, and the suffix to the name was added some time in the first half of the 19th century.

Llanfairpwllgwyngyllgogerychwyrndrobwllllandysiliogogogoch, village, Gwynedd, Wales.

The famous Anglesey name, the so-called longest place-name in Britain and described by Morgan (1887) as 'a rather pretty and inviting word to a Saxon tourist', seems to have been devised as a joke by a tailor who lived in the town of Menai Bridge in the early part of the 19th century. Doubtless prompted by the already existing lengthy name of the village, Llanfair Pwllgwyngyll ('St. Mary's church in [the township of] Pwllgwyngyll'), the tailor took the name of a neighbouring parish, Llandysilio, altered this to the name of another place in Cardiganshire, Llandysiliogogo (thus combining the names of two adjoining parishes, Llandysilio, 'St. Tysil's church', and Gogo, 'the cave'), and then inserted a middle section and a final, meaningless '-goch'. The middle section does not exist as an independent name, but seems to allude to a swirling pool called the Pwll Ceris in the narrow section of the Menai Straits near the village: *goger y chwyrn drobwll*, 'near the fierce whirlpool'. Including the original second element of the name (Pwllgwyngyll), added to distinguish this particular Llanfair from the many other places so called, the whole name can thus be (unrealistically) translated as: 'church of [saint] Mary [near the] white hazel near the fierce whirlpool [and the] church of [saint] Tysil(io) [by the] cave'. Some guidebooks and other sources, e.g. the *Guinness Book of Records*, also translate the final *goch* of the name as 'red', although this syllable seems to have been added merely to round the extravagant name off. Morgan gives the name with an extra syllable *go*, but this appears to be a slip, forgivable in the circumstances. The name is often abbreviated to 'Llanfair P.G.', a form described by Richards (1972) as 'quite unacceptable'. The recommended Post Office form of the name is Llanfairpwllgwyngyll.

Llangrove, village, Hereford and Worcester, England.

The name originated as 'Longgrove', and is so recorded in 1372 (as *Long grove*). The village is close to the Welsh border, four miles north of Monmouth, and at some stage in the 19th century its name was adapted to what was felt to be a more appropriate or even more 'correct' form, with Welsh *llan*, 'church', substituted for English 'long'. This modification may have been made by the Post Office. *Cassell* (1896) enters the name as '*Long Grove*, or *Llangrove*'.

Loch Thom, lake (near Greenock), Strathclyde, Scotland.

The small loch and reservoir is named after the engineer who constructed it in 1827, Robert Thom.

Londonderry see **Derry**.

Long Lane see **Coalville**.

Longside, village (near Peterhead), Grampian, Scotland.

The village was founded in 1801 by James Ferguson of Pitfour who also founded **New Deer**. Its name is apparently descriptive for the village, which is laid out on a hill.

Longtown, village, Hereford and Worcester, England.

The village is only two miles from the Welsh border, and the original locality here had a Welsh name, *Ewyas Lacy*, 'sheep district [belonging to Roger de] Laci'. In 1540 the settlement had developed sufficiently for it to be separately identified as *Longa villa in Ewias Lacy*, and a record made in *c*.1670 notes that the village 'hath lately taken the name of Longtown'. The name refers to the location of the village, which extends up the Olchon Valley.

Lossiemouth, town and port, Grampian, Scotland.

The town was laid out at the mouth of the river Lossie five miles north of Elgin in 1698, when construction of the harbour also began. A place named *Port of Lossy* is recorded in 1383, but this seems to have been further up the river.

Louisburgh, village, Mayo, Ireland.

The village was named commemoratively for the capture of Louisburg, Nova Scotia, by English forces under General Amherst and Admiral Boscowen, in 1758. Henry Browne, uncle of the 1st Marquis of Sligo, had been present at the capture as a young officer. The marquises, whose family name is Browne, had long been landowners in the locality. Their title of Sligo was created in 1800. The village's Irish name is *Cluain Cearbán*, 'Carban's meadow'.

Louisburgh, district of Wick, Highland, Scotland.

The name commemorates that of Lady Louisa Dunbar, who was a landowner here in the second half of the 18th century.

Lowther, village, Cumbria, England.

The name derives from the Lowther family, long resident in the locality. The Lowthers first attempted to found a model village here in 1683–4, but the carpet manufacturing business they had planned met with financial failure and Lowther New Town, as it was named, did not achieve success as an industrial centre. Sir James Lowther, Earl of Lonsdale (1736–1802), commissioned the architect brothers Adam to draw up plans for a new village in 1765, but although building took place until 1773 the village was not completed. See also **Newtown** (Cumbria).

Lowtherstown see **Irvinestown**.

Lowthertown, village (near Annan), Dumfries and Galloway, Scotland.

The village arose in *c*.1840 and took its name from the landowners here, the Lowther family, long resident in the neighbourhood.

Lowtherville, district of Ventnor, Isle of Wight, England.

The name derives from a local doctor here, Horace Lowther (1840–1916), who developed property in the district under the Poor Law Authorities in the 1880s. The name is rarely used officially, and the local name for the district is Upper Ventnor.

M

Macduff, town and port, Grampian, Scotland.

The settlement was originally named Doune or Down when it was acquired in 1733 by William Duff, 1st Earl of Fife. In 1783 George III granted a charter to James Duff, 2nd Earl of Fife (1729–1809), erecting the town to a burgh of barony, and the second earl renamed the town on rebuilding it this year. The form of the name was a compliment to his father: William Duff had been created Earl of Fife and Viscount Macduff in 1759 on proving his descent from the semi-mythical Macduff, Earl of Fife, who is said to have lived in the 11th century (and who figures in Shakespeare's *Macbeth*). For a similarly derived name, compare **Dufftown**.

Maesteg, town, Mid Glamorgan, Wales.

The name means 'fair field' (Welsh *maes*, 'field' and *teg*, 'fair') and was originally the name of a farm here divided into three parts: 'Maesteg Isaf' ('lower Maesteg'), 'Maesteg Canol' ('middle Maesteg'), and 'Maesteg Uchaf' ('higher Maesteg'), these referring to the open field system that was practised in the valley of the river Llynfi here in medieval times. Documents of the 15th century record the name generally as *Maesteel*, with *Maes tege issa* (for 'lower Maesteg') noted in 1543. Today 'Maesteg Uchaf' has its site in the centre of the modern town, where the County Library and Church Street stand. The unified name of Maesteg was adopted for the growing industrial town in 1887, when an enlarged urban district was formed comprising the former townships of Cwmdu and Llangynwyd Uchaf. An alternative name for the town, still in use by local Welsh-speakers, was *Y Llwyni*, 'the bushes'. This was the name of the farm where industrial development first took place in the Llynfi valley. The name is first recorded in 1631, as *y llwyney*. Yet another (English) name for the new industrial development was *Bowrington*, after Sir John Bowring (1792–1872), a director of an ironworks here in the 1840s. This name was soon abandoned in favour of the Welsh ones, however. At an eisteddfod held in the town in 1839, the suggestion was made that *Y Llwyni* should be changed to *Y Llyfnwy*, but this name, of unauthenticated origin, was not adopted and remained in use only among local literary and musical figures. 'Llyfnwy' was the name taken, however, as the bardic name of Thomas Morgan, a 19th-century local historian and antiquarian.

Maida Vale, district of west London, England,

The name, strictly that of the main street here, is first recorded in 1868, and is commemorative for the battle of Maida in Calabria, Italy, in 1806, when Sir John Stuart defeated the French forces under General Régnier. The street is called 'Vale' rather than 'Street' or 'Road' since the houses were built along the Edgware Road at the foot of a hill, this being originally Maida Hill (today Maida Avenue). Maida Vale Underground station opened in 1915 to secure the name for the residential district.

Maindee, district of Newport, Gwent, Wales.

The name derives from that of a house here in the 17th century, 'Maendy' ('stone house').

Maitland Park, district of north-west London, England.

An estate here was purchased in 1847 as a site for an orphanage and was named after its treasurer, Ebenezer Maitland.

Mannofield, district of Aberdeen, Grampian, Scotland.

The district arose on an estate so named in *c*.1790 by its owner, Robert Balmano.

Manorhamilton, village, Leitrim, Ireland.

The name is that of a castle built here in 1638 by Sir Frederick Hamilton, to whom Charles I had granted confiscated Irish lands in the district. The Irish name of the village is *Cluainín*, 'little meadow'.

Marino, suburb of Dublin, Ireland.

The name derives from Marino House, the seaside retreat here of James Caulfeild, 4th Viscount and 1st Earl of Charlemont (1728–99), which he started to rebuild in *c.*1770.

Markham, village, Gwent, Wales.

The mining village took the name of its colliery owner in the 19th century, George Markham.

Maryborough, former name of Port Laoise, town, Laois, Ireland.

The town became the county town of **Queen's County** in 1556 when the Leinster territory of Leix (Irish *Laois*) was shired, taking its name from Mary Tudor, whose husband gave his name to **Philipstown**. The town reverted to its Irish name in 1920. This does not mean 'port of Laois' but 'fort of Laois', Laois (formerly rendered in English as Leix) being the name of the district held by the O'Mores. Compare **King's County**, which was the territory of the O'Connors. The original name of the fort round which Maryborough grew was *Fort Protector*.

Maryburgh, village (near Dingwall), Highland, Scotland.

The village seems to have been founded during the reign of Mary II, wife of William III, thus in the six-year period 1689–94. For other places at one time called Maryburgh, see **Blairadam** and **Fort William**.

Maryhill, district of Glasgow, Strathclyde, Scotland.

The district was named in 1760 after its proprietress, Mary Hill of Gairbraid.

Maryland, former village, Brownsea Island, Dorset, England.

The village was built in *c.*1852 for pottery workers here by the owner of Brownsea Island, Colonel William Petrie Waugh, who named it after his wife Mary. The pottery business failed in the early 1880s and the village collapsed soon after.

Marylebone, district of west central London, England.

The original name of the district was 'Tyburn', recorded in the 'Domesday Book' of 1086 as *Tiburne*, this being the name of the river here (now entirely below ground). From the early 14th century, the name came to be associated with the Middlesex Gallows here, and for this reason some time in the 15th century was changed to 'Maryburn' (recorded as *Maryburne* in 1453), this meaning 'Mary's stream' after the church of St. Mary that stood here. At some stage in the 17th century the meaningless -le- was inserted in the name, perhaps on an analogy with St. Mary le Bow, with the result that the modern name of Marylebone has popularly been taken to be of French or Norman origin, and to mean 'Mary the Good' (or 'Mary the Blessed').

Maryport, town and former port, Cumbria, England.

The town was originally known as 'Ellenfoot' (*Ellnesfoote* 1566, *Elnefoot* *c.*1745), for its position at the mouth of the river Ellen. (Compare the name of Ellenborough, a district of Maryport.) A new harbour was built here over the ten-year period beginning in *c.*1750, and its founder, Humphrey Senhouse, named the subsequent coalport that developed after his wife Mary. Although the origin of the new name is well attested (for example, in the *Transactions of the Cumberland and Westmorland Antiquarian and Archaeological Society, Old Series*, 1866), local legend still persists that the name was given because Maryport was 'where, or near where, Queen Mary landed in her flight from Scotland, 1568' (Johnston, 1914).

Maxwelltown, district of Dumfries, Dumfries and Galloway, Scotland.

The district was originally called *Bridgend*, for its location by the river Nith. The former town was then erected into a free burgh of barony in 1810, when it was renamed Maxwelltown in honour of its proprietor, Marmaduke Constable Maxwell, of Nithsdale.

Mayfair, district of central London, England.

This part of London was open land until the end of the 17th century, and here in the reign of Charles II (1660–85) an annual fair came to be held in the first week in May. The first occurrence of the name seems to be recorded in a document of 1702 which refers to 'a fair held in the parish of St. Martin in the Fielde, commonly called May Fair'. The fair was suppressed in 1709, then revived, and finally abolished in 1760 after an existence of a hundred years. Meanwhile building had begun in the district as early as 1704. The actual site of the old fair was Shepherd Market, just south of Curzon Street.

Medina, administrative district, Isle of Wight, England.

The district takes its name from the river Medina, whose ancient name means 'middle'. It divides the Isle of Wight roughly into two parts as it flows north into the sea.

Melandra (Castle), Roman fort (near Glossop), Derbyshire, England.

The original name of the fort seems to have been *Ardotalia*, meaning 'high edge'. The present name is not found before 1772, and appears to be an artificial pseudo-Greek creation. Perhaps it was devised as a learned pun on the name of the creator, who thus may have been called Blackman (Greek *melas*, 'black', *aner*, *andros*, 'man'). There does not seem to have been any Greek character so called, whether historical or mythological. How in any case could a Greek name have come to be given to a Roman fort? In spite of the spuriousness of the name, it is quoted in some scholarly works as authentic, for example in I. D. Margary, *Roman Roads* (1967), where it is printed in italics as if a genuine Romano-British name.

Meirionydd, administrative district, Gwynedd, Wales.

The district has taken the old name of Merioneth, which former territory and county approximate to the present district in area. The name means 'territory of Meirion', this ruler being, like Ceredig (see **Ceredigion**), one of the sons of Cunedda in the 5th century. See also **Gwynedd**.

Menai Bridge, town, Gwynedd, Wales.

The present name was taken by the town (then a village) after the completion of Telford's suspension bridge across the Menai Straits here in 1826. The original name, and still the present Welsh one, was *Porthaethwy*, from *porth*, 'ferry' and the tribal name Daethwy. This name was first recorded in 1291 as *Porthatheu* and in 1795 was noted as *Porthaethwy Ferry*, something of a tautology. Some local Welsh-speakers use the shortened form of the name, *Y Borth*, 'the ferry'.

Middlestown, village, West Yorkshire, England.

The original name of the village, in use in some form down to the 19th century, was 'Middle Shitlington'. This was changed, however, for reasons of propriety, with the present name first recorded in 1556, as *Midlestowne* (so that the two names were in parallel use for some time). The old name simply meant 'Scyttel's farm', i.e. derived from the name of a person. For similar name changes, compare **Littleworth**, **Netherton**, and **Overton**.

Middletown, village, Powys, Wales.

The name is first recorded in *c*.1570, as *Middletoune*, this being the English translation of the Welsh name *Treberfedd*, 'middle homestead' (from *tref*, 'farm', 'homestead', 'town', and *perfedd*, 'middle').

Midlands, central area of England.

The name seems to have been first used in Michael Drayton's *Polyolbion* of 1622, where it appears as *the Mid-lands*. In 1675 the name appears as *the Midland Countries* (sic). It originally applied to the counties in central England, defined by the *Oxford English Dictionary* as 'the counties south of the Humber and Mersey and north of the Thames, with the exception of Norfolk, Suffolk, Essex, Middlesex, Hertfordshire, Gloucestershire and the counties bordering on Wales'. The name also has application in hunting terms, since some of England's longest established hunts are based in the Midlands. In this narrower sense, the name is defined by the *Oxford English Dictionary* as pertaining to 'the champaign [i.e. open] country including parts of the counties of Leicester, Rutland, Northampton, Warwick, Nottinghamshire, and Derbyshire'. Today, partly as a result of the reorganization in 1974 of local government boundaries, and the abolition of some counties (such as Huntingdonshire and Rutland) altogether, the name has become somewhat vaguer, and the area has tended to polarize into the two industrial regions of East Midlands and West Midlands. East Midlands, thus, is now understood as the area including the cities of Nottingham, Derby, Leicester, and Northampton, and **West Midlands** (the official name from 1974 of a new metropolitan county) as centring on Birmingham but also including Coventry, Walsall, Wolverhampton, and West Bromwich. Both these names, East Midlands and West Midlands, are also used in an official sense for two of the 'standard' regions of England delimited for statistical purposes, with West Midlands covering a wider area than that of the metropolitan county. The general name Midlands has also been obscured geographically by its use for the names of

commercial organizations, such as the Midland Bank and the London Midland region of British Rail.

Midleton, town, Cork, Ireland.

The town was founded in *c.*1670 by the Brodericks or Brodricks, later the Earls of Midleton, who had greatly profited by the confiscation of Irish lands. The name seems to refer to the town's location, roughly halfway between Youghal and Cork. The first Lord Midleton was Alan Brodrick (?1660–1728).

Midlothian, administrative district, Lothian, Scotland.

The name was originally that of a county here that centred on Edinburgh, and that was thus called Edinburghshire. After the local government reorganization of 1975, the new district of Midlothian was formed, somewhat smaller in area than the original county.

Midville, village, Lincolnshire, England.

The village was formed as a township in 1812 by act of parliament on the draining of a large area of fenland here, and seems to be named for its position halfway between 'the Hob-hole and Catch-water drains' (*White's Directory of Lincolnshire*, 1842). Other townships formed this same year were **Carrington**, **Eastville**, **Frithville**, **Langriville**, **Thornton-le-Fen**, and **Westville**. Although *White's Directory* mentions the location of Midville halfway between two drains, it is more obviously situated midway between Westville and Eastville.

Milford-on-sea, town and resort, Hampshire, England.

The name is basically an old one, with *Melleford* ('ford by a mill') recorded in the 'Domesday Book' of 1086. When the town began to develop as a seaside resort after World War I, the owner of some estates here tried to introduce the name 'Melleford-on-Sea', based on the 1086 spelling, for his sale brochures, but the name was not popular and was dropped. The suffix '-on-sea', however, was adopted and came into regular use some time after 1930.

Mill Hill, district of north-west London, England.

The name is first recorded in 1547, as *Myllehill*, although there is no evidence that a mill ever existed here. The present Underground station of Mill Hill East (there is no 'Mill Hill West') originated as Mill Hill station on the Great Northern Railway line in 1867. The station was renamed Mill Hill East in 1928 and the line was first used by Underground trains in 1941, by which time the station name had become firmly established for the surrounding district.

Milliken Park, village (near Johnstone), Strathclyde, Scotland.

The village was founded in 1856 and was named after a Major Milliken who bought the original estate here in 1733.

Millport, port and resort (Great Cumbrae), Strathclyde, Scotland.

The island port was named for the grainmill here that formerly stood above the harbour. The town grew up from c.1805 when stone was quarried on the island for shipping to the mainland. Millport first developed as a resort at about the same time, when also a harbour was built.

Millwall, district of east London, England.

The name means '(river) wall on which a mill has been built'. The name 'walls' was given to embankments which ran along the river Thames here, such as Blackwall, Wapping Wall and Bermondsey Wall. Millwall is recorded as being called Marsh Wall in 1754, and in fact had several mills on it to about this year. According to Rawlings (c.1925) such walls may have been Roman or even pre-Roman.

Moira, village, Leicestershire, England.

The village is in the parish of Ashby-de-la-Zouch, which was the property of Francis Rawdon-Hastings, 2nd Earl of Moira (1754–1826), when fireclay and coal were discovered here at the end of the 18th century. The first pits were sunk in 1804, and the Earl built cottages for the miners here in 1811, with the village name first recorded in 1831. The Earl's title in the Irish peerage comes from Moira, Down, Northern Ireland.

Mole, river, Devon, England.

The name seems to be a back formation of 'Molton', with both North Molton and South Molton on the river. It may also be connected with the village of Molland, east of South Molton. The name was first recorded in 1553, as *Moll*. The river's earlier name was probably the 'Nymet', preserved in the villages of George Nympton, Kings Nympton, and Bishops Nympton, all close to the Mole.

Mole, river, West Sussex/Surrey, England.

The river name is a back formation of 'Molesey', with both West Molesey and East Molesey situated close to the point where the Mole runs into the Thames. The name is first recorded in 1577, as *Moule water*, and in its present spelling in 1612. The river's former name was the 'Emel', preserved in the Surrey administrative district of **Elmbridge**. Another early name for the Mole may also have been the 'Dork', surviving in Dorking. The local legend is still popular that the Mole is so called because it runs underground in some places, with this explanation being the one offered by Johnston (1914). (An alternative to this is that the mole inhabits the banks of the river (Edmunds, 1872).) See also **Mole Valley** (below).

Mole Valley, administrative district, Surrey, England.

The district takes its name from the river **Mole**, which flows north through the towns of Dorking and Leatherhead here.

Monkstown, resort and suburb of Cork, Cork, Ireland.

The name seems to derive from Monkstown Castle, also known as Castle Mahon, built here in 1636 by Anastasia Archdeacon (or Cody), née Gould. On the other hand, *Cassell* (1896) says that the name may originate in a small Benedictine monastery established here in the 14th century as a cell for St. John's, Waterford.

Montaguetown see **Bucklers Hard**.

Morecambe, town and resort, Lancashire, England.

The town is on Morecambe Bay, which came to be so called in 1771 when it was identified with the place *Morikámbē* indicated on Ptolemy's map of the British Isles of *c*.150. In fact the name recorded by Ptolemy, and apparently deriving from Celtic meaning 'great bay' (not 'curved bay' as often explained), seems to refer more specifically to the estuary of the river Lune, or even the Leven. Morecambe the town was originally known as *Poulton-le-Sands*, and by 1844 had become an established seaside resort. This earlier name continued officially down to 1870, with Morecambe simply a minor and alternative name. The new name, however, was promoted by The Morecambe Bay Harbour and Railway Company (later The Morecambe Harbour and Railway Company), which was established here in the latter half of the 19th century and which encouraged a new area of residential and commercial development away from Poulton. Even so, as late as 1896 *Cassell* enters the town as '*Morecambe* (sometimes called *Poulton-le-Sands*)'. The present name is thus not a genuine survival of the very old name, but an antiquarian revival. Field (1980) sees an advantageous touristic pun in the name, if interpreted as 'more come'.

Morice Town, district of Plymouth, Devon, England.

The name derives from the family of Sir William Morice, who is recorded as having purchased the manor of Stoke here in 1667 from Sir Edward Wise.

Morriston, district of Swansea, West Glamorgan, Wales.

The district arose as an industrial village built in *c*.1790 by Sir John Morris of Clasmont for the workers at his copper works here, founded in *c*.1768. The Welsh name is the same as the English in meaning, *Treforys*.

Mountain Ash, town, Mid Glamorgan, Wales.

The original name of the place was 'Aberpennarth', recorded in 1570 as *Aber Pennarthe* ('mouth of the Pennardd'). The town grew up in the industrial expansion of the 19th century. Local tradition says that the name was given arbitrarily by the landowner here, John Bruce Pryce. The best account of the origin is given by Morgan (1887): 'A man named David John Rhys went to Mr Pryce one day to ask him for a lease on a certain piece of land, on which he proposed building a public-house and a private house. They went together to measure the land, and, in reply to a question of Mr Pryce with regard to the name of the new public-house he was asked to name, seeing a *cerdinen* (mountain ash) close by, he turned to Mrs Pryce, and said—"We shall call this place Mountain Ash".' The Welsh name of the town today remains *Aberpennar*.

Mount Batten, district of Plymouth, Devon, England.

The name derives from Admiral Sir William Batten (d. 1667), governor of the fort here in the Civil War (1642–9). The earlier name of the place was 'Hoestart', recorded in 1296 as *Hostert* and in 1598 as *Hoe Stert*. This means 'end of the ridge' (*Hoe* as in Plymouth Hoe, *Start* as in Start Point). The name seems to have come into use during the governorship of Admiral Batten. Compare **Mount Gould** (below).

Mount Gould, district of Plymouth, Devon, England.

The name is that of Colonel William Gould, who was governor of the Plymouth garrison in the Civil War (1642–9). The name appears in some sources as Mount Gold (e.g. in the plan of Plymouth in *AA England & Wales*, 1963).

Mountnorris, village, Armagh, Northern Ireland.

The name derives from a fort built here in the second half of the 16th century by General Sir John Norris (?1547–97) to protect the pass between Armagh and Newry.

Mount Stewart see **Fivemiletown**.

Mount Vernon, village (near Glasgow), Strathclyde, Glasgow.

Most sources say that the name was introduced in *c*.1787 by George Buchanan, one of the so-called 'Virginia dons' (who traded extensively with Virginia in tobacco), after Mount Vernon, the Washington estate in Virginia, United States. This was so named by Lawrence Washington, the half-brother of George Washington, after Admiral Edward Vernon, under whom Lawrence Washington had served, with 'Mount' for the hill by the river Potomac on which the estate stands. Earlier, the Scottish Mount Vernon was known as *Windyedge*.

Murrayfield, district of Edinburgh, Lothian, Scotland.

According to Johnston (1934), the name is apparently that of Archibald Murray, an advocate who was a landowner here in the early 18th century.

N

Nant-y-glo, village, Gwent, Wales.

The name, meaning 'the coal stream' or 'the coal valley' (Welsh *nant*, 'stream', 'valley', *y*, 'the', *glo*, 'coal'), was first recorded in 1752, as *Nantygloe*. The 19th-century industrial development grew up round an iron furnace here from c.1795.

Nar, river, Norfolk, England.

The name is a back formation from the villages of Narborough and Narford, which stand on the river. The name first occurs in *Icenia, sive Norfolciae Descriptio topographica* ('Icenia, or a Topographical Description of Norfolk'), a posthumous work by the historian and antiquarian Sir Henry Spelman (?1564–1641), and it is possible that he invented it. Earlier names for the river recorded are *Castel Acre river* in c.1540 and *Linus* (also a back formation, from **King's Lynn**) in 1577.

Nazareth, village, Gwynedd, Wales.

The name originated in the first half of the 19th century as that of a Congregationalist chapel here. The biblical name, occurring several times in the New Testament (e.g. Luke 4: 16) was believed to mean 'abounding in flowers', and was specially chosen as the name of the town where Christ was brought up and where he preached.

Nebo, village, Dyfed, Wales.

This is an early 19th-century chapel name, taken from the name of the mountain where Moses died (Deuteronomy 32: 49) and understood as meaning 'he who utters prophecy'. There are several villages of the name in Wales, including at least three in Gwynedd.

Nelson, town, Lancashire, England.

The town grew up in the early 19th century round the Lord Nelson inn here. This, together with many other inns of the name, would have been built some time after 1805, the year of Nelson's victory at Trafalgar. The name first appears on a map dated 1818, and a local board is recorded as having been formed in 1864 for 'the district of Nelson'. The township formerly here was called *Marsden*.

Nelson, village, Mid Glamorgan, Wales.

The original name of the locality was *Ffos y Gerdinen*, 'mountain ash ditch' (compare **Mountain Ash**). When the village began to grow at the beginning of the 19th century, an inn was built here called the Lord Nelson, and this subsequently transferred to the village. Compare **Nelson**, Lancashire (above).

Netherton, village, West Yorkshire, England.

The name of the village down to the early 19th century was one form or another of 'Nether Shitlington'. This was gradually changed to 'Netherton', presumably for reasons of delicacy, until the latter name took over altogether. See also **Middlestown** and compare **Overton**.

New Aberdour, village (near Fraserburgh), Grampian, Scotland.

The village was founded in 1798 near to Aberdour Bay. It was 'New' as distinct from the 'old' Aberdour in Fife.

New Addington, district of Croydon, London, England.

The name derives from the nearby district of Addington, with development begun here in 1934–5 by the First National Housing Trust. According to the *Croydon Official Guide* (1964), the name is 'not officially recognised by the Post Office or the General Register Office'.

New Ash Green, village, Kent, England.

The village, named for the nearby village of Ash, arose in 1965 as an 'urban village', built by the Span development company.

New Birmingham, village, Tipperary, Ireland.

When coal mines were first developed near here, the resulting settlement was named after Birmingham, the industrial city in England, itself surrounded by coal mines. Lewis (1837) records that New Birmingham is 'indebted for its origin and name to the late Sir Vere Hunt, Bart.'.

New Bolingbroke, village, Lincolnshire, England.

According to *White's Directory of Lincolnshire* (1842), the village was founded by John Parkinson, lessee of crown lands here, in c.1817 'upon that part of the West Fen which was allotted at the enclosure to Bolingbroke parish'. New Bolingbroke is five miles south-west of Bolingbroke (now officially Old Bolingbroke).

Newborough, former name of Gorey, town, Wexford, Ireland.

Doctor Thomas Ram, Bishop of Ferns, who had a sizeable estate here and who lived here, obtained a charter of incorporation for the inhabitants from James I in 1620 under the designation 'the sovereign burgesses and free commons of the borough and town of Newborough'. The name never came into general use, however, and the Irish name *Guaire*, 'sandbank', anglicized as Gorey, prevailed.

New Bradwell, district of Milton Keynes, Buckinghamshire, England.

The district was designed as a village for railway employees some time before 1850, basing its name on Bradwell, just south of it (and now also part of Milton Keynes New Town).

Newbridge see **Droichead Nua**.

New Brighton, village, Clwyd, Wales.

The village was originally known as *Pentre Cythraul*, 'Devil's village'. Presumably from the undesirable associations, the name was changed to New Brighton some time in the second half of the 19th century, with the new name apparently taken from **New Brighton**, Merseyside. There are two villages of the name in Clwyd: this one is near Mold, the other near Wrexham.

New Brighton, district of Emsworth, Hampshire, England.

The residential district developed some time in the 19th century, when Emsworth was a popular bathing resort (partly as a result of a visit here to 'take the waters' made in 1805 by Princess Amelia, daughter of George III), and the name was almost certainly a reference to the already established resort of **Brighton**, further east along the coast in Sussex. An additional link with the older resort was made when Emsworth came to be located on the Portsmouth to Brighton railway line, opened in the mid-19th century.

New Brighton, resort and district of Wallasey, Merseyside, England.

The district owes its development to James Atherton, a retired merchant from Liverpool, who purchased about 170 acres of sandhills and heathland here in 1830 and named the future resort New Brighton after the already established resort of **Brighton** in Sussex. Building on the site began in c.1832, and the resort is named and in fact advertised in a prospectus entitled 'Eligible Investment at New Brighton, Cheshire' probably published this same year (E. C. Woods and P. C. Brown, *The Rise and Progress of Wallasey*, 2nd rev. ed., 1974).

New Byth, village (near Turriff), Grampian, Scotland.

The village was laid out as a planned settlement in 1764 by Joseph Cumine of Auchry (see **Cuminestown**) for his neighbour, William Urquhart, who had granted various estates on which it could be built. The village was named after nearby Byth.

Newcastle, port and resort, Down, Northern Ireland.

The town derives its name from the castle built here in 1588 by Felix Magennis. This replaced an older castle, probably on the same site, that was recorded as existing here in 1433. The castle was itself demolished in the first half of the 19th century to make way for a hotel, also subsequently demolished.

Newcastleton, town, Borders, Scotland.

The town was created in 1793 by Henry Scott, 3rd Duke of Buccleuch (1746–1812), on the site of the former village of Castleton, whose castle had been destroyed by Cromwell in the first half of the 17th century.

Newchapel, suburb of Kidsgrove, Staffordshire, England.

The name refers to the church of St. James here, which was built in c.1760 on the site of an Elizabethan chapel and which was rebuilt in 1880. The district name seems to have come into general use late in the 19th century, recorded as *New Chapel* 1891, *Newchapel* 1896, *Thursfield, now New Chapel* 1902.

Newchurch, village (near Aberystwyth), Dyfed, Wales.

The former Welsh name, and the present one, was *Llanfihangel-y-Creuddyn* (*-Uchaf*), '(Upper) St. Michael's church by the pigsty'. The new name dates from some time after 1803, when Colonel Thomas Johns, of Hafod Ichtryd, built a new church here.

Newchurch, village (near Carmarthen), Dyfed, Wales.

The name is the English translation of the Welsh 'Eglwys Newydd' (now *Llannewydd*). The Welsh name is an old one, first recorded in 1129, as *Eglusnewit*. The English name is first recorded in 1535, in its present form.

Newchurch, village, Gwent, Wales.

The name is the English translation of the Welsh 'Eglwys Newydd' (now *Eglwys Newydd ar y Cefn*, 'new church on the ridge'). The English name was first recorded, with its present spelling, in 1537. The village was formerly in Monmouthshire.

Newchurch, village, Powys, Wales.

The former name of the village, and the present one, was *Llan-ddulas-tir-yr-Abbad*, 'church [by the river] Dulas [on the] land [of] the abbot'. A new church was built here in 1716, and the new (English) name came into use as a result.

New Cross, district of south-east London, England

The name seems to derive from New Cross Heath, recorded here in the 15th century. This was so named for the crossroads formed where the road from east to west passed through Camberwell, intersecting the road from Kent and the south. Later, a coaching inn called the Golden Cross was built here. In his *Diary*, Evelyn says he went to 'New Crosse' in the entry dated 10 November 1675. The name became established for the district when the East London Line railway station opened here in 1880.

New Deer, village (near Peterhead), Grampian, Scotland.

As a parish, New Deer was separated from Old Deer in the early 17th century, but the name became fully established with the founding of the village in 1805 by James Ferguson of Pitfour (1734–1820), together with **Longside** four years previously.

New Earswick, suburb of York, North Yorkshire, England.

The suburb arose as a garden village, founded in 1902 for the workers at Rowntree's cocoa factory and named after the nearby village of Earswick.

New Elgin, district of Elgin, Grampian, Scotland.

The village arose in 1850, when it was founded by the Incorporated Trades of Elgin one mile south of Elgin. New Elgin was the last of the many 'planned villages' in Scotland.

New Galloway, town, Dumfries and Galloway, Scotland.

Estates here had been held for many years by the Gordon family of Kenmure when in 1629 Charles I conferred on Sir John Gordon, later 1st Viscount Kenmure and Lord Lochinvar (?1599–1634), the charter of a royal burgh. Shortly after, this became known as New Galloway, after the family ties with Lochinvar, in the county of Galloway. The name seems to have been first recorded in 1682, as *The New Town of Galloway*.

New Geneva, former village, Waterford, Ireland.

The village arose in 1785 when an attempt was made to found a settlement for watchmakers, gold- and silver-smiths, and a number of intellectuals from Geneva, Switzerland, with plans for a university here. The attempt failed, largely through the unreasonable demands of the *émigré* craftsmen, and by the end of the 18th century the place had been abandoned.

Newham, district of north London, England.

The district was formed as a borough in 1965 when the two towns of East Ham and West Ham were united, together with other areas, and the name was intended to reflect these two, now forming a 'new Ham'. The choice of name was the final one of ninety suggested. Davies & Levitt (1970) note that 'the Town Clerk hoped that people would take care to pronounce the middle "h"'.

Newhaven, town and port, East Sussex, England.

The town was originally known as 'Meeching', this name being first found, as *Mechingas*, in 1121. In a year variously stated as 1570 or *c*.1580 there was a violent storm in the region, as a result of which shingle sealed off the mouth of the river **Ouse** where it entered the sea at Seaford, and forced it to find a new

exit some two miles to the west. This therefore became the 'new haven' while Seaford was thus the 'old haven', and apparently even known as this for a while. Both *EPNS Surrey* (1934) (in the Addenda) and Johnston (1914) give the earliest record of the name Newhaven as 1563, but this seems to be an error. In the *Survey of the Sussex Coast* (1587) the village is named as *Michin* and the port as *Newehaven*. In 1685 the name is recorded as *Meetching alias Newhaven*. It is perhaps significant that the English name of the French port Le Havre was *Newhaven* for some years in the 16th century after it had been established as a port by Francis I in 1517. Le Havre ('the harbour', 'the haven') lies on the opposite coast of the English Channel, due south of Newhaven. The name Newhaven, too, had its precedents (see next entry, for example).

Newhaven, district of Edinburgh, Lothian, Scotland.

The district arose as a fishing port founded by James IV in *c*.1500, with its name recorded in 1510 as *the new haven lately made by the said king*, and in 1536 as *The New Havin*. The harbour built here was 'new' by contrast with the 'old' harbour at Leith.

New Holland, village, Humberside, England.

The settlement arose in the 1830s as a terminus for passengers crossing the river Humber to Hull by ferry, having reached the end of the Manchester, Sheffield, and Lincolnshire railway line. The village was formerly in north Lincolnshire, and was named for the resemblance of the surrounding region to the district called Holland in the south east of the county.

New Houghton, village, Norfolk, England.

The village was built in *c*.1729 to replace the old village of Houghton that had been demolished to allow the construction of Houghton Hall, built over the period 1722–35.

Newhouse see **Avonwick**.

Newington, district of Edinburgh, Lothian, Scotland.

According to J. Anderson, *Calendar of the Laing Charters 854–1837* (1839), the name was in use in 1720 for lands here purchased by one Alexander Pitcairn, and first appears on a map in John Laurie's *Plan of the County of Midlothian* (1763). The name appears to be a semi-arbitrary one to suggest 'new town', 'new property'.

New Invention, village, Shropshire, England.

The name seems to have derived from an inn so called, itself being a semi-punning name for a public house (a 'new inn-vention'). The inn name is fairly common (see next entry).

New Invention, district of Walsall, West Midlands, England.

The name, as in the previous entry, almost certainly derives from an inn here so called. Inevitably, however, local legends abound, among the most ingenious (or ingenuous) being the following: 'New Invention is a place-name which originated not from any connection with the local industries, as one might be led to expect, but from nothing more serious than a nickname of derision. The tradition is that many years ago an inhabitant from the centre of the town [of Walsall] was strolling out that way [on the road to Wolverhampton], when he was thus accosted by an acquaintance living in one of the few cottages which then comprised the neighbourhood, and who was standing on his own doorstep to enjoy the cool of the evening: "I say, Bill, hast seen my new invention?" "No, lad; what is it?" "That's it!" said the self-satisfied householder, pointing up to a hawthorn bush which was pushed out of the top of his chimney. "That's it! It's stopped our o'd chimdy smokin', I can tell thee!" And ever after that the locality which this worthy honoured with his ingenious presence was slyly dubbed by his amused neighbours the "New Invention", by which name it afterwards became generally known.' (F. W. Hackwood, *The Annals of Willenhall*, 1908). Norman Tildesley comments on this tale, and adds further possible origins of the name, in *A History of Willenhall* (1951): 'We face another problem in the name New Invention and here again the present name may be a corruption of an earlier one. It is certainly of early origin for we find it mentioned in the seventeenth-century parish registers. In the baptism of one of his children in 1663 John Poole is described as of "the New Invention near the Snead." At that time New Invention consisted of less than a dozen cottages. The suggestion by F. W. Hackwood, in his *Annals of Willenhall*, that the name New Invention was derived from the invention of a new chimney pot by a man of the district is, of course, absurd for chimney pots were almost unknown in 1660.' (As a matter of record, chimneys could have existed here then because of the clay mining carried on locally.) Yet another explanation says that the village was named after a 'new invention' produced for pumping water out of mines. Even so the inn name seems the likeliest derivation.

New Keith, district of Keith, Grampian, Scotland.

Plans for a new town near to the old town of Keith were laid down in 1750 by James Ogilvy, 6th Earl of Findlater and 3rd Earl of Seafield (?1714–70). Compare **Fife-Keith**.

New Lanark, village (near Lanark), Strathclyde, Scotland.

The settlement arose in 1784, originally as a cotton-milling village founded by the industrialist David Dale (1739–1806), who was its first proprietor. In 1963 the village was taken over by the New Lanark Association for a scheme of restoration and rehabilitation. The initial recommendation to found a village with factories here had been made by the inventor and manufacturer Richard

Arkwright, who even predicted that such a village would 'in time become the Manchester of Scotland'. The village is named after nearby Lanark.

Newmarket, village, Cork, Ireland.

The village was founded by the Aldsworth family in the time of James I (reigned 1603–25), who granted them a market here. The former name of the place was 'Ahahasne' ('place of the ford') or 'Ahtrasne' ('oblique ford'). Its current Irish name is *Áth Trasna*, the latter of these.

Newmarket (Clwyd, Wales) see **Trelawnyd**.

New Merchiston see **Laurieston** (Central, Scotland).

New Milford, alternative name for Neyland, town and port, Dyfed, Wales.

The name is said to have arisen as a result of industrial rivalry with Milford Haven to the west: 'the inhabitants, aspiring hard to compete with their neighbours in Milford, abandoned the old name, and called the place New Milford' (Morgan, 1887). Today both names remain in use, but Neyland is the preferred name on maps and by the Post Office.

Newmill, village (near Keith), Grampian, Scotland.

The village was laid out in 1759 as a rival to **New Keith** by James Duff, 2nd Earl of Fife (1729–1809) (compare **Macduff**).

New Mills, town, Derbyshire, England.

The town grew up round a mill known as 'Berde Mill' or 'New Mill', in operation here in 1565. A further mill was built in the 18th century, and the present (plural) name may come from this. Another theory, however, maintains that there were mills established here for iron-smelting as early as 1285, and that the name may be older than it appears.

Newmills, village, Tyrone, Northern Ireland.

The original name of the location seems to have been 'Tullaniskin'. This was changed to Newmills some time after 1758, when two corn-mills were built here. The Irish name is *An Muileann Úr*, 'the new mill'.

New Milton, village, Hampshire, England.

The village arose round the railway station opened here in 1888. The station was named Milton, which caused confusion with the Milton that is now a district of Portsmouth. At the suggestion of Mrs Newhook, postmistress at the sub post office near the station, therefore, the station was renamed New Milton after 'old' Milton, half a mile away, where Mrs Newhook had earlier managed the post office in the village centre. The name then came to apply to the new development here, two miles from the sea. In the early 20th century, an estate agent's brochure attempted to promote the village as 'New Milton-on-Sea', but this failed to be adopted: first, New Milton is not 'on sea'; second, there would have been confusion with the developing seaside resort nearby of **Milford-on-Sea**.

New Pitsligo, village (near Fraserburgh), Grampian, Scotland.

The village was founded in c.1780 by Sir William Forbes of Pitsligo (1739–1806) on the site of the upper barony of Pitsligo, which was one of the forfeited estates of Alexander Forbes, 4th and last Baron Forbes of Pitsligo (1678–1762).

Newquay, town and resort, Cornwall, England.

The name dates back to 1439, when Bishop Lacey of Exeter granted an indulgence for the *Kaye* at *Tewen Blustry* to be repaired. Presumably the quay was regarded as 'new' after this work. The earliest note of the name is in c.1480. In his *Survey of Cornwall* (1602) the antiquarian Richard Carew gives the name as *Newe Kaye*, but mentions that the quay is unserviceable. The Cornish name is *Towan Blistra* (see above), with *towan* meaning 'sand dune' and an uncertain second word. Johnston (1914) gives the name as *New Quay* and, presumably speculatively, says it is of 19th-century origin.

New Quay, town and resort, Dyfed, Wales.

The town grew up here with the construction of the harbour in 1835, this apparently being a replacement for an earlier, smaller harbour. The Welsh name of the town, with the same meaning, is *Ceinewydd*.

New Quay see **Connah's Quay**.

New River, river, Hertfordshire/London, England.

The name is that of an artificial river constructed in the period 1606–13 by Sir Hugh Myddelton (?1560–1631). The 'new' river flows south, roughly parallel to the river Lea, from Ware, Hertfordshire, to two reservoirs in Hackney, London, a total distance of some 40 miles.

New Scone, village (near Perth), Tayside, Scotland.

The village arose as a planned settlement in 1805, when the then Earl of Mansfield had the former village moved to allow an extensive park to be laid out round the Palace of Scone. The former village, or Old Scone, thus no longer exists, and since there is no longer an 'old' village, New Scone is usually known generally as Scone.

New Stonehaven, district of Stonehaven, Grampian, Scotland.

The district was founded by Robert Barclay of Ury in 1797 and united with Old Stonehaven in 1880. See also **Stonehaven** itself.

Newton Aycliffe, town, Durham, England.

The residential development arose as a New Town designated in 1947 for workers on the nearby Aycliffe Industrial Estate, itself originating in 1940 as the Royal Ordnance factory in the village of Aycliffe. The name both reflects the town's status as a New Town and preserves the old name of Aycliffe, while at the same time distinguishing the town from the old village, one mile away.

Newton Douglas see **Newton Stewart**.

Newton Stewart, town, Dumfries and Galloway, Scotland.

The town is named after William Stewart, third son of the 2nd Earl of Galloway, who had built a few houses here and who in 1677 obtained a charter from Charles II for the settlement to be erected to a burgh of barony. In c.1778 the town became the property of Sir William Douglas, founder of **Castle Douglas**, and he changed the name to *Newton Douglas*. The name did not catch on, however, and Newton Stewart prevailed. The original name of the location had been Black Ford o' Cree, for its location on the river Cree. (Compare **Creetown**.)

Newtown, district of Widnes, Cheshire, England.

The district arose in the mid-19th century as a settlement for workers at the alkali plant here, with the name a conventionally descriptive one.

Newtown, district of New Mills, Derbyshire, England.

The district was formed from Disley, Cheshire, in 1894 and transferred to Derbyshire that same year. In 1934 it united with **New Mills**.

Newtown, village, Cumbria, England.

This is the same village as **Lowther**, here considered separately so that the course of its other name can be charted. The name 'Newtown' has been recorded from the early 18th century as follows: *The New towne* 1709, *Lowther New Town* 1741, *Lowther New Village* 1769, *Newton* 1859. In *A Six Months' Tour through the North of England* (1770) by the writer and agriculturalist Arthur Young, the village

is described as 'the new town of Lowther where Sir James Lowther is building a town to consist of 300 houses for
the use of such of his domesticks and
other people, as are married'. Many of
the 'other people' would have been
workers at the carpet factory built earlier
that century here. The earliest recorded
name above (of 1709) refers to the
original attempt by the Lowthers to
found a village here in 1683–4.

Newtown, district of Ebbw Vale, Gwent,
Wales.

The district, formerly known by its
Welsh name Trenewydd, arose as a
settlement built by the Ebbw Vale
Company over the period 1828–40 to
house its furnace workers. The name
was designed to distinguish the place
from the older houses to the west of the
river Ebwy, the so called Colliers'
Rows.

Newtown, village (near Balfron), Central, Scotland.

The village arose when a cotton mill
opened here in c.1796. The name is a
conventional one for a new settlement.

Newtown, town, Powys, Wales.

The settlement here has had a somewhat complex development over the
centuries, since it was a 'new town' in
the 13th century, long before it was
designated a 'New Town' in 1967. With
some justification, Lewis (1849) comments that the name is 'evidently in
allusion to a somewhat recent date, but
whether with reference to its origin, or
to any more ancient town that previously existed near the site, has not yet been
ascertained'. The town originated as a
fortress begun here by Llewellyn the
Last in 1273. This was destroyed by
Edward I of England who in 1279
granted a charter for a new town to be
built round an existing village here
called *Llanfair in Cedewain* (more correctly *Llanfair-yng-Nghedewain*, 'St. Mary's
church in Cedewain'). The Welsh name
continued alone for the place until the
16th century, when it was first recorded

as 'Newtown' in the form of *Nova Villa*
(or according to other sources *Villa
Nuova*). In the early 19th century the
settlement was growing considerably in
size and expanding as an industrial
town, and when the 'privileges of
corporation were bestowed upon it'
(Morgan, 1887) in 1832 the English
name of Newtown was finally adopted,
with the present Welsh name, Y
Drenewydd, being a translation of this.
By this constant process of 'renewal'
in one form or another, the town has
thus justified its name in a unique
manner.

Newtownards, town, Down, Northern
Ireland.

The town was founded by Sir Hugh
Montgomery, laird of Braidstone in
Scotland, who obtained lands here in
the period 1605–16 as part of the plantation of Ulster. The name is first recorded
in 1613, as *Newtowne*, and in its present
form, as *Newtown-Ardes*, in 1837. The
district here is called Ards, from Irish
ard, 'height', and Newtownards is at the
head of Strangford Lough and the Ards
peninsula. The Irish name of the town is
Baile Nua na hArda, 'new town of the
Ards'.

Newtownbarry, former name of Bunclody, town, Wexford, Ireland.

The original name of the town, as at
present, was Bunclody (Irish *Bun Clóidí*,
'mouth of the [river] Clody'). In 1708 it
came into the possession of James
Barry, Sovereign of Naas, and was
renamed after him. The town reverted
to its Irish name after World War I.

Newtown Forbes, village, Longford,
Ireland.

The name is that of Sir Arthur Forbes of
Corse, Scotland, who in 1619 went to
Ireland with the Master of Forbes's
regiment, of which he was lieutenant-
colonel, and was granted large estates in
Longford and elsewhere by James I.
Forbes began to build his residence
here, Castle Forbes, that same year, and
the village grew up round it.

Newtownhamilton, village, Armagh, Northern Ireland.

The village dates from 1770, when it was founded by Alexander Hamilton, a local landowner and Member of Parliament who was descended from Hugh Hamilton, who had settled in Ireland from Scotland in the early 16th century. The Irish name of the village is simply *Baile Úr*, 'new town'.

Newtownmountkennedy, village, Wicklow, Ireland.

The name comes from Mount Kennedy House, called earlier Ballygarney, built in c.1785 and in turn named after Sir Robert Kennedy who was granted the manor here in 1671. The former name of the house and estate seems to derive from Irish *baile Ó gCearnaigh*, 'town of Kearny', this being a surname.

Newtown Pery, district of Limerick, Limerick, Ireland.

The district was built in the 18th century and was named after a landowner here, Edmund Sexton Pery (1719–1806), otherwise Viscount Pery, Speaker of the Irish House of Commons.

Newtownstewart, town, Tyrone, Northern Ireland.

The original name of the estates here was Lislas, apparently meaning 'ring fort', after an ancient circular earthen fort on the site. On the English settlement of Ulster, these lands were granted by James I, in c.1610, to Sir James Clephane (or Clapham). He did not comply with the conditions of the grant, however, so the property was forfeited to the Crown and subsequently re-granted to Sir William Stewart in c.1628 by Charles I on the occasion of Stewart's marriage to a daughter of Sir Robert Newcomen. The latter landowner had built the castle here, now in ruins, in c.1618. Stewart's name ultimately transferred to the town, which in Irish is simply *An Baile Nua*, 'the new town'.

New Tredegar, town, Mid Glamorgan, Wales.

The settlement was founded in the mid-19th century as an industrial village and was named after the landowner here, Lord Tredegar, whose own title comes from the Morgan family's seat at Tredegar Park, near Newport (see **Tredegar**). The Tredegar baronetcy was created in 1859. New Tredegar was formerly known for a time as *Elliotstown*, after a local coal owner, George Elliot.

New Village, district of Newport, Humberside, England.

The district came into being in 1780 when it was enclosed as part of Walling Fen. Newport itself is a village seven miles east of Howden.

New York, village, Lincolnshire, England.

According to Stokes (1948), an 'apparently reliable informant' claimed that 'the builder who began the place had such high hopes of its development that he rashly boasted of being about to produce a new and superior version of his home town, which was York'. Although emulation of an established town or city can be a distinctive feature of 'New' names (see, for example, **New Birmingham**, **New Brighton**, **New Geneva**), New York seems much more likely to have received its name by association with the town of Boston, only eight miles away. (Indeed, Stokes has a photograph of a sign-post indicating the B1192 road and worded 'NEW-YORK. BOSTON.') New York may even have been named by residents of Boston when they were reclaiming the Wildmore Fen here in the 18th century. If it were not for the special 'American' connection New York might have originated as a field name here, since many fields (and often the farms that owned them) came to have North American names to denote their remoteness. Apart from New York, such field names as Baltimore, Labrador, Newfoundland, Nova Scotia, and Pennsylvania can be found in various parts of Britain.

Nine Elms, district of south-west London, England.

The name is first recorded as *ix elmes farme* in 1646, no doubt after a prominent clump of trees. Walford and Thornbury (1873) say that there were nine elms here until the South Western Railway cut them down in the mid-19th century to utilize the land.

Normandy, village, Surrey, England.

The name is first recorded, as *Normandie*, in 1656, from an inn here, the Duke of Normandy. The place must have had an earlier name, since in 1664 it is described as having been a tithing of Ash. 'Duke of Normandy' was the title of William the Conqueror, and local legend is keen to associate the village with the Norman Conquest, mentioning a group of monks who built a chapel-of-ease here.

Norristhorpe, village, West Yorkshire, England.

According to Goodall (1914), 'Norristhorpe is a name of modern creation, the hamlet being formerly called Doghouse'. What seems more likely, however, is that both names have been in simultaneous use since the mid-19th century, possibly earlier, with Doghouse a local name referring to some kennels here, and Norristhorpe not conclusively explained. The *Norristhorpe Primary School Centenary Brochure* (1977) notes that in the 1870s the village was one of five hamlets forming the dispersed village of Liversedge, and that it comprised 'the Congregational Church, two public houses, a co-op, a brewery . . . and the dog kennels, from which the village got its local name of "Doggus" (Doghouse)'. The local name of Doghouse is still in use today.

Norriston, village (near Dunblane), Central, Scotland.

The village is named after the founder of the chapel-of-ease here in 1674, one Gabriel Norrie. The name was spelt *Norriestown* regularly to the 19th century.

Northavon, administrative district, Avon, England.

The district is both in the north of the county and to the north of the river Avon. In many administrative district names, the element 'North', where it occurs, is usually separate, as North Devon, North Wolds.

North Camp, district of Aldershot, Hampshire, England.

The district arose in 1854, when, at the time of the Crimean War, Field Marshal Sir Henry Hardinge, a commander-in-chief during the War, suggested that the government should make land available for military training, as there was no existing camp or garrison in the country where troops could be trained on a wide scale. The government chose Aldershot Heath, north of the Basingstoke Canal, near Aldershot, and erected a hutted camp for troops here, originally known as just 'The Camp'. When shortly after the camp was extended south of the Canal, the two areas became known as North Camp and South Camp, with North Camp subsequently acquiring its own railway station on the Guildford to Reading line, and developing into an established residential district.

Northchapel, village, West Sussex, England.

The name is first recorded in 1514, as *North-Chapell*. The place had formerly been a chapelry situated north of Petworth.

Northwick Park, district of Harrow, London, England.

The name derives from the Northwick family, lords of the manor of Harrow since 1797. The Underground station of Northwick Park and Kenton was opened here in 1923, and renamed Northwick Park in 1937. This served to establish the district as a residential area.

Northwood, district of Hillingdon, London, England.

The town grew up after the railway

came here in *c.*1880. The name originally applied to a wood that lay to the north of Ruislip, recorded in 1435 as *Northwode*.

Norwood, district of south-east London, England.

The name originally applied to a wood to the north of Croydon, recorded in 1176 as *Norwude* and in 1272 as *Northewode*. The wood was still here down to at least the 17th century, when the antiquarian John Aubrey wrote of it as 'the great wood, called *Norwood*'. The wood was finally cut down in the 19th century.

Notting Hill Gate, district of west London, England.

The name derives from a turnpike gate here, removed in 1864, which stood close to the present Underground station of Notting Hill Gate (opened 1868). Notting Hill itself is an old name, recorded in 1356 as *Knottynghull'*, perhaps referring to a hill where a family named 'Knotting' lived. The district was earlier called *The Gravel Pits*.

Nunhead, district of south London, England.

The name appears to derive from an inn here, the Nun's Head, and is first recorded in 1680, spelt as today. Later versions of the name to be noted are *None Head c.*1745, *Nun or None Head* 1777, and *Nonehead Hill* 1789.

O

Oakleigh Park, district of north London, England.

The name seems to have been established some time in the 19th century. It may be of conventional origin: street names prefixed 'Oak-' (such as Oakdale, Oakdene, Oakfield, Oakhurst, Oaklands, and Oakleigh itself) are common in London, as elsewhere in Britain. In this case, however, the name may have been suggested by Oak Hill Park, just east of here.

Oatlands Park, district of Weybridge, Surrey, England.

The name, as 'Oatlands', was originally that of a palace built here in the first half of the 16th century by Henry VIII for Anne of Cleves. After housing a number of royal owners, the palace was converted in 1857 to the Oatlands Park Hotel, with extensive rebuilding. Today the district, still locally called Oatlands, is a superior residential area. The hotel still exists, although original remains of the palace are scarce.

O'Connorville, village, Hertfordshire, England.

The name derives from the Irish Chartist Leader Fergus O'Connor (1794–1855), who bought an estate here to be let to members of the Chartist Co-operative Land Company, later the National Land Company, formed in 1846. Today the name is rarely used, and the village is known by its earlier name of **Heronsgate**.

Ogwr, administrative district, Mid Glamorgan, Wales.

The name, better known in English as *Ogmore*, is an old one, and is that of the river Ogwr that flows to the sea east of Porthcawl here, of the village of Ogwr on the river, and of the village of Aberogwr (English *Ogmore-by-Sea*) at the river's mouth. The name, meaning 'sharp river', also occurs as an element in the Welsh name of **Bridgend**, where the district's local government offices are located.

Old Swan, district of Liverpool, Merseyside, England.

The district is named after an inn here called the Three Swans down to 1824 but then renamed the Old Swan to distinguish it from a newly-opened rival inn called the Swan.

Old Town, district of Barnsley, South Yorkshire, England.

The district was known as Old Barnsley down to the 17th century when it assumed the name Old Town that had been in parallel use from the 12th century. The district is thus an old one, and may originally have been a pre-Norman settlement.

Olympia, district of west London, England.

The district took its name from the exhibition building erected here in 1886 by the National Agricultural Hall Company, and modernized and extended in 1930. The name was chosen as a typical late-Victorian 'grand classic' designation for an architectural showpiece. Olympia Underground station (properly Kensington (Olympia)) was opened by the West London Railway as Kensington station in 1844. It was resited to the north in 1868, renamed Kensington (Addison Road) in 1868, and again renamed Kensington (Olympia) in 1946.

Omoa, district of Cleland (near Motherwell), Strathclyde, Scotland.

The settlement arose as a development round an iron-works so named, built here in 1787. This in turn was named Omoa by a local landowner, Captain John Dalrymple, who had been a commander at the capture of Omoa, Honduras, in 1779.

Ore, estuary of river Alde, Suffolk, England.

The name is a back formation of Orford, which town is on the estuary. The earliest record of the name is as *Orus* in 1577. See also **Alde**.

Ouse, river, West Sussex/East Sussex, England.

It is possible that the name may be a corruption of Lewes, which stands on it, since an early record of *c.*1270 notes the river as *aqua de Lewes*, and this could later have been wrongly understood as 'aqua del Ewes', with the latter word becoming Ouse. Again, the name may derive from English 'ooze', or from its Old English equivalent. The first precise record we have of the name is in Michael Drayton's topographical poem *Polyolbion* of 1612. Apart from the earlier name mentioned, the river was also known as 'Midwin', meaning 'middle winding', possibly since the river divides Sussex roughly into two halves as it flows east and south to enter the sea at **Newhaven**. A record of 1577 has the name as *Isis*, which may be a back formation from Isfield, a village in the Ouse valley. This name was almost certainly devised by the topographer William Harrison (1534–93).

Overton, village, West Yorkshire, England.

The name was recorded as both 'Overton' and 'Over Shitlington' down to the 19th century, the latter name referring to a farm-owner here but abandoned through reasons of propriety on the same grounds as **Middletown** and **Netherton**.

P

Padanaram, village (near Forfar), Tayside, Scotland.

In his chapter on the parish of Kirriemuir in *The Third Statistical Account of Scotland* (1951 onwards), the Revd John M. Skinner describes Patanaram as 'an unusual Biblical place-name, for which no-one can satisfactorily account, supplanting the original "Ellenorton" and insinuating itself into the parish records about 1850'. In the Bible (Genesis 25: 20, 28: 2) the name is said to mean 'the plain of Syria', and presumably arose here for a Nonconformist chapel of some kind. Also near Forfar are the localities of Jericho and Zoar.

Paddington, district of Warrington, Cheshire, England.

The name, first recorded in 1844, was invented by Robert Halton who established a soap factory here in 1820. Although obviously influenced by Paddington, London, the name could also be a blend of the suburb of *Pad*gate and Warr*ington* itself.

Palatine(town), village, Carlow, Ireland.

The name is said to derive from a colony of German refugees who settled here for religious reasons in the early 18th century. Compare The Palatinate, an area in central Limerick, so named after the Calvinist refugees planted here also in the early 18th century by Thomas Southwell, 1st Baron Southwell (1667–1720), after the French conquest of the Rhenish Palatinate.

Palfrey, district of Walsall, West Midlands, England.

The name is first recorded as *Palfraye Green*, in *c*.1600. This probably had associations with the lady's riding-horse called a palfrey which was 'tender' as payment for a fine or was given to a king or a superior in return for land.

Palmers Green, district of Enfield, London, England.

The name is first recorded in 1608, as *Palmers grene*, this taking its name from a family called Palmer who lived here. Matthew le Palmere was known to have been here in 1341, and Richard Palmer in 1598.

Pang, river, Berkshire, England.

The river name is a back formation from Pangbourne. This town stands on the Thames at the point where the Pang flows into it. Pangbourne itself derives its name from the former name of the river, recorded in 956 as *Panganburna* and in 1271 as *Pangeburn*. The second half of this name is the 'burn' or 'stream' that is now the Pang.

Parkgate, district of Neston, Cheshire, England.

The name is first recorded in 1707 as that of a settlement here. This arose as a result of the passenger traffic to Ireland and, as a resort, developed simultaneously for sea bathing. Parkgate almost certainly derives from the name of the entrance to Neston Park, now no longer in existence. Harrison (1898) quotes from Mrs Gamlin, *'Twixt Mersey and Dee* (1897), with regard to the name: 'The name Parkgate is said to have been given by the labourers who were engaged in making the sea-wall, and its proximity to Leighton Park originated it; before that it was called New Quay or New Haven'. This seems plausible, but Leighton Park (the park of Leighton Hall) is further inland than Neston Park was, and it would have been more likely for the settlement to be named after the nearer gate.

Park Royal, district of Willesden, London, England.

The name was chosen for an area of land here at the end of the 19th century where a fixed site was to be laid out for the annual shows of the Royal Agricultural Society. The attempt was unsuccessful, however, and in c.1910 the area was gradually built over and became the present residential district. The name was presumably intended to suggest a 'park' held by the *Royal Agricultural Society*.

Park Village, district of Wolverhampton, West Midlands, England.

The development here so called must have arisen some time in the mid-19th century. It does not appear on the tithe map for Wednesfield dated 1842, and on the Ordnance Survey map of 1889 is shown as three streets north of the Cannock Road, and thus originally outside the borough of Wolverhampton. Estates of suburban villas called Park Village existed elsewhere in the country, with the Park Villages built by John Nash and Sir James Pennethorne on the edge of Regent's Park, London, dating from 1824.

Parsonstown, former name of Birr, town, Offaly, Ireland.

The town took its name from Sir Lawrence Parsons of Leicestershire, England, to whom James I assigned Birr 'and its appendages' in 1620. Lawrence Parsons was the brother of Sir William Parsons (?1570–1650), surveyor-general of Ireland from 1602. The original and present Irish name, more accurately *Biorra*, means 'watery place'.

Patna, village (near Ayr), Strathclyde, Scotland.

The village was built as a mining settlement in c.1810 on the Skeldon Estate owned by William Fullarton, Provost of Ayr, who named it after his birthplace, Patna in India.

Peacehaven, town and resort, East Sussex, England.

The name was chosen as the result of a competition held just after World War I. The location had earlier had military connections, since New Zealand and Australian troops had been stationed nearby at the start of the war, and for this reason the town was known for a time as *Anzac-on-Sea*. The present name, however, was intended to symbolize peace after war and to echo the name of nearby **Newhaven**, of which today it is virtually a suburb. Land for development as a resort had been bought here in 1914 by Charles Neville, a local businessman.

Pease Pottage, village, West Sussex, England.

A persistent local legend maintains that 'pease pottage' (a mash of boiled dried peas eaten with a piece of pork) was provided here for the guards who preceded the Prince of Wales, the future George IV, on his way to **Brighton** in 1783. This attractive story must be discounted, however, since the name was first recorded some time before this, in 1724, when George IV had not even been born. In this earlier year the name appeared as *Peaspottage Gate*. And even though Pease Pottage had an earlier reputation as a place for a meal—taken by prisoners on their way to Horsham gaol—it seems highly unlikely that the place was named after this dish, or even that the dish was named after the place; as was suggested by the writer of a letter to the editor of *The Times* (10 May 1980). The *Oxford English Dictionary* records the earliest instance of 'pease pottage' as found in 1605 (and 'pease porridge' in 1538), and it thus seems likely that the *Peaspottage Gate* noted in 1724 was so named since it stood at a point on the road where the mud was deep, and like pease pottage in consistency. The origin, therefore, may well lie in this descriptive nickname.

Peckham Rye, district of south London, England.

The district is just south of Peckham, and the 'Rye' was a former brook here, now underground. The name was first recorded, in its present spelling, in 1512.

Peel Town see **Cliftonville**.

Pembroke Dock, port, Dyfed, Wales.

The port was originally a small village—'a farm, one house, and a church', according to Morgan (1887)—called *Pater* or *Paterchurch*, i.e. 'St. Patrick's church'. In 1814 a government dockyard (the Royal Dockyard) opened here, and the place was renamed Pembroke Dock shortly after, for its location one mile west of Pembroke. The Royal Dockyard closed in 1926. The Welsh name remains with the original meaning, *Llanbadrig*.

Penk, river, Staffordshire, England.

The river name is a back formation of the village of Penkridge, located on it. The name was first recorded in *c*.1540, as *Pen*.

Pennines, mountain range, central England.

The name was invented some time before 1765 by the literary forger Charles Bertram (1723–65), who perhaps based it on either the Old British root *penno*, 'top', 'hill' (as found in Welsh and Cornish names starting *Pen*-) or even 'imported' the Apennine Mountains, Italy. Bertram produced an account of Britain by 'Richard of Westminster', an imaginary monk, who was 'identified' by the antiquarian William Stukeley as being the real monk Richard of Chichester, who was known to have lived at Westminster in the 14th century. The forgery was exposed in the *Gentleman's Magazine* in 1866.

Penns, district of Sutton Coldfield, West Midlands.

The district was named for the Penn family, with John Penn recorded as living here in 1618. A mill was already in existence nearby at this time, and the Penn family held the tenancy of it almost to the end of the 17th century. The mill ('Penn's' mill, hence the final *s* of the name) was originally a flour mill, but became a wire mill in 1773 and was eventually destroyed in 1859. Meanwhile Penns Hall had been built here some time before 1759, when it is first mentioned, and still stands, having

been converted into a hotel in 1947. The district of Penns grew with the coming of the railway in 1879. The railway company had originally intended to name the station Walmley, after the district here so called, but a similar name was already in use for a station on the Midland Railway—Warmley on the Bristol to Bath line (now a village in Avon just east of Bristol). The company therefore named the station Penns, which established the name for the district. The station closed in 1964.

Penny Bridge, village, Cumbria, England.

The 'Bridge' of the name is over the river Crake and was built in the late 16th century. It took its name from the Penny family of Crake Side who settled by the old ford of the Crake, called Tunwath, in *c*.1587. The village grew up round the bridge.

Pentonville, district of north London, England.

The district was named after Henry Penton (d. 1812), a Member of Parliament for Winchester who held land here that he first leased for building in *c*.1773. The name of the district became well established with the construction of Pentonville prison here in 1842. The '-ville' seems to have been added some time in the 1790s.

Penwith, administrative district, Cornwall, England.

The name is that of an old hundred here, and is also the old Cornish name of Land's End, which is in the district. This was first recorded in 997, as *Penwihtsteort* (*sic*) (i.e. 'Penwith Start', with the final element meaning 'promontory', as in Start Point, Devon). From Land's End the name passed to the whole peninsula, now West Penwith, then to the hundred.

Perivale, district of Greenford, London, England.

The name arose as an alternative name for Little Greenford, recorded in 1254 as

Greneforde Parva, in 1508 as *Pyryvale*, and in 1524 as *Peryvale*. The name seems to mean 'pear-tree valley', referring to a meadow or orchard here. It is just possible, however, that Perivale could have derived from the *Parva* of the 1254 name, or at least been suggested by it.

Peterhead, town and port, Grampian, Scotland.

The town was founded in 1593 by George Keith, 5th Earl Marischal (?1553–1623), and the English name of Peterhead came to be adopted to replace the original Scottish name of Inverugie ('mouth of the Ugie', from its location). The name, meaning 'St. Peter's headland', was already in use for the locality, and is recorded as *Petyrheid* in 1544. The headland in turn was named after a church here dedicated to St. Peter. The remains of this church are today at Kirkton of Peterhead.

Peterlee, town, Durham, England.

The town arose as a New Town, designated in 1948 and named after the mining trade union leader Peter Lee (1864–1935), born locally in the village of Trimdon Grange and spending most of his life here as miner and administrator. The name seems to have been proposed by C. W. Clark, engineer and surveyor to Easington Rural District Council, who in his report *Farewell Squalor*, subtitled 'A design for a NEW TOWN and proposals for the RE-DEVELOPMENT of the EASINGTON RURAL DISTRICT' (1947), writes:

At the moment, the naming of the new town has not been considered. Many names have come to my mind; some having their derivation from local history, some coined from the names of our present villages and others from the names of members of the Government. I have reviewed each one of them from all angles and have come to the conclusion that this new town should bear the name of some local man who, during his life time, went fearlessly and courageously forward for the good and uplift of the people of the district. [. . .] Having all these virtues in one single frame seems well nigh impossible. I am convinced, however, that there was one

person whose life was moulded on these virtues and whose memory could be appropriately perpetuated by the naming of the New Town—PETERLEE.

Philipstown, former name of Daingean, village, Offaly, Ireland.

The original name of the place, and the present one, was *An Daingean*, 'the fortress', referring to the medieval fortress of the O'Connors here. After a number of campaigns by the English against the O'Mores and the O'Connors in Offaly, and the capture of a number of key forts, including this one, the O'More territory was shired in 1556 as **Queen's County**, with its capital at **Maryborough**, and the O'Connor territory became **King's County**, with its capital here at Daingean, renamed Philipstown in honour of Philip II of Spain, the husband of Queen Mary, who was then reigning. The village reverted to its Irish name in 1920.

Phillipstown, village, Mid Glamorgan, Wales.

The name derives from Nehemiah Phillips, colliery agent here in the 19th century for the Powell Duffryn Company.

Phoenix Park, district of Dublin, Ireland.

The district originated as lands belonging to the priory here of the Knights of St. John of Jerusalem. On these lands in the early 17th century was built a country residence for the Viceroy, with a royal deer park laid out round it in 1662. The park took its name from a spring just outside the grounds, known in Irish as *fionn uisg*, 'clear water', with the full Irish name of the park being *Páirc an Fhionnuisce*. This should have been understood as 'Clearwater Park', but instead was believed to mean 'Phoenix Park', from the resemblance of this English word to the Irish. The error even received official sanction when in 1745 the 4th Earl of Chesterfield, viceroy for eight months that year, erected a Corinthian pillar near the house, the so-called Phoenix Column, surmounted by a phoenix rising from the ashes. (Some sources claim that it was the Earl who promoted the name when he was unable to understand the Irish words.) The original spring or rivulet is now underground, and the viceregal residence is the residence of the President.

Pilgrims' Way, ancient British track, Hampshire/Surrey/Kent, England.

The track follows the southern slope of the North Downs, and came to be used by pilgrims journeying to Canterbury in medieval times. It first seems to have received its name, from this association, in the second half of the 18th century. In Hasted's *History of Kent* (1778) it is called *the Upper Pilgrim Road* near Otford, Kent, and *Pilgrim Road* near Halling, Kent.

Pimlico, district of south-west London, England.

The name is first recorded in 1630, as *Pimplico*, and is said to have been that of an inn here in turn named after one Ben Pimlico, innkeeper at another inn in Hoxton, north London. Bebbington (1972), however, sees the name transfer the other way round, with the Hoxton inn named after the Pimlico one. According to Johnston (1914), 'old Ben Pimlico' was mentioned as early as 1598. The district here was also known by the name, as well as the inn, from the early 17th century, although it remained sparsely inhabited until the 19th century. The name became widely known as a result of the popular 'Ealing comedy' film *Passport to Pimlico*, produced in 1948, and was even more firmly established for the district with the opening of Pimlico Underground station in 1972. The Hoxton Pimlico is still commemorated in the name of Pimlico Walk there.

Pitsmoor, district of Sheffield, South Yorkshire, England.

The name is first recorded in 1618, as *Pitsmore*, this being the name of a moor that had ore pits here as early as the 14th century, when they have been noted as *Orepittes*.

Pittville, district of Cheltenham, Gloucestershire, England.

The district is named after its developer, Joseph Pitt (1759–1842), a local attorney. Pitt bought a considerable amount of land in Cheltenham in 1800 and in the 1820s laid out the new estate that bore his name. The most important feature of the estate was the Pump Room, the largest and grandest of Cheltenham's spas, built in 1830, and Pitt originally envisaged building a whole new town to rival Cheltenham. Financial difficulties prevented this, however, and most of the planned development was never realized.

Plaistow New Town see **Canning Town**.

Plantation, district of Glasgow, Strathclyde, Scotland.

The name seems to derive from its association with one John Robertson, who had made his fortune in West Indian plantations and who bought the house of Craigiehall here in 1783.

Plymouth, city and port, Devon, England.

The original name of the settlement here, down to c.1450, was Sutton ('southern settlement') recorded in this latter year as *Sutton Prior vulgariter Plymmouth nuncupatur* ('Sutton Prior is now commonly called Plymmouth'). The manor at Sutton was held by the priory of Plympton, whose own name gave that of the river Plym, an early back formation from it (recorded in 1238 as *Plyme*). From the name of this river in turn came the name of Plymouth, standing at its mouth, first recorded in 1231 as *Plimmue*, and also in 1235 as *Plummuth*. The name originally applied only to the river mouth, then to the harbour, then finally to the town and port that grew up here. Plymouth's harbour is still called Sutton Harbour. See also **Devonport**.

Ponders End, district of Enfield, London, England.

The name implies an 'end' or section of a parish held by the family of Ponder, and is first recorded in 1593, as *Ponders ende*. A document of 1373 mentions John Ponder as living here, with his surname perhaps meaning 'keeper of the pond'.

Pontardawe, town, West Glamorgan, Wales.

The settlement probably took its name from a house built at the end of a bridge over the river Tawe here, since the name, in its present form, means 'bridge over the Tawe', and it was recorded in 1706 as *Ty pen y bont ar tawey*, meaning literally (word for word) 'house end the bridge over Tawe'. The earliest dating of the name is 1578, as *Ar Dawy*, 'over the Tawe'. Morgan (1887) says that the bridge was built here in c.1757 by one William Edwards, but there seems to have been an earlier bridge, judging by the place-name evidence. Compare the following entry for a similar development.

Pontarddulais, town, West Glamorgan, Wales.

In its present form, the name means 'bridge over the Dulais'. The settlement must have grown up at the end of a bridge over this river here. The earliest dating of the name is 1557, as *Ponte ar Theleys*, with the same meaning as the modern name.

Ponthir, village, Gwent, Wales.

The name means 'long bridge', according to Morgan (1887) after the long bridge over the river Llwyd was built here in c.1800. The name before this, when tin works had been built here, was *Gwaith Newydd*, 'new works'. This name was superseded by Ponthir some time after c.1820.

Pontllanfraith, village, Gwent, Wales.

The name means 'bridge of the multi-coloured lake', with the settlement having grown up by this bridge. *Llan* in Welsh names normally means 'church', but here, as can be seen by the early forms of the name, it originated as *llyn*, 'lake', becoming *llan* by popular association with this common element. The name was first recorded in 1492, as *tre penybont llynvraith*, 'farm [at the] end [of] the bridge [by the] lake [that is] speckled'. By 1713, this had become *Pontllynfraith*, and in 1782 is noted as *Pontlanfraith*.

Pontyates, village, Dyfed, Wales.

According to Morgan (1887), the name may mean 'bridge built by a Mr Yates', but the Welsh name, properly spelt *Pont-iets*, seems much more likely to mean 'bridge [of the] gates', this referring to a former toll gate here.

Pontypool, town, Gwent, Wales.

The name means 'bridge of the pool' (modern Welsh *Pont-y-pwll*). This was recorded in 1614 as *Pont y poole*. The town is on the river Llwyd, and the 'pool' thus seems to refer to a stretch of the river here.

Pontypridd, town, Mid Glamorgan, Wales.

The name means 'bridge of the earthen house', i.e. a 'wattle and daub' house. The name is first recorded in c.1700 as *Pont y Tŷ Pridd*, this possessing the *tŷ*, 'house' that later became assimilated in the name as a whole and disappeared. Another bridge was built over the river here, the Taff, by the self-taught architect, William Edwards (compare **Pontardawe**), in 1755, and for some time the place had two names: Newbridge and Pontypridd. The former (English) name was eventually dropped, however, doubtless because of the proximity of the other town of Newbridge only 14 miles away (north-west of Newport).

Port Allen, village (near Perth), Tayside, Scotland.

The village was planned in c.1840 by John Allen of Errol to export potatoes and grain from his estate here. Port Allen is on the north shore of the Firth of Tay.

Portarlington, town, Laois, Ireland.

The town is named after Henry Bennet, 1st Earl of Arlington (1618–85), an Englishman who after the Eleven Years' War (ended 1652) was given lands confiscated from the O'Dempseys here in 1641. The original name of the place was Coltodry (or Cooletetoodra, or Cooletooder), these being approximations of the present Irish name of the town, *Cúil an tSúdaire*, 'the tanner's corner'. The town is a 'port', i.e. a landing place, on the river Barrow.

Port Bannatyne, village and resort (Isle of Bute), Strathclyde, Scotland.

The Bannatyne family came here from Ayrshire in *c.*1220 and made their home at Kames Castle. Macnie and McLaren (1977) give the subsequent development of the name as follows: Kames Castle was sold in 1812 and the name of the settlement was changed to Kamesburgh. When, however, the Marquis of Bute bought the lands in 1863 he wished to preserve the original family name so renamed the village Port Bannatyne. But this date is suspect, since the 3rd Marquis of Bute, John Stuart, the only Marquis of Bute alive in 1863 (the 2nd Marquis had died in 1848), was then still a 16-year-old Harrow schoolboy. Lewis (1824), moreover, gives the name, which thus must have originated some time before this, possibly shortly after the sale of Kames Castle in 1812.

Port Carlisle, village, Cumbria, England.

The village was built 11 miles west of Carlisle on the estuary of the river Eden in the early 19th century, to serve as a port for this city by means of a newly-built canal. With the coming of the railway, however, the canal was filled in, and the fate of the port was finally sealed when it was discovered that the Glasgow and South-Western Railway Company had built a viaduct between the village and the sea through which only a rowing-boat could pass. The expected trade therefore went to the port of Silloth, ten miles to the south.

Port Charlotte, village (Islay), Strathclyde, Scotland.

The village was planned in 1828 and named after Lady Charlotte Campbell, mother of the Islay Gaelic scholar, W. F. Campbell. See also **Port Ellen**.

Port Clarence, port and district of Stockton-on-Tees, Cleveland, England.

The port took its name from the Clarence Railway which ran here. This railway, an extension to Middlesbrough of the Tees and Weardale Railway, was constructed in 1827 and named after the Duke of Clarence, the future William IV, who was Lord High Admiral of the British navy at the time. The name was adopted for the district, formerly known as Samphire Batts, in *c.*1834.

Port Dundas, district of Glasgow, Strathclyde, Scotland.

The district was laid out by Sir Lawrence Dundas of Kerse in the late 18th century as a port at the eastern end of the Forth and Clyde Canal. The site chosen was the narrow neck of land between Sealock (as which Port Dundas was known to 1784) and a newly cut stretch of the river Carron. See also **Laurieston** (Central).

Port Ellen, town and port (Islay), Strathclyde, Scotland.

As with **Port Charlotte**, the name was created by the Gaelic scholar W. F. Campbell, and the new settlement was named in 1821 after his first wife, Lady Ellenor Campbell of Islay.

Port Elphinstone, village (near Inverurie), Grampian, Scotland.

The village was named some time before 1834 after Sir Robert Elphinstone, who had financed the construction of the Aberdeen Canal here, opened in 1807. Port Elphinstone was the terminus of the canal, which closed in 1854.

Port Glasgow, town and port, Strathclyde, Scotland.

The town was founded in 1668 on the
site of a fishing village called Newark,
below Newark Castle (dated 1597
although with some parts much older).
The aim was for the new port to be a
centre for the export of fish, near the
rapidly expanding town of Glasgow, as
well as a main anchorage and harbour
for Glasgow. With the increased fishing
trade, Port Glasgow (originally called
Newport Glasgow) prospered, but the
deepening of the river Clyde prevented
it from becoming Glasgow's main port,
as planned. The town therefore turned
to shipbuilding in the late 18th century
when Glasgow itself became a port. Port
Glasgow was constituted a free port and
burgh of barony by George III in 1775.

Portgordon, village (near Buckie), Grampian, Scotland.

The village, on Spey Bay, was created in
1797 by Alexander Gordon, 4th Duke of
Gordon (1743–1827) as a trading port for
the export of grain.

Porthcawl, town and resort, Mid Glamorgan, Wales.

The name seems to mean 'port of
sea-kale', and was recorded in 1632 as
Portcall. Perhaps there was plenty of
sea-kale growing here at some time.

Port Laoise see **Maryborough**.

Portlaw, village, Waterford, Ireland.

The village arose as a model settlement
built by the Quaker family of Malcolm-
son for workers at the cotton mills here,
the first of which was built in 1818. The
name refers to the hill at the end of the
village, with the Irish original, *Port Lágh*,
thus meaning 'landing place of the hill'.
The village is on the river Clodiagh.

Portmadoc (more correctly, **Porth-
madog**), town and resort, Gwynedd,
Wales.

The name derives from that of the
Member of Parliament for Boston, Lin-

colnshire, William Alexander Maddocks (1772–1828), who in *c*.1800 enclosed a large area of the reclaimed tract
of land here known as Traeth Mawr
('great shore') and in 1821 obtained an
Act of Parliament to construct a harbour
for the shipping of slate from the
quarries at Ffestiniog. The name is thus
a deliberate creation, and not genuinely
Welsh: the true Welsh name of the town
or port would be 'Trefadog' or 'Porth-
fadog'. Locally, Portmadoc is known
simply as *Port*. Compare **Tremadoc**.

Port Mary, house and estate (near Kirkcudbright), Dumfries and Galloway,
Scotland.

The original name of the place was
Nether Reswick, but the estate, on the
Solway Firth, was renamed in honour of
Mary, Queen of Scots who embarked
here for Workington, England, after her
flight from the battle of Langside in
1568.

Portmeirion, village and resort,
Gwynedd, Wales.

The Mediterranean-style resort was
built in 1926 by the Welsh architect
Clough Williams-Ellis, who began his
venture by purchasing the old mansion of Aber Ia and adding Castle
Deudraeth and its grounds to his
property. Williams-Ellis has explained
how he came to devise the name in his
account of the village, *Portmeirion: The
Place and its Meaning* (1963):

And here, before passing on to the actual
building of Portmeirion and no later, I should
perhaps explain why I dropped its old Welsh
place name of Aber Ia—thereby inevitably
somewhat offending local traditionalists. First
I disliked its chilly sound; and I was aiming
even then at a world public and I thought my
new name for a new thing both euphonious
and indicative of its whereabouts, "Meirion"
giving its county [of Merioneth] and "Port"
placing it on its coast. Also it was a little in
affectionate memory of Portofino [a pictures-
que fishing village and resort in north-west
Italy], . . . to which I had immediately and
hopelessly lost my heart.

The name also happily echoes that of
nearby **Portmadoc**.

Port Montgomery see **Portpatrick**.

Portobello, district of Edinburgh, Lothian, Scotland.

Local legend, which may well have a sound historical basis, maintains that the name derives from a house here, Portobello Hut, built in *c.*1750 by a sailor who claimed he had been present at the capture of Portobello, Panama, by Admiral Vernon in 1739. The name is thus apparently a commemorative one, first recorded in 1753 as *Porto-Bello*. The original name of the district here, described by Lewis (1846) as having been a 'dreary tract of unproductive land covered with furze', was Figgate, or Figgate Whins. There are a number of other places named Portobello in Britain, including present-day districts of Wolverhampton (see next entry) and Wakefield. Some of these may have been inspired by the Scottish Portobello; others may have been similarly commemorative of the victory in Panama.

Portobello, district of Wolverhampton, West Midlands, England.

The district is said to have taken the name of its Edinburgh equivalent (see previous entry), since both places had a bed of rich clay that led to the development of local industries, and moreover since the Wolverhampton Portobello was near a coal-pit named Bunker's Hill, a name similarly commemorative of a victory (of the British over the Americans in 1775 at Bunker Hill, Boston, Massachusetts, in the American War of Independence). Inevitably, local legends are found to explain the name, one of the more preposterous being quoted in F. W. Hackwood, *The Annals of Willenhall* (1908): 'A man once passing a solitary farmhouse in that locality [. . .] called and inquired if the farmer had any beer on tap. The reply was, as the man pointed cellarwards, "No—only porter below!"'

Portpatrick, town and resort, Dumfries and Galloway, Scotland.

The crossing from Ireland to Britain is at its shortest here, and local legend claims that the town was named after St. Patrick, who 'strode from Ireland' the 21½ miles across to Portpatrick. In fact the name comes from an old chapel dedicated to St. Patrick here, and the settlement became fully established as Portpatrick when it was chartered as a burgh of barony in 1620. Earlier, Sir Hugh Montgomerie had acquired the barony in 1608 by purchase from Sir Robert Adair of Kinhilt, and he altered the name to Port Montgomery. But as Maxwell (1930) states, 'that did not long endure', and the place resumed its former name in *c.*1628 when it was separated from the parish of Inch. Until the mid-19th century Portpatrick had been the main port for crossings to Ireland, but because of the strong southwest gales it was superseded in this role by Stranraer, sheltered in Loch Ryan six miles north east of Portpatrick.

Port Penrhyn, former port, Gwynedd, Wales.

In *c.*1782 Richard Pennant, Baron Penrhyn (?1732–1808), began to develop a slate quarry at the entrance to Nant Ffrancon, the valley of the river Ogwen between **Bethesda** and Llyn Ogwen, and built a quay at the mouth of the river Cegin to ship the slate from it. The quay was linked with the quarry by a tramtrack in 1801 and developed as Port Penrhyn. Later, however, the importance of the settlement declined and today it is simply a dock.

Portree, town and port (Isle of Skye), Highland, Scotland.

A keen local legend derives the name from Gaelic *port righe*, 'port royal', from the visit of James V here in 1540 when he was sailing through the Hebrides to Skye in an endeavour to control these outlying islands of his kingdom. Local pronunciation of the name, however, proves it to be *Port-righeadh*, 'harbour of [the] slope'. The name was first recorded in 1549, as *Portri*. The earlier name of the port has been variously recorded as *Kiltragleann*, 'church at the foot of the glen' (Booth and Perrott, 1981), *Loch Chaluim Chille*, 'loch of Columba of the cells' (Forbes, 1923) and *Ceilltarraglan*, 'burial ground at the bottom of the glen' (and basically the same as Booth and Perrott above) (Lewis, 1846). Some sources give Portree as an early name of **Portpatrick** (see above).

Portsea, district of Portsmouth, Hampshire, England.

The district owed its growth to the rapid development of government establishments here. It was originally known as Portsmouth Common, but took its present name by Act of Parliament in 1792 from Portsea Island, the island on which most of modern Portsmouth is situated. (The definition 'island' is disputed by some, since Portsmouth is separated from mainland Hampshire merely by a tidal creek and is, moreover, joined to it by three road bridges and a railway bridge.)

Portstewart, town, Londonderry, Northern Ireland.

The town originated in the mid-18th century and is named after the Stewarts, to whom the surrounding lands belonged.

Port Sunlight, district of Bebington, Merseyside, England.

The district arose as an industrial estate built in 1888 by William Hesketh Lever, 1st Viscount Leverhulme (1851–1925), for workers making Sunlight soap at his factory here. Compare **Leverburgh.**

Port Talbot, town and port, West Glamorgan, Wales.

The town arose in 1836 when docks were built on the site of what was then known as Aberavon Harbour, and this same year the settlement and harbour were renamed Port Talbot after the Talbot family of Margam Abbey, who owned most of the land on which the town and docks were built and who sponsored its industrial development. Margam and its abbey site had passed to the Talbots, from Lacock, Wiltshire, in

1750. The last of the Talbots here, Captain Andrew Talbot-Fletcher, sold the estate in 1941 and left for Saltoun, Scotland.

Port Tennant, district of Swansea, West Glamorgan, Wales.

The district was named after George Tennant (1765–1832) of Cadoxton Lodge, Neath, who built the Tennant Canal from Neath to Swansea, opened in 1824. Shortly after this the name Port Tennant came to be applied to the new dockland and shipping area at the Swansea terminus of the canal.

Port William, town and resort, Dumfries and Galloway, Scotland.

The town was founded in 1770 by Sir William Maxwell of Monreith.

Postbridge, village, Devon, England.

The name was originally that of a bridge here, recorded in 1675 as *a stone bridge of three arches called Post Bridg*, and in 1720 as *Poststone Bridge*. Presumably the bridge was first so named when it began to take the post road between Exeter and Plymouth, or two other towns. The village has an old clapper bridge believed to date from the 13th century.

Potters Bar, town, Hertfordshire, England.

The name is first recorded in 1509, as *Potterys Barre*, this perhaps referring to a gate leading into Enfield Chase, and a man named Potter who guarded it. The *Hertsmere Official Guide* (1980), however, regards this explanation as 'fanciful', and suggests that the name may have referred to local potteries here: one such pottery stood near the junction of the Great North Road and Southgate Road, and another was near Heath Road. In such case the 'bar' could have been a toll bar or gate on the road leading to the pottery. The precise origin is still uncertain.

Poulton-le-Sands see **Morecambe**.

Powys, county, Wales.

The name is an old one, of an ancient

territory here in medieval times that approximately corresponded to the area of the modern county, formed in 1974 out of the former counties of Montgomery and Radnor and most of Brecknock (Brecon). The origin of the name is said to lie in Latin *pagenses*, 'country people' (thus related to English 'pagan'). Perhaps this can be understood as 'territory of dwellers in open country': the county consists almost entirely of exposed uplands, with mountains to the north, west, and south.

Poyntzfield, village (near Cromarty), Highland, Scotland.

The village was named after Charlotte Poyntz, wife of the 1st Laird of Poyntzfield, whose seat was at Poyntzfield House. The name is that preferred by the Post Office for **Jemimaville**.

Poyntz Pass, village, Armagh, Northern Ireland.

The village dates from 1790 and is named after the castle formerly here where Lieutenant Sir Toby Poyntz of the English army fought in 1598 to prevent Hugh O'Neill, Earl of Tyrone, from entering Down. The Irish name of the village, with the same meaning, is *Pas an Phointe*.

Prestonpans, town, Lothian, Scotland.

The name was recorded in 1587 as *Saltprestoun*, and in 1654 in its present spelling. The reference is to salt pans near a village called Preston ('priests' village'). The 'priests' were monks of Newbattle Abbey here, who laid out the salt pans early in the 13th century.

Primrose see **Carrington** (Lothian).

Primrose Hill, district of north-west London, England.

The name was first recorded in 1586, when a song was published called 'A Sweete and Courtly Songe of the Flowers that grow on Prymrose Hill'. The name thus appears to be a descriptive one. For some time the wooded hill was also known as *Green Berry Hill*.

Princetown, town, Devon, England.

The name refers to the Prince of Wales, the future George IV, who owned Dartmoor as part of his Duchy of Cornwall. The origin of the town lies, historically if not quite geographically, with a farm here in 1780, Prince Hall, also named after the Prince Regent. In 1785 Sir Thomas Tyrwhitt, Lord Warden of the Stannaries and a friend of the Prince of Wales, set about improving this part of Dartmoor. He laid out an estate half a mile south east of Prince Hall and built a house here, Tor Royal, in 1798. He then proposed building a prison nearby to accommodate French and American prisoners taken in the Napoleonic wars. The Prince gave him the necessary land, and the prison was built over the period 1806–13. The town of Princetown grew up round the prison.

Princetown, village, Mid Glamorgan, Wales.

The village arose round a former inn here, the Prince of Wales.

Prosperous, village, Kildare, Ireland.

The American-style name proved to be an ironic one. The village was founded in 1776 by Robert Brooke (d. ?1802) as a cotton manufacturing centre, Brooke using the fortune he had made as a captain in the East India Company in India for the purpose. At first, he received considerable support and patronage for his enterprise, but as a commercial venture his undertaking proved a failure, and after Parliament had rejected Brooke's appeal for support in 1786, he was obliged to close the business finally in 1798 when the government announced that it could no longer finance the venture. Brooke, however, was fortunate enough to be appointed governor of St. Helena while his business was in increasing difficulties, and held the post from 1787 to 1801. The Irish name of the village is *An Chorrocoill*, 'the projecting wood'.

Prussia Cove, village and resort, Cornwall, England.

The village is named after a cove here, itself said to have been so called since in the 18th century the landlord of the local inn, King of Prussia, was a noted smuggler, using the cove for his contraband imports.

Pulteneytown (or **Pultneytown**), district of Wick, Highland, Scotland.

The district, today usually known as Old Wick, was founded in $c.$ 1808 by the British Fisheries Society, who named it after their chairman, Sir William Pulteney.

Q

Quakers' Yard, village, Mid Glamorgan, Wales.

The land here was given in *c.*1670 or 1680 as a 'suitable repository for the dead' by the wealthy Quaker, Lydia Fell, who owned the north portion of the Llanfabon estate. The Welsh name of the village is *Mynwent y Crynwyr*, 'graveyard of the Quakers'.

Queensbury, district of north-west London, England.

The name derives from the Underground station here, opened in 1934. This was chosen in an arbitrary manner to match the next station of Kingsbury, whose own name dates back to before the 'Domesday Book' of 1086.

Queensbury, town, West Yorkshire, England.

The original village here was at first known as *Queenshead*, from an inn here, the Queen's Head, with this name recorded in 1821. At a public meeting held on 8 May 1863, however, the decision was taken to change the name to Queensbury, presumably as this was more fitting for the name of a town. Compare **Triangle**.

Queen's County, former name of Laois, county, Ireland.

The name was given to the county in 1556 when the territory of Leinster was shired, with the 'Queen' being the reigning monarch, Queen Mary. The old Irish name of Laois was resumed in 1920. Compare **King's County** and **Philipstown**, and see the name of the capital of Queen's County, **Maryborough**.

Queensferry, town, Clwyd, Wales.

The town, on the south bank of the river Dee, was originally *King's Ferry* (so recorded in a directory of 1835), but after Queen Victoria came to the throne in 1837 the name was changed to Queensferry, this found in a directory of 1850. Any direct royal connection with the place seems uncertain.

Queen's Nympton, village, Devon, England.

The village seems to have been so named in *c.*1900 in honour of Queen Victoria, but on what occasion is not clear. There may also have been a wish to distinguish between this village and the older King's Nympton to the south-west of it (compare **Queensbury**, London).

Queenstown, former name of Cobh, town and port, Cork, Ireland.

The name was assumed by the town in 1849, after a visit here by Queen Victoria that year. Before this, it had been known as *Cove*, or *Cove of Cork*. In 1922 it resumed this (English) name, but in the Irish spelling *Cobh*. (See *Cóbh*.)

R

Randalstown, town, Antrim, Northern Ireland.

The settlement was originally called *Mainwater*, for its location on the river Main, as well as *Ironworks*, for its forges and furnaces that smelted the iron ore found near by. In 1683 Charles II constituted the town as a borough and granted the manor of Edenduffcarrick to Rose O'Neill (d. 1695) after her marriage in c.1653 to Randal MacDonell, 2nd Viscount Dunluce, 2nd Earl and 1st Marquis of Antrim (1609–83), and she named it after her husband. The better-known name of Edenduffcarrick, and the one preferred today, is Shane's Castle, after Shane O'Neill, Rose O'Neill's grandfather, who had built it in the 16th century. According to some sources, it was not Rose O'Neill who named Randalstown, but Charles II himself, since his charter of 1683 'further appointed, ordained, and declared the town of Ironworks *alias* Mainwater, with its right, members, and appurtenances [. . .] should be called for ever by the name of the borough of *Randalstown*' (J. A. Pilson, *History of the Rise and Progress of Belfast and Annals of Co. Antrim*, 1847). The Irish name of the town, *Baile Raghnaill*, has the same meaning as the English.

Rathcogan see **Ráthluirc**.

Ráthluirc, town, Cork, Ireland.

The town was founded in c.1659 by Roger Boyle, Baron Broghill and 1st Earl of Orrery (1621–79), who named it *Charleville* after Charles II. Before this it had been called *Rathcogan* or *Rathgoggan*, 'Cogan's fort'. In the 20th century, some time after World War I, it again took an Irish name, this time *Ráthluirc*, 'Lorc's fort', a name that had been in alternative use (to Rathcogan) before the mid-17th century.

Ravenscourt Park, district of west London, England.

The original name of the district was 'Padderswick', recorded in 1270 as *Palyngewyk*. Some time in the 18th century, or possibly earlier, it became known as Ravenscourt Park, with this name first recorded in 1765, as *Ravenscourt formerly known by the name of Paddingswick*. The precise origin of the modern name is not known, although in 1819 there was known to be a Raven's Court House here. Ravenscourt Park Underground station, opened in 1873, was originally called Shaftesbury Road (to 1888). The station name established the district name.

Rayners Lane, district of Harrow, London, England.

The district developed some time after 1930 as a residential area. Local legend claims that the name derived from an old shepherd called Rayner, who is said to have lived in an isolated cottage here till c.1905. Rayners Lane railway station opened as a halt on the Metropolitan Railway in 1906, and this established the name for the district.

Raynes Park, district of south-west London, England.

The name is that of Edward Rayne (1778–1847), a sheep farmer who owned land here on which the South Western Railway Company built in 1837. Raynes Park railway station opened in 1871, and the district developed round it. There was no actual 'park' as such: the land here between **Nine Elms** and Woking was the pastureland of West Barnes Farm, owned by Rayne. It seems surprising that the origin of the name has not been satisfactorily explained in place-name sources: *EPNS Surrey* (1934) reported that officials of the Southern Railway 'who made search on our behalf were unable to throw any light on it', and even Field (1980) says that although there seems to have been a family named Rayne here, it has not been identified. Yet the family is listed in local directories, and Rayne's co-operation with the railway is well known.

Redbridge, borough of north-east London, England.

The borough was created in 1965 out of the former boroughs of Ilford and of Wanstead and Woodford together with parts of Chigwell and Dagenham. The name is first mentioned in a map of 1746, but the original 'red bridge' probably existed a century earlier. The bridge crossed the river Roding at a point formerly called Redbridge Lane, where today Eastern Avenue crosses the river with a modern bridge. The bridge was so called since apparently it was built of red brick to carry vehicles, by contrast with the nearby White Bridge, which was a wooden foot-bridge. The name does not seem to have any connection with that of the river Roding, in spite of the similarity. The bridge was originally on the boundary between the two boroughs of Ilford and Wanstead and Woodford.

Redhill, district of Reigate, Surrey, England.

The name seems to have originated as that of a field on a hill, referring to the colour of the soil. As such, it is first recorded in 1301 as *Redehelde*, with a more recent version of the name noted in 1588 as *Redd hyll*. The town arose here in the mid-19th century with the coming of the London and Brighton Railway. This opened in 1841, and Redhill Junction was built soon after.

Regent's Park, district of north-west London, England.

The district was originally known as Old Marylebone Fields or Marylebone Park. The area was re-laid by John Nash in 1812 for the Prince Regent, the future George IV, and named in his honour. Nash planned to take one of the country villas to be built here, but in the event only a few villas were built and the district remains better known today for its Park, one of the largest open spaces in London, than for its residential character. While Nash was working on the Park he also built Regent Street, similarly named after the Prince, as part of a 'royal mile' connecting the Park with the Prince's house in **St. James's**.

Renton, town, Strathclyde, Scotland.

The owner of the original estate here was Commissary James Smollett, cousin of Tobias George Smollett, the novelist. When James Smollett died in 1775, the estate should have passed to Tobias George, but he had predeceased him in 1771. The property therefore went to Tobias Smollett's sister, Jean Telfer. On succeeding to the estate, she resumed her maiden name of Smollett, and in 1782, when various bleaching and other works grew up here in the vale of Leven, named the industrial settlement Renton, after her daughter-in-law, Cecilia Renton, daughter of John Renton of Blackadder. Cecilia, who appears as 'Miss R.', one of the belles of Edinburgh, in Tobias Smollett's *Humphry Clinker* had married Jean Smollett's son, Alexander Telfer, and was the mother of Lieutenant-Colonel Alexander Smollett, killed at the battle of Alkmaar in 1799 (see **Alexandria**).

Rest and Be Thankful, tourist location (near Arrochar), Strathclyde, Scotland.

The location is nearly 900 feet up at the summit of the pass from Glen Croe to Loch Fyne, and is marked by a stone slab inscribed with its name. This replaces what was said to have been a rough seat set up here in the 1740s by soldiers building a military road from Dumbarton to Inveraray on the orders of General Sir John Cope, commander-in-chief of the forces in Scotland during the Jacobite rebellion of 1745 (the ' '45').

Rhydgwilym, village, Dyfed, Wales.

The name means 'William's ford', and is said to derive from the Revd William Jones, the first Baptist minister here, who conducted his first baptism in the river at this point.

Richmond(-upon-Thames), town and borough, London, England.

The original name of the settlement here was 'Sheen', recorded in *c*.950 as *Sceon*, and subsequently as *Sceanes* 1130 and *Shene* 1230. The place had long been popular with royalty, and Henry VII, on succeeding to the throne in 1485, rebuilt and enlarged the palace here originally built by Edward I in the 13th century. In 1501 the palace was burnt down, and when Henry rebuilt it he ordered the name to be changed to Richmond, after his previous title of Earl of Richmond, this being taken from Richmond in Yorkshire. The new name was first recorded in 1502 as *Shene otherwise called Richemount*. The former name is preserved in North Sheen and East Sheen in the borough of Richmond, as well as in East Sheen Common and Sheen Road, now part of the A305. Field (1980) suggests that Henry may have been partly motivated into changing the name since he regarded 'Sheen' as not being sufficiently dignified. It is a coincidence that the Yorkshire Richmond is itself a transferred name, from a place called *Richemont* in France.

Richmondshire, administrative district, North Yorkshire, England.

The name comes from Richmond, the administrative centre of the district, and 'shire'. The district was an ecclesiastical area in Norman times.

Ripleyville, district of Bradford, West Yorkshire, England.

The name derives from Sir Henry William Ripley (1813–82), dyeworks manager and builder, who established homes for his dyeworkers here in 1863–4. The district became a slum area and was demolished in 1969.

Riverhead, suburb of Sevenoaks, Kent, England.

The original name of the village here was 'Rotherhithe', recorded in 1292 as *Reydrythe* and subsequently as *Readride* 1313, *Retherhead* 1619, *Retherhed alias Riverhead* 1656. In 1778 it was referred to as 'Rotherhith, or Rethered, now called Riverhead'. The old name means 'cattle landing-place'. The modern name, which resembles it quite closely, seems to have arisen to denote the location of the place at the head of the river Darent, or to differentiate between this Kent location and the Rotherhithe that is now a dock area of east London. The two places are only 17 miles apart.

Riverstown, village, Cork, Ireland.

The name seems to have arisen in the first half of the 19th century to denote the location of the place on two rivers here. Its earlier name was Ballynarosheen, Irish *Baile Roisín*, 'town of the little wood'. According to Lewis (1837), the village at one time was also formerly known as *Sadlierstown*.

Roach, river, Essex, England.

The river name is a back formation of Rochford, and the Roach rises to the west of this town. Before it acquired its present name, perhaps as late as the 18th century, the river was known as the 'Wallfleet', and was also marked on late 18th-century and early 19th-century maps as 'Broom-hill River'.

Robin Hood's Bay, village and resort, North Yorkshire, England.

The village is named after the bay on which it stands. This was recorded in *c*.1550 as *Robyn Huddes Bay*. This is only one example of the several cairns, crosses, caves, oaks and other locations in Britain named after Robin Hood, with this the most northerly. Robin Hood himself was a folk hero of doubtful historicity who featured in English ballads at least as early as the 14th century. His particular geographical associations are with Nottinghamshire and Yorkshire.

Rob Roy Town, former district of Plaistow, London, England.

The name arose as that of a development to the east of West Ham in 1855, comprising Leabon Street, John Street, Plaistow Grove, and the north end of Plaistow Road. It was short-lived, and although suggesting Scottish associations, is of uncertain origin.

Rochfortbridge, village, Westmeath, Ireland.

The village acquired its name from Robert Rochford (1652–1727), Member of Parliament for Westmeath and speaker of the Irish House of Commons, who owned property here in the second half of the 17th century. Its former name was Irish *An Droichead*, 'the bridge', or English *Beggar's Bridge*. A fanciful story was told that a beggar had died here and in his pockets was found enough money to build the bridge.

Rockvilla, district of Glasgow, Strathclyde, Scotland.

The name derived in 1783 from Rock Villa, the house of Robert Graeme, the sheriff substitute.

Roding, river, Essex, England.

The river name is a back formation, first recorded in 1576 as *Rodon*, from all the nine 'Roding' villages that stand on or near it: Abbess Roding, Aythorpe Roding, Barwick Roding, Beauchamp Roding, Berners Roding, High Roding, Leaden Roding, Margaret Roding, and White Roding. The original name of the river was 'Hyle', preserved in the name of Ilford.

Rom, river, Essex/London, England.

The name is a late back formation from Romford, standing on it. Below Romford, the river is called the Beam. Its earlier name was recorded in 1300 as 'Wythedenbrok'.

Rosebank, village (near Larkhall), Strathclyde, Scotland.

The village seems to have arisen some time between 1811 and 1846, with its name either descriptive or arbitrary.

Rose Lands, suburb of Eastbourne, East Sussex, England.

The name is first recorded in 1587 as *Rowesland*, by 1612 having been assimilated to *Roseland*. The origin lies in a man named Rowe who owned land here.

Rosherville, suburb of Gravesend, Kent, England.

The name derives from that of Jeremiah Rosher, who created a pleasure site here in *c.*1845. On the Ordnance Survey one-inch map of 1880 the name appears as *Rosherville Garden*.

Rother, administrative district, East Sussex, England.

The name is that of the river **Rother**, which flows through the district from west to east.

Rother, river, Hampshire/West Sussex, England.

The river name is a back formation from the former hundred of Rotherbridge, which lay to either side of the river, probably with a bridge over it. The name is preserved in Rotherbridge Farm, south west of Petworth, West Sussex. The former name of the river was 'Shire', apparently meaning 'clear', 'bright'. The 'Rother' of Rotherbridge is from an Old English word meaning 'ox', 'cattle' (compare the next entry).

Rother, river, East Sussex/Kent, England.

The river name is a back formation from the village of Rotherfield, East Sussex, near which the Rother rises. It was recorded as *Rocter* in 1572 and in its present spelling in 1575. The former name of the river was 'Limen', preserved in Lympne, Kent, which village used to stand on the river, and took its name from it. (The Rother now enters the sea three miles east of Rye; at one time it flowed into the English Channel at Lympne, its course following what is now, though disused, that of the **Royal Military Canal**.) The 'Rother' of Rotherfield means 'ox', as for Rotherbridge (see previous entry). The link between the two Rothers is purely a semantic one, and there is no geographical connection, in spite of the proximity of the two rivers to each other. The river Rother in South Yorkshire has an old name that is not a back formation.

Roundtown see **Terenure**.

Royal British Legion Village, village, Kent, England.

The village was set up here as a residential and rehabilitation centre for ex-servicemen shortly after the founding of the British Legion in 1921, and was originally known as *British Legion Village*. When the organization was granted the prefix 'Royal' in 1971, however, the name of the village was similarly changed. The administrative headquarters of the Village are at Preston Hall, a mansion built in the mid-19th century and formerly the home of the Brassey family. (The headquarters of the Royal British Legion itself are in London.)

Royal Canal, canal, Dublin/Kildare/Westmeath/Longford, Ireland.

The Canal was built over the period 1789–1802, although not completed until 1817, and was named in honour of the reigning monarch, George III. The Irish name of the Canal, with the same meaning, is *An Chanáil Ríoga*. The Canal is now disused. Formerly it ran from the river Liffey, in the outskirts of Dublin, to the Shannon at Richmond Harbour.

Royal Military Canal, canal, Kent, England.

Construction of the Canal began in 1807, with the aim for it to be part of the land defences here during the Napoleonic War. It was named after the reigning monarch, George III. The Canal is now disused (see **Rother**, Kent, above).

Royal Oak, district of west London, England.

The name derives from that of an inn here so called, near the location of the present Paddington railway terminus,

with entrance to the inn made by means of a wooden plank over the river Westbourne (which became the 'Ranelagh Sewer'). Royal Oak Underground station opened in 1871 and served to establish the name for the district. The inn no longer exists.

Royal Oak, village, Carlow, Ireland.

According to Lewis (1837), the name derives from 'an old and well-known inn in its vicinity, which was established previously to the erection of the village'. The Irish name of the village is *Cloch Rúsc*, 'stone [building in the] marsh'.

Rushcliffe, administrative district, Nottinghamshire, England.

The name is that of a former hundred here in the south of the county, meaning 'brushwood hill'.

Rushmoor, administrative district, Hampshire, England.

The name is that of Rushmoor Bottom, a natural feature to the west of Aldershot military camp. 'Rushmoor' means what it says, 'waste land overgrown with rushes'.

Rutland Island, island, Donegal, Ireland.

The name derives from that of Charles Manners, 4th Duke of Rutland (1754–87), who was appointed Lord Lieutenant of Ireland in 1784 and in that year attempted to establish a port here. Traces of the port still remain. The former name of the island was Innismacdurn, an English corruption of its present Irish name *Inis Mhic an Doirn*, 'Mac an Doirn's island'. Compare **Burtonport**.

Rydal Water, lake, Lake District, Cumbria, England.

The original name of the lake was 'Routhmere', recorded in 1589 as *Rothemyer* and meaning 'lake of the river Rothay' (which flows through it). Some time in the 16th century, possibly earlier, the name was altered to Rydal Water, first recorded in 1576 as *the*

Rydal-water, after the village of Rydal ('rye valley', an old name), at the east end of the lake.

Ryton, river, South Yorkshire/Nottinghamshire, England.

The river name is a back formation from the small village of Ryton (now Rayton) on the river east of Worksop. The former name of the river was 'Blyth', so recorded in 1677, with the village of Blyth, on the river, taking its name from it.

S

Saffron Walden, town, Essex, England.

The original name of the town was simply 'Walden', with the prefixed form of the name first recorded in 1582, as *Saffornewalden*. It is known that saffron was first cultivated in England in *c*.1340. The earliest reference to it at Walden is in 1545, when it was recorded that the town made a gift of a pound of saffron to 'my ladye Pagett', the wife of one of the secretaries of state. The prefix was doubtless also added to distinguish this Walden from the village of Little Walden just north of the town. If it had not been for the distinctive saffron, the town might have been called 'Great Walden'.

St. Anne's(-on-Sea), district of Lytham St. Anne's, Lancashire, England.

The name is that of a church dedicated to St. Anne here, built in 1872–3 and the first building to be constructed in the new planned town. The original name of the site was *Kilgrimol*, 'Kelgrim's hollow'. Lytham and St. Anne's were two separate towns until they were incorporated in 1922 as Lytham St. Anne's.

St. Budeaux, district of Plymouth, Devon, England.

The original name of the village was 'Budshead', recorded in the 'Domesday Book' of 1086 as *Bucheside*, 'hide of land of St. Budoc'. The name then gradually altered to its present form, being recorded as *Seynt Bodokkys* in 1520 and *Saint Budeaux (or Saint Buddox)* in 1796. The name looks French, but the church is dedicated to the Celtic saint Budoc, whose name is related to that of Boudicca (still popularly known as Boadicea).

St. Edmundsbury, administrative district, Suffolk, England.

The name is a modern version of the old, pre-Domesday name of Bury St.

Edmunds, the district's administrative centre. This was recorded in 1038 as *Sancte Eadmundes Byrig*.

St. George, district of Bristol, Avon, England.

The name was recorded in 1638 as *St. George's*, and the district was described in 1779 as 'a newly-erected parish'. In 1784 St. George was the name given to a civil parish created from parts of several parishes here, and was later called Euston St. George for a while.

St. Helens, town, Merseyside, England.

The name derives from a chapel dedicated to St. Helen and first mentioned here in 1552. This was probably a medieval chapel-of-ease, and stood at the junction of the roads from Warrington to Ormskirk and Prescot to Ashton. There have been four different churches on the site since, of which the third, here from 1816 to 1916, was dedicated to St. Mary. The present industrial town began its development in the 17th century with coal-mining, while glass-making was introduced in 1773.

St. James's, district of south-west London, England.

The district, famous for its royal and diplomatic associations, came to acquire a 'blanket' name to refer to St. James's Palace, Park, Street, and Square. St. James's Park, the oldest of the so-called 'Royal Parks' in London, was recorded in 1555 as *Seynt James Newe Parke*. It was originally a marshy meadow belonging to the old leper hospital of James the Less, whose own name was recorded in 1204 as *hospital' leprosis puellis de şcī Jacobi extra London justa Westm̃* ('hospital for leprous girls of Saint James outside London next to Westminster'). The hospital was dissolved in 1532 and in its place Henry VIII built a royal palace, subsequently laying out the adjoining meadow as a deer park. St. James's

Street was so named in 1624, and St. James's Square in 1682.

St. Johnstown, village, Donegal, Ireland.

The village arose during the English settlement ('plantation') of Ulster, when lands were granted by James I to Ludovick Stuart, 2nd Duke of Lennox and Duke of Richmond (1574–1624). The settlement was designed to accommodate English and Scottish artisans and mechanics, and to build the town, the Duke was pledged to assign 60 acres of property. The town was incorporated in 1618 under the designation of the 'Provost and Burgesses of the Borough and Town of St. Johnstown'.

St. Leonards(-on-Sea), town and resort, East Sussex, England.

The town, recorded in 1557 as *Seynt Leonards*, was originally named after the church dedicated to St. Leonard here, itself recorded in 1279 as *ecclesia Leonardi de Hastynges*. The resort, which adjoins Hastings to the west, developed after 1838, when the London builder James Burton, and his son Decimus Burton, the architect, bought land here on which to establish a fashionable watering-place similar to the one at **Brighton**. The original church of St. Leonard was washed away by the sea in *c*.1430.

Salem, village, Dyfed, Wales.

The name derives from a chapel so called here in the early 19th century, with its own name understood to be a form of 'Jerusalem' and to mean 'peace'. The biblical city of Jerusalem is referred to in the Bible as Salem, in for example Genesis 14: 18 and Hebrews 7: 1.

Salop, former name of Shropshire, county, England.

Salop was the official name of Shropshire from 1974 to 1980. The name has long been in unofficial use for the county, however, if only as an abbreviated form, postal or otherwise. In this sense it has been as common as 'Hants' for Hampshire and 'Oxon' for Oxford-

shire. All three abbreviated county names have sound linguistic and historical precedent, since Salop can be regarded as a contraction of the Norman name of the county, recorded in 1094 as *Salopescira* and itself a 'smoother' variant of the Old English *Scrobbesbyrigscir* (i.e. 'Shrewsburyshire'), recorded in 1006 and regarded as too much of a mouthful by the Normans. It was this earliest form of the name that was to produce modern 'Shropshire' (with the central section of the long name omitted). Both names for the county have thus a similar antiquity. Of the two, however, 'Shropshire' has always been the preferred form among the inhabitants, and the official change to 'Salop', made in 1974 with the reorganization of local government boundaries, was resented by many, who saw the name as a 'foreign' one imposed by central government. As the result of a campaign organized by a county councillor, therefore, the County Council re-adopted Shropshire as the official name of the county in 1980. (One additional reason for preferring the former name is said to have been tabled by the European Member of Parliament for Salop and Staffordshire, who had been embarrassed by the similarity of 'Salop' to French colloquial *salope*, 'slattern', 'slut'.) In spite of the reversion to the older name, 'Salop' continues to be used as before, with Shrewsbury, the county town, still referred to as 'Salop' by some inhabitants, and the adjective Salopian used in a number of respectable and positive contexts (former members of Shrewsbury School, founded in 1552, are known as 'Old Salopians', for example).

Salsburgh, village (near Airdrie), Strathclyde, Scotland.

The name was recorded in 1839 as *Sallysburgh*. According to Johnston (1934), the name is a '19th century freak, named from some forgotten Sally'. She appears to have been Sally Young, wife of the proprietor of the lands on which the village arose in the late 18th century, a Mr Young of Craigshead.

Saltaire, district of Shipley, West Yorkshire, England.

The village was founded as a new town for the manufacture of alpaca by Sir Titus *Salt* in 1850, with his surname and the river *Aire*, on which Saltaire stands, forming the name. Sir Titus had been mayor of Bradford until 1849, and resigned his office that year in order to establish the new settlement. The first houses were built here in 1853.

Saltcoats, town and resort, Strathclyde, Scotland.

The name means 'salt-workers' houses', and was first recorded in 1528, as *Saltcottis*. The manufacture of salt from saltpans here has been recorded at various periods before this date. Compare **Prestonpans**.

Saltdean, village and resort, East Sussex, England.

The name derives from *Saltdean Gap*, so recorded in 1740. This was a 'gap' or cleft in the cliffs that runs up from the sea here. Such 'deans' are a feature of this part of the Sussex coast: also here are Ovingdean and Rottingdean, with Roedean (since 1885, a girls' school) above the cliffs between Rottingdean and **Brighton**.

Sandhaven, village and port (near Fraserburgh), Grampian, Scotland.

The village arose in *c.*1839 as a planned settlement, with its name apparently self-descriptive (a haven or port on the sands).

Saron, village (near Ammanford), Dyfed, Wales.

The name is that of a Nonconformist chapel set up here some time in the early 19th century. It is a biblical name (better known as Sharon) usually understood to mean a fruitful place and metaphorically to indicate the Church itself. It occurs several times in the Bible, for example in Isaiah 35: 2 and 65: 10 and Song of Solomon 2: 1. There are other villages of the name in Wales, including another in Dyfed (near Llandyssul) and two in Gwynedd (near Caernarfon and near Llanwnda).

Saundersfoot, town and resort, Dyfed, Wales.

The town has grown up since 1821, with only two or three houses here before this. Even so, the name has been recorded as early as 1602, as *Sannders foot*. The first part of the name seems to be a personal one, perhaps Alexander or Saunders; the second element may refer to the foot of a hill or cliff, or perhaps be a corruption of 'ford'. If the latter, the reference could be to a ford across the stream at the rear of Milford Street. The usual local legend tells of a Norman family named Saunders who first set *foot* here when they landed in Britain!

Savile Town, district of Dewsbury, West Yorkshire, England.

The name came into use for the district some time after 1863, when a bridge was built over the river Calder. The owner of the district was Lord Savile.

Seaforde, village, Down, Northern Ireland.

The name derives from Colonel M. Forde, who initiated development here in 1819 by rebuilding his 18th-century residence, Seaforde House. Most of the remaining houses in the village were built in the 1820s.

Seaforth, district of Crosby, Merseyside, England.

The district took its name from Seaforth House, the home of Sir John Gladstone (1764–1851), who so named it in 1813 when his wife moved there, as she was a member of the Mackenzie clan whose head at the time was Francis Humberston Mackenzie, Baron Seaforth and Mackenzie (1754–1815). The Baron's own title was taken from Loch Seaforth, Isle of Lewis, Scotland. Sir John Gladstone was the father of William Ewart Gladstone, the British prime minister.

Sealand, village, Clwyd, Wales.

The region here was originally part of

Saltney Marsh, but in 1732 Nathaniel Kenderley and Company (from 1740 the River Dee Company) obtained an Act of Parliament to cut a canal through the marsh, thus forming a new channel for the river. They carried out this project in 1737, with the result that over 600 acres of land here, purchased from the lord and freeholders of Hawarden, were formed into a new village under the name of Sealand.

Seathwaite, village, Cumbria, England.

The village arose in the 16th century, first recorded as *Seathwot* in 1592, and took its name from Seathwaite Tarn, one of the smallest lakes in the **Lake District**. The village lies five miles south of Seathwaite Tarn, and must not be confused with the Seathwaite, also in the Lake District, that is further north in Borrowdale, near Seatoller.

Seaview, village and resort, Isle of Wight, England.

The name apparently originates from a lodging house so called here, built early in the 19th century.

Sebastopol, village, Gwent, Wales.

The village, now part of **Griffithstown**, owed its name to the major operation of the Crimean War, in which British and French troops captured the main naval base of the Russian Black Sea Fleet at Sebastopol in 1854. This victory was commemorated by one John Nicholas, who built a group of houses here in *c.*1858 and named them after the Russian port (whose own name, more correctly Sevastopol, derives from the Greek, meaning 'majestic city'—a highly favourable connotation of which many inhabitants of the Welsh mining village may be unaware).

Selly Oak, district of Birmingham, West Midlands, England.

The original name of the settlement was 'Selly', so recorded (as *Escelie*) in the 'Domesday Book' of 1086. 'Oak' appears to have been added some time in or after the 16th century, with reference to a prominent oak-tree that is said to have stood in the village.

Selsey Bill, headland, West Sussex, England.

The name is first found on a map of 1740, and there is no evidence that the name is much older than this. The first part of the name is old, meaning 'seal island'. 'Bill' suggests 'beak-like', i.e. a headland shaped like a bird's beak. Selsey Bill, however, is rounded, not pointed, and it is possible that this part of the name was given on an analogy with Portland Bill, Dorset, which is sharp-pointed and much more deserving of its name. (Perhaps significantly, no earlier forms of this name have been found either: the first recorded appearance of the name is *the Bill* in 1649, with *Portland Bill* first noted in 1773.)

Seven Dials, district of Central London, England.

The name is first recorded in 1707, as (*les*) *Seven Dials*. However, the place is mentioned earlier, in the entry in Evelyn's *Diary* for 5 October 1694: 'I went to see the building near St Giles where seven streets make a star from a Doric pillar placed in the middle of a circular area'. This building was by Thomas Neale on Cock and Pye Fields (so named after an inn), and the 'Doric pillar' was the column with seven dials which stood at the junction of seven streets here until 1773 when it was removed to Weybridge, Surrey. The district was formerly notorious for its poverty and thieves' quarters.

Seven Sisters, chalk cliffs, East Sussex, England.

The name is recorded as *The Seven Cliffes or hills* in *The Mariners Mirror* of 1588. It cannot have been much later that the present name came to be established for the seven chalk cliffs: 'Seven Sisters' has long been a popular name for any group of seven natural objects, originating with the seven stars of the Pleiades. In modern place-names, the reference can also be to seven real sisters, see **Seven Sisters**, West Glamorgan (below).

Seven Sisters, district of Tottenham, London, England.

The name originates from Seven Sisters Road here, constructed in the 1830s, and itself said to be named after seven elm trees near Page Green. The name was first recorded in 1754 as *Seven Sesters*, and became established for the district with the opening of Seven Sisters Underground station in 1968.

Seven Sisters, village, West Glamorgan, Wales.

The village arose with the coming of the railway in the mid-19th century, and the name originated from that of a coal pit here, one of the first to be sunk in the area. The pit owner was one David Bevan, and it was his eldest daughter, Isabella Bevan, who cut the first turf of the new mine on 11 March 1872. There had been some discussion as to what the name of the pit should be: some suggested Bryncae ('meadow hill'), after the location of the pit on Nant Melyn Farm, while others proposed Isabella Pit, after the young woman who had cut the first sod. It was David Bevan's son, however, Evan Evans Bevan, who apparently suggested the eventual name: since he had seven sisters, they should all be equally honoured in the name of the pit. The new pit was thus called the 'Seven Sisters Colliery', and the village that grew up round it came to acquire the name in due course. The seven sisters themselves were (married name in brackets): Nancy Isabella (Thomas) (1849–84), Mary Diana (Marsden) (1851–1920), Sarah Jane (1852–1930), Margreta (Aylwin) (1855–1930), Frances Matilda (Sutton) (1858–1903), Maria Louisa (Ritson) (1862–1928), and Sophia Annie (1862–1947). The original name of the location has been disputed. It may have been *Blaendulais* ('source of the [river] Dulais'), *Cwmdulais* ('valley of the Dulais') or *Bryndulais* ('hill of the Dulais').

Shellhaven, industrial anchorage site, Essex, England.

The site is today virtually part of **Coryton**, and forms a point on the west bank of the estuary of Holehaven Creek. The Shell Oil Company opened a refinery here in 1912, but the identity of the two names is simply a happy coincidence, for 'Shellhaven' was already in existence as a name for the location at the time. According to an article in the *PLA Monthly* of November, 1963, the name appears on 16th-century maps and is also mentioned by Pepys in his *Diary*. On the Ordnance Survey one-inch map of 1884, a Shellhaven House appears here near Shellhaven Creek, at the mouth of which is even Shellhaven Haven. If the name is a genuinely old one, it may derive from Old English *scylf*, 'bank', as does the name of the village of Shelley, also in Essex. Compare **Thameshaven**.

Shepherds Bush, district of west London, England.

The name is first recorded in 1635, as *Sheppards Bush Green*. It seems likely that this was named after a family called Sheppard or Shepherd (or some similar spelling) who lived here, although there was a type of tree known as a 'shepherd's bush'—defined by Rawlings (c.1925) as a 'thorn-tree clipped so as to afford a raised standing-place whence a shepherd could keep watch over his flock'—and there could possibly have been a prominent one here. The name became established for the district with the opening of Shepherds Bush railway station on the Hammersmith and City Line in 1864. This was resited and a new station opened in 1914, while in 1900 Shepherds Bush Underground station was opened.

Shepherdswell, village, Kent, England.

The name was originally *Sibertswold*, this being a pre-Domesday name meaning 'Swithbeorht's forest', but in the 19th century the name was popularly altered to Shepherdswell, largely as a result of the opening of Shepherd's Well station on the East Kent railway. Presumably the railway company believed it was 'correcting' a corrupt name. *Cassell* (1897) enters the name as '*Shepherd's Well*, a local form of *Sibertswold*'.

Shepway, administrative district, Kent, England.

In Saxon times Kent was divided into five so-called lathes, one of which was named 'Shepway', whose territory approximated to the present administrative district. There also existed an ancient 'Court of the Cinque Ports', known as the 'Court of Shepway', which included the two Cinque Ports of Hythe and Romney, now in the modern district. The old name, meaning 'sheep way', was recorded in 1227 as *Shepweye* and in 1254 as *Shypwey*. With its local territorial and historical associations, the name was an obvious choice for the district formed in 1974.

Shillingstone, village, Dorset, England.
Since the 'Domesday Book' of 1086, the name of the village has changed from 'Okeford' to its present name. The original name, meaning 'oak-tree ford', was recorded in 'Domesday' as *Acford*. This then came to acquire 'Shilling' as first a suffix, then a prefix: *Acforde Eskelin* 1155, *Okfordskelling* 1302, *Ockford Shilling* 1664, and *Skillyng Okeford* 1407, *Shilling Okeford* 1795. Meanwhile the present name first appeared as *Shillyngeston* in 1444, and the name was recorded in 1774 as *Shillingston, vulgarly Ockford-Shilling*. The 'Shilling' is one Schelin who held the manor here at the time of the 'Domesday' record, and the element was added to the early name of the village to differentiate it from nearby Child Okeford and Okeford Fitzpaine. At the same time 'ford' became 'town' (i.e. 'village').

Shortstown, village, Bedfordshire, England.
The place arose as a garden village outside Bedford built by the aircraft manufacturing firm of Short Brothers

from 1917. The village subsequently became the property of the Royal Air Force.

Shottermill, village, Surrey, England.
The name is first recorded in 1537, as *Shottover*, and in its present form as *Schotouermyll* in 1607. The derivation probably lies in a family name Shotover, who owned the mill here. A local favoured explanation is that the mill was so called since the water went over it ('shot over') rather than going under. (This is offered as a serious possibility by, for example, Pamela Edwards in *Surrey Villages*, 1968.)

Silver End, village, Essex, England.
The village was built in the late 1920s by the firm of F. H. Crittall, who produced metal windows for houses at Braintree. The name presumably refers to the 'silvery' appearance of the windows of houses built in the new village.

Silvertown, district of east London, England.
The name derives from the firm of S. W. Silver & Co., who in *c.*1852 opened a factory here to produce rubber goods. The workers' houses built round the factory came to be known as Silvertown. Sir Samuel Canning was associated with the firm (see **Canning Town**).

Sinclairtown, district of Kircaldy, Fife, Scotland.
The district arose as a planned village in *c.*1780, and was named after the St. Clair family, the earls of Rosslyn, whose seat at Dysart House was nearby.

Sion Mills, village, Tyrone, Northern Ireland.
The settlement arose as a model industrial village founded in 1835 by James Herdman to provide housing for the workers at the flax-spinning mill here. The name appears not to have religious connotations, but to derive from Irish *sidheán* (pronounced approximately 'sheeawn'), 'fairy mount', with the full modern Irish name being *Muileann an*

tSiáin, 'mill of the fairy mount'. The village was enlarged in 1888.

Six Bells, village, Gwent, Wales.

The name originates from an inn here, whose own name may refer to the silver bell that was formerly won in horse-racing.

Smithborough, village, Monaghan, Ireland.

According to Lewis (1837), the village was named after 'a gentleman named Smith, who here established monthly fairs, in the latter part of the last [i.e. 18th] century'. The Irish name of the village is *Na Mullai*, 'the hilltops'.

Sodom, village, Clwyd, Wales.

There is some dispute as to how the village came to acquire the biblical name with its undesirable connotations of 'iniquity and destruction'. Local tradition claims that the name was given as a nickname because of the quarrelsome nature of the inhabitants. There may be some truth in this if one allows the following possibility: the village was founded round a chapel named Salem (a common chapel-name in Wales); the members of this chapel were contentious; their dissent provoked the semi-facetious conversion of 'Salem' to 'Sodom'; this name then became adopted for the village. The village does not appear under this name on the Ordnance Survey one-inch map of 1840.

Soho, district of west London, England.

The usual explanation given for the name is that it originated as a hunting cry, with 'So-ho!' used for hunting the hare just as 'Tally-ho!' was used for hunting the fox. This may be possible, since it is known that there were fields here before the area was built over in the 18th century. It has also been recorded that hunting took place here in 1562. The district name is first recorded in 1632 as *So Ho*, with later versions of the name appearing as *place called So Howe* 1634, *Sohoe* 1636, *Soe-Hoe in St. Martins in the Fields*, and *Soe Hoe feildes* 1684. It may

be that the name spread to the district not directly from the hunting cry itself but from an inn so called, with hunting names a popular theme for names of inns (such as the Huntsman, Hare and Hounds, Hunted Stag, Dog, and the like). The old legend that the name was originally the battle-cry of the Duke of Monmouth at the Battle of Sedgemoor cannot have any basis, since the names above pre-date the battle of 1685. (The legend seems to have arisen since the Duke of Monmouth had his residence here.)

Solent Breezes, village and resort, Hampshire, England.

The village consists of a permanent caravan site for yachtsmen and holiday-makers located on Southampton Water. It arose as a development of the 1960s, with a typical 'seaside' name. The village is inhabited only in the summer season, but appears as a permanent feature on Ordnance Survey maps and in gazetteers such as Mason (1977).

Somerleyton, village, Suffolk.

The settlement arose in the early 1850s as a model village built for the employees of Somerleyton Hall by the hall owner Sir Samuel Morton Peto (1809–89), Member of Parliament for Norwich and contractor.

Somers Town, district of north London, England.

Building of the district began in 1786 on the estate of John Somers, Lord Somers (1651–1716), Lord Chancellor of England, which after his death passed to his family. The name is first recorded in 1795, as *Sommers Town*, this being one of the earliest uses of the suffix 'Town' to denote an urban development on an estate. The district was notorious for its poverty, and for a while earned the nickname 'Botany Bay', from the large number of French refugees who came to live here after the Revolution.

Southborough, town, Kent, England.

The earliest record of the name is in

1450, as *la South Burgh in Tunbrigge*. It remained part of the parish of Tonbridge to 1894, when it became an independent town.

Southbourne, district of Bournemouth, Dorset, England.

The name was originally used for a terrace of shops near The Square, Bournemouth, and was subsequently selected by a Dr Compton for his seaside residential development three miles east of the town centre in *c*.1870. The obvious name for the development would have been 'Eastbourne', but this was unusable because of the Sussex resort so named. Presumably the name of the terrace was intended to refer to its location in the *south* of *Bourne*mouth, or at a point *south* on the river *Bourne*, near its outflow to the sea.

Southend(-on-Sea), town and resort, Essex, England.

The resort was originally part of Prittlewell, and was established at the southern end of this settlement (now itself a district of Southend). The earliest record of the name is *Southende* in 1481, but this was many years before the resort began to develop, in *c*.1800. Before this, the place seems to have been called 'Streetend' (*Stratende*, 1309), meaning 'end of the Roman road'. Such a road could have linked the Romano-British settlements at Billericay, Wickford, and Prittlewell and reached the sea at this point. As a resort, Southend first gained prominence with the visit here in 1804 of Queen Caroline and her eight-year-old daughter Princess Charlotte.

South Hams, administrative district, Devon, England.

The name is an old one (*Southammes*, 1396) revived for administrative use. The meaning of the name is 'southern riverside land', since the district is between Plymouth and the estuary of the river Dart, with Dartmoor to the north. The area was divided into two parts, each known as 'Hamme'. The name continued in semi-official use down to the 19th century, and the district was nicknamed the 'Garden of Devonshire' for its rich pastures, meadows, cornfields, and orchards.

Southport, town and resort, Merseyside, England.

The original name of the site was South Hawes. Here in 1792 one William Sutton of North Meols (the main settlement) built a hotel out of driftwood. This was replaced by a stone building in which at a public dinner in 1798, a 'housewarming' for the hotel, the place was named 'South Port' by a Dr Barton of Hoole. The reason for the choice of name has not been conclusively established. Among possible motives may have been: (1) a port that was 'south' of Preston; (2) a modification of the former name of South Hawes; (3) a port 'south' of Blackpool; (4) a generally favourable name suggesting a resort in the south, such as **Southsea**; (5) a tribute to William Sutton, whose surname could be understood as 'south town'. The hotel, subsequently called Duke's Folly, stood near the point where Duke Street joins Lord Street.

Southsea, resort and district of Portsmouth, Hampshire, England.

The origin of the district is in the castle that Henry VIII planned here in 1538 to protect the entrance to Portsmouth Harbour. This 'goodlie and warlyk castill' was to be built on the southern tip of land one mile east of Portsmouth, and so was to be a 'south sea castle'. The castle was originally called 'Chaderton Castle' after its first governor, John Chaderton, the present castle being a reconstructed version of the first. The town of Southsea, now part of Portsmouth, began to develop in the early 1800s. The earliest record of the name, referring to the castle, is in 1545, as *le South Castell of Portesmouth*.

Spa (of Tralee), village, Kerry, Ireland.

The village arose in *c*.1746, when a well with a mineral spring was discovered. The name, as for all places called 'Spa', was taken from the Belgian resort of Spa whose mineral springs were known in Roman times. The village is near Tralee.

Spelthorne, administrative district, Surrey, England.

The district council was formed in 1972 by joining the former urban districts of Staines and Sunbury-on-Thames, and was granted borough status in 1974. The name was originally that of one of the six hundreds of Middlesex, meaning 'speech thorn tree'.

Spenborough, district, West Yorkshire, England.

The district is an industrial borough which in 1915 was formed into an urban district and in 1937 enlarged to include Cleckheaton, Gomersal, Liversedge, Birkenshaw, Hansworth, Hartshead, and part of Clifton. The 'borough' of the name indicates its status, with the base of the name taken both from the river Spen, in the valley of which Spenborough is located, and from the former village of Spen, east of Cleckheaton. A similar name is the urban district of *Aireborough*, in the valley of the river Aire, north of Bradford.

Spital, district of New Windsor, Berkshire, England.

The name means 'hospital', and the district arose on the site of a former hospital for lepers here. The earliest record of the name is in 1535, as *Le Spitall*, with a document of 1573 giving the name as *the Spittle*. (In spite of the dates, 'spital' as an ordinary noun in English was a later spelling of 'spittle'.)

Spithead, roadstead, Hampshire, England.

The name means literally 'head of the spit of land', in this case referring to the end of the sandy spit that today is mostly built over and extends eastwards from Haslar Royal Naval Hospital, Gosport. The original Spithead (first recorded with this spelling in 1629) was thus a very precise point. A document of 1635 states that a ship had 'come to

anchor near the Spithead'. At one time the name Solent was used for the whole length of the channel between the Isle of Wight and the mainland. Later, 'Spithead' came to be used as the name of the whole roadstead off the entrance to Portsmouth Harbour and even, as today popularly understood, to the entire channel between the Isle of Wight and the mainland from Ryde across to Portsmouth, with a certain amount of 'leeway' to east and west. Because of this extended use, 'Solent' is today understood to denote the channel here from Hurst Castle (Hampshire) and Cliff End (Isle of Wight) in the west to Spithead in the east. According to the *Oxford English Dictionary*, 'spit' meaning 'reef', 'point of land' dates no earlier than 1673.

Springfield, village (near Gretna Green), Dumfries and Galloway, Scotland.

The village was founded by weavers in 1791 on the estate of Sir William Maxwell, whose residence was at Springkell, seven miles north west of here.

Springhead, district of Oldham, Greater Manchester, England.

The name was originally that of a weaver's house here, still in existence and today located on the corner of Cooper Street and Oldham Road, Springhead. The name passed from the house to the district, but only became official in 1895 when an urban district was established. Prior to this, the official name of the district was 'The Middle Division of Quickmere'. The origin of the name is uncertain: the house, however, was built in a field called Little Hurst Head, and 'spring' may have been a local term for a wooded area (the *Oxford English Dictionary* gives the word in this sense, with specific reference to local place-names). The house is mentioned in a deed dated 1809, but existed some time before this.

Stalybridge, town, Greater Manchester, England.

The original name of the settlement was

'Staveley' or 'Stayley', with 'Staly-bridge' in use as the name of a hamlet in Lancashire across the river Tame. In the 18th century the name extended to the Cheshire side of the river and eventually replaced the original 'Staveley' ('Stayley') for the whole town. The name can today thus be understood as 'bridge over the river Tame at a place that was once called Stayley'. The earlier name may derive from a family called Stayley or Stavelegh who were known to own land here in the 14th century.

Stanley, village (near Perth), Tayside, Scotland.

The village was named in c.1700 after Lady Amelia Sophia Stanley, the fourth daughter of James Stanley, 7th Earl of Derby. She married John Murray, 2nd Earl and 1st Marquis of Atholl (1631–1703), a prominent landowner here.

Stanstead St. Margarets, village, Hertfordshire, England.

The earliest record of the name of the village is as (de) Ponte Tegule in 1200, this being medieval Latin for 'tile bridge'. The name then developed and changed as subsequent records show: Pons de Thele 1269, Thele 1296, ecclesia Sce Margarete de Thele c.1400, Stanstead Thele 1540, Stanstead Thele or St. Margarett 1604, Stanstead St. Margarete 1559, with Stanstead Theel or Stantheel recorded as late as 1769. 'St. Margaret' was the dedication of the church, with 'Stanstead' being assumed as the basic name of the village (meaning 'stony place'). 'Stanstead Thele' altered to 'Stanstead St. Margaret' to distinguish the village from Stanstead Abbots on the other side of the bridge here over the river Lea.

Starcross, village, Devon, England.

The name is first recorded in 1689, as Star Crosse. The precise origin is not clear; possibly there was a cross of a particular shape here, as at **Handcross**.

Staylittle, village, Powys, Wales.

The name derives from an inn here so called, its own name devised as an invitation to travellers to 'stay a little' or 'rest a while'. The Welsh name of the village is Penfforddwen, 'top of the white road'. The village is at the head of the Clywedog Reservoir. (On the map in AA England & Wales [1963] the name of the village appears as Stay-a-little.)

Stewartry, administrative district, Dumfries and Galloway, Scotland.

The name is the ancient one for the district here, a 'stewardship', of which Kirkcudbright was the capital (and today is the administrative centre). There were two stewartries in Scotland, that of Orkney and Shetland, and the present one, of Kirkcudbright, which were identical with the former counties, and in both of these districts the official title was 'stewartry', not 'county'. As an administrative division, the stewartry was abolished in 1748. In the case of Kirkcudbright, the steward, who held jurisdiction over the stewartry, was the Earl of Douglas.

Stewartstown, village, Tyrone, Northern Ireland.

The village was named after Sir Andrew Steuart (according to Killanin and Duignan [1967], Sir Alexander Stewart), who was granted lands here by James I and who built a castle near here in c.1608. The village, whose name is also found in the spelling Steuartstown, was once a flourishing market town.

Stiffkey, river, Norfolk, England.

The river name is a back formation, of uncertain date, from the village of Stiffkey located on it.

Stocksbridge, town, South Yorkshire, England.

Stocksbridge arose as a 19th-century township formed out of Bradfield, and takes its name from a bridge over the river Little Don marked on the Ordnance Survey one-inch map of 1841 as Stocks Br., i.e. 'bridge made of logs'. The town grew rapidly as a steel manufacturing centre.

Stonebridge Park, district of north-west London, England.

A stone bridge was first recorded here in 1745, over the river Brent. A document of 1875 notes that a group of sixty or eighty villas had been built here on an estate called Stonebridge Park. The name became established for the district in 1912, when the London and North Western Railway opened a station here. In 1917 Stonebridge Park Underground station opened.

Stone Chair, village, West Yorkshire, England.

The name seems to date back to coaching days, when a double milestone here, north-east of Halifax, had a flat stone forming a seat. Goodall (1913) notes that the inscription on the modern stone reads, 'Stone Chair. Erected 1731. Re-erected 1891. Halifax–Bradford.'

Stonehaven, town and port, Grampian, Scotland.

The name was recorded in 1587 and 1592 as *Stanehyve* and in 1629 as *Steanhyve*. 'Stonehaven' suggests 'stone harbour', but the 'hyve' of the early forms of the name does not support this, and even the 'stone' is suspect because of the 1629 spelling, which approximates to the modern pronunciation, with the stress on the second syllable. According to Macnie and McLaren (1977), the town was created by George Keith, 5th Earl Marischal (?1553–1623), who founded **Peterhead**. See also **New Stonehaven**.

Stort, river, Essex/Hertfordshire, England.

The river name is a back formation from **Bishop's Stortford**, situated on it. The name was recorded as *Stour* in 1576, *Stort* in 1586, and *Sturt* in 1612.

Stourport(-on-Severn), town, Hereford and Worcester, England.

The industrial town is located at the confluence of the rivers Stour and Severn. It has its origins in the new town that was built round the basin that linked the Stour with the canal first planned here in 1756 by James Brindley. The canal was constructed over the period 1766–71 and opened in this latter year as the Staffordshire and Worcestershire Canal, connecting the Trent and Mersey Canal at Great Heywood Junction, Staffordshire, with the river Severn here at Stourport. Before the town grew up here, the settlement was known as Lower Mitton. Upper Mitton is still the name of a northern suburb of Stourport. The town seems to have been the only one in Great Britain to arise on a canal.

Stow-on-the-Wold, town, Gloucestershire, England.

The original name of the settlement here was 'Edwardstow', recorded in the 'Domesday Book' of 1086 as *Eduudesstou*, with variants of this occurring down to 1585. A parallel name of 'Stow' also developed, recorded in 1213 as *Stoua* and first in its present extended form in 1557 as *Stow super le Olde*. The 'Domesday' name was for St. Edward's church. Stow is the highest town in the Cotswolds, as reflected in its modern suffix of '-on-the-Wold'. 'Stow', meaning basically 'place', here by extension means 'place for religious gatherings', so 'church'.

Stragglethorpe, village, Nottinghamshire, England.

Although at first appearance an old name, *Straggelthorpe* was first recorded as late as 1796. A connection with the Lincolnshire village of Stragglethorpe seems unlikely: perhaps the name arose more as a nickname for some farms here, a 'straggling thorp'.

Strand on the Green, district of Chiswick, London, England.

The basic name was first recorded, as *Stronde*, in 1353, with the form *Stronde in parochia de Cheswyck* noted in 1412. The present form of the name is first documented in 1593, as *Strand Green*, with later versions of this recorded as *Strand under Green* 1760, and *Strand on*

Green 1795. The name means 'strand or bank beside a green place': the district lies along the north bank of the river Thames.

Stratford-on-Slaney, village, Wicklow, Ireland.

The village was laid out in c.1785 and built for Edward Stratford, 2nd Earl of Aldborough (d. 1801), who provided houses for workers at the cotton mills and linen printworks here. The industrial enterprise failed in 1846 and the village is now decayed. The name, referring to the location of the village on the river Slaney, may well have been influenced by that of Stratford-on-Avon, England.

Strathkelvin, administrative district, Strathclyde, Scotland.

The name, modelled on that of the region in which it is situated, means 'valley of the river Kelvin'. Kelvin is also an industrial estate in the southern part of the new town of East Kilbride, Strathclyde.

Strawberry Hill, district of Twickenham, London, England.

The name was originally that given to a house here by the writer Horace Walpole, 4th Earl of Orford (1717–97), when he bought it in 1748. Walpole's choice of name was prompted by a local field name, Strawberry Hill Shot, which he found in some old deeds on buying the house. The previous name of the house, which had been built by a retired coachman, was Chopped Straw Hall, although this was more of a nickname than a house name proper. Walpole extensively rebuilt the house, now a theological college.

Strelitz, former village (near Coupar Angus), Tayside, Scotland.

The village was laid out on the farm of Whitely in 1763 with the aim of providing accommodation for disbanded servicemen after the Seven Years War, which ended that year. By the end of the year seventy houses had been built, and on 27 February 1764 the name of the village was changed from Whitely to Strelitz, in honour of Queen Charlotte of Mecklenburg-Strelitz, wife of George III. The population reached 291 in 1766 but when the estate on which the village stood was restored in 1784 to the heir of the previous owner, Lord James Drummond, from whom it had been confiscated in 1752, Strelitz was neglected and the villagers gradually moved to Burrelton, less than a mile away.

Stuartfield, village (near Peterhead), Grampian, Scotland.

The village was created in c.1772 for the local weaving community by John Burnett, laird of Crichie, who named it after his grandfather, Captain John Stuart. The local name for the village is Crichie, after the estate.

Summerstown, district of south-west London, England.

The land here was built on by a man named Sumner or Summers, and a family of the name is recorded as having lived here in the 17th and 18th centuries. The first mention of Summerstown, however, is as late as 1823.

Summertown, district of Oxford, Oxfordshire, England.

The name is said to derive from a signboard displayed by the first man to make his home here in the late 18th or early 19th century. The sign read, 'James Lambourn horsedealer Somers Town', and Lambourn is said to have chosen the name because the place seemed so pleasant to him. The name appears on the Ordnance Survey map of 1822 as *Summerstown*. It is probably no more than a coincidence that Somerton is the name of an Oxfordshire village thirteen miles north of here.

Sunk Island, village, Humberside, England.

The name first appears on a map of 1678, where the place is shown as a small island rising out of a sandbank in the river Humber. The northern arm of the river Humber has now filled up and

Sunk Island is part of the mainland. The original island seems to have been part of the mainland that had been washed away some time earlier.

Sunningdale, residential district, Berkshire, England.

The district is an ecclesiastical parish formed in 1841 from parts of Old Windsor, Sunninghill, and the Surrey parishes of Windlesham, Egham, and Chobham, becoming a civil parish in 1894. On William Eden's *Map of Windsor Park and part of the New Forest*, published in 1800, the place appears as *Sunning Hill Dale*, and the present name appears to derive directly from this, and thus indirectly from Sunninghill.

Surrey Heath, administrative district, Surrey, England.

The district, formed as a county borough in 1974 from the urban districts of Frimley and Camberley and the rural district of Bagshot, is named after Bagshot Heath, located in it.

Swale, administrative district, Kent, England.

The name is that of The Swale, a branch of the estuary of the river Medway, which separates the Isle of Sheppey from mainland Kent. This name is a pre-Domesday one, probably meaning 'rushing river', as the river Swale in Yorkshire.

Swift, river, Leicestershire/Warwickshire, England.

The name of the river is first recorded in 1577. It does not appear to mean 'swift', since the river is slow and winding, so it may have a dialectal sense 'sweeping' (with 'swift' and 'sweep' words of common Indo-European origin). An earlier name of the river seems to have been 'Waver', preserved in the 'over' of Brownsover, Cesterover, and Churchover, all in Warwickshire, and all on or near the Swift.

Swiss Cottage, district of north-west London, England.

The name originated in a chalet-style inn, the Swiss Tavern, built here in 1803–4 on the site of a tollgate keeper's cottage. The inn name was subsequently changed to Swiss Cottage, and the building was reconstructed in 1965. The name was used for the railway station built here in the late 19th century, and this then spread to the district.

Sydenham, district of south-east London, England.

The name should be something like 'Chippenham', since it was recorded in 1206 as *Chipeham*, in 1315 as *Shippenham*, and in 1494 as *Syppenham*. At some stage, however, it appears that a copyist wrote the name with *d* instead of *p*, and this produced the present spelling. The first record of the modern name is in 1690, as *Sidenham*. The *y* in the present spelling of the name may derive from the 1494 variant, or have been prompted by the personal name Sydney.

T

Taibach, village, West Glamorgan, Wales.

The name means 'small houses', and referred to four small thatched cottages that stood at the end of the present Water Street in this virtual suburb of **Port Talbot**.

Talbot Village, village, Dorset, England.

The name is that of a model village built by two sisters, Georgina Charlotte Talbot and Mary Anne Talbot, in the 1860s for poor families who had been dispossessed of land on the hills outside Bournemouth by the enclosures of 1802 and 1805. The village consisted of nineteen cottages, six farms, a church, a school, and almshouses with accommodation for seven couples or single inmates.

Tallistown, village, Gwent, Wales.

The name comes from a family of coal owners here, Tallis.

Tameside, administrative district, Greater Manchester, England.

The name derives from that of the river Tame, which flows through east Manchester to join the Mersey at Stockport. The river name is an old one, and probably of the same origin as the Thames.

Tas, river, Norfolk, England.

The river name is a back formation from that of the village of Tasburgh, located on it. The name was first recorded in 1577, as *Tas*, with a variant of 1801 spelt *Tase*. The Tas is a tributary of the **Yare**.

Tayport, town and port, Fife, Scotland.

The town is located on the south side of the Firth of Tay opposite Broughty Ferry on the north bank, and a ferry across the Tay at this point is known to have existed from the earliest historic times.

(A local legend tells that Macduff, Thane of Fife, crossed the firth by this ferry when he escaped from Macbeth's court to England.) In the 13th century the site was granted on a perpetual lease ('feued') to Sir Michael Scott of Balwearie, and while held by this family became known as *Scotscraig*. In 1588 James VI gave the town, ferry and lands of *South Ferry of Portincraig*, as it had become, to Sir Robert Melville of Murdocairney. Ten years later the town was erected into a burgh of barony as *South Ferry of Port-on-Craig*. By the 17th century the name of the settlement had become established as *Port-on-Craig*, or more fully *Ferry-Port-on-Craig*, with subsequent variations on this name recorded in the 19th century as *Port-on-the-Tay*, *Port-on-the-Craig*, *Ferry-Port-a-Craig*, and *South Ferry*. All these names served to distinguish the place from other ferries and ports in this part of Scotland, with *South Ferry* distinguishing from the 'north ferry' of Broughty Ferry. However, some sources claim that *Port-on-Craig* was an early name for Broughty Ferry. The full name is explained in the *First Statistical Account of Scotland* (1791–9): 'This passage was named Ferry-Port-on-Craig to distinguish it from the many other ferries in this part of Scotland. There being no pier or quay on either side of the river where the boats might ship passengers or horse, it was the custom to boat horses at the point of a craig, or rock, whence the name "Ferry-Port-on-Craig".' With the building of the railway bridge, the Tay Bridge, across the river in 1878 (rebuilt by 1887) from Wormit on the south bank to Dundee on the north, the importance of Tayport as a ferry port began to decline, and in 1888, when also the town was reconstituted as a police burgh, its name was officially changed from *Ferry-Port-on-Craig* to *Tayport*, apparently by the railway company.

Teignbridge, administrative district, Devon, England.

The name relates to the river Teign and its many bridges in the district, as well as to villages containing the river name (Bishopsteignton, Kingsteignton, Drewsteignton) and the town of Teignmouth, all of which are on or near the river or its estuary.

Teise, river, Kent, England.

The river name is a back formation from Ticehurst, near which one arm of the river rises. The name is recorded as *Theise* in 1577 and *Teise* in 1612.

Telford, town, Shropshire, England.

When the new town here was first designated in 1963, it was named Dawley, after an existing village. On 24 October 1968, with the expansion of the town to include the communities of Wellington and Oakengates, the name was changed to Telford, in honour of the Scottish civil engineer Thomas Telford (1757–1834), appointed surveyor of Shropshire in 1786, and agent and engineer to the Ellesmere Canal Company (see **Ellesmere Port**) in 1793. Telford was also responsible for the **Caledonian Canal** and for the suspension bridge over the Menai Straits (see **Menai Bridge**).

Templeborough, Roman fort, Rotherham, South Yorkshire, England.

The name appears to have been invented by some antiquarian in the 16th century, and was first recorded in 1559 as *Templebarrow*, with later versions of the name noted as *Temple Brough* in 1800 and *Burgh Green* on the Ordnance Survey one-inch map of 1841. The fort is sited just south-west of Rotherham on the south bank of the river Don.

Tendring, administrative district, Essex, England.

The name is a revival of the old 'Domesday Book' name of 1086, there recorded as *Tendringa* and possibly meaning 'dwellers by the beacon'. The name also exists in the villages of Tendring, Tendring Green and Tendring Heath, all in Tendring.

Ter, river, Essex, England.

The river name is a back formation of the village of Terling, situated on it.

Terenure, suburb of Dublin, Ireland.

Until the second half of the 19th century, the district was named *Roundtown*, for the circular group of cottages at the crossroads on the Harold's Cross–Rathfarnham road. *Terenure* is a revival of a former Irish name here, *Tír an Iúir*, 'land of the yew'. Joyce (1875) notes approvingly: 'The village [. . .] was called from its shape, Roundtown; but the good taste of the present proprietor has restored the old name Terenure, and "Roundtown" is now falling fast into disuse'.

Thamesdown, administrative district, Wiltshire, England.

The name comprises the two chief topographical features of the district: the river Thames, which forms its northern boundary, and the Wiltshire Downs, which form the boundary in the south.

Thameshaven, industrial district of Coryton, Essex, England.

The name of this oil-refining district, like that of **Shellhaven**, pre-dates the present specialized industrial activity of this Thames-side site, and the Ordnance Survey one-inch map of 1884 shows *Thames Haven* Dock here and the *Thames Haven* Branch Railway running to it, from the main London, Tilbury, and Southern Railway line, to reach its terminus at *Thames Haven* Station. The name thus simply means 'harbour on the Thames'. The branch railway line is now closed, and Thameshaven is currently an oil storage depot owned by Thames Terminal Ltd. See also **Coryton** (Essex).

Thamesmead, residential district, east London, England.

The name seems to be a conventional

combination of *Thames* and 'mead'. The district arose in the late 1960s as a new residential district for 60,000 Londoners on the Erith Marshes to the south of the river Thames.

The Old Meuse, village, Surrey, England.

The place arose as a period-style village built in 1975 near Weybridge, with 'Meuse' an (authentically but ostentatiously) old spelling of 'Mews'.

Thet, river, Norfolk, England.

The river name is a back formation from Thetford, where the Thet joins the Little Ouse. It is first recorded, in this spelling, in 1586.

Thornaby-on-Tees, town, Cleveland, England.

The town is part of the Teesside complex, south of the river Tees from Stockton-on-Tees. It was incorporated as a borough in 1892, before which it was known as South Stockton. Thornaby is an old name, recorded in the 'Domesday Book' of 1086 (as *Tormozbi*).

Thornton Heath, district of Croydon, London, England.

The place was originally the common of Norbury Manor, and sometimes called Grandon Heath. Its name, first recorded in 1511 as *Thorneton hethe*, means 'heath by Thornton', the latter word meaning probably 'thorn tree farm' (from Old English *tūn*) or possibly 'thorn tree hill' (Old English *dūn*) or perhaps even 'thorn tree valley' (Old English *denu*). As if to support the second of these, the name was recorded in 1749 as *Thornhill Heath*. The former common was next to Thornton Heath Pond on the London Road. With the coming of the railway, and especially the opening of Thornton Heath station in 1862, the whole district to the east became known as Thornton Heath.

Thornton-le-Fen, village, Lincolnshire, England.

The village was one of seven townships created by Act of Parliament in 1812 when Wildmore Fen and the East and West Fens here were drained, the others being **Carrington**, **Eastville**, **Frithville**, **Langriville**, **Midville**, and **Westville**. The name of the location, as Thornton, seems to be an old one, recorded (as *Thorenton*) in 1218, with '-le-Fen' added to distinguish the new township from other places of the name locally, such as Thornton-le-Moor, Thornton-by-Horncastle, and Thornton Curtis, all in Lincolnshire. However, as pointed out in an article in *Lincolnshire Life* (July 1980), 'one tradition states that the name Thornton was chosen in honour of the largest landowner in the Fen'. It is perfectly possible, of course, that the name of this landowner itself derived from the old place-name.

Thornville, estate, West Yorkshire, England.

The name was first recorded in 1771, as *Thornvill*. The estate was originally a detached portion of the village of Whixley. The name seems to have been invented by a Colonel Thornton, who in 1789 bought the estate of Allerton Mauleverer nearby from the Duke of York and changed its name to Thornville Royal. In 1805 the estate passed to Lord Stourton, and some time after this the former name was restored.

Thorpeness, village and resort, Suffolk, England.

The village arose as a model resort in the 1920s, and was named after the headland of Thorpe Ness nearby. Originally, the village seems to have been known simply as Thorpe.

Three Bridges, district of Crawley, West Sussex, England.

The place arose as a residential development after the opening of the Brighton railway here in 1841 and the building of Three Bridges station. A document of 1534 (*Letters and Papers Foreign and Domestic*) refers to 'two bridges called the Three bridges leading from Charlewood to Crawley', and in 1598 the location is noted as 'three bridges between Worth and Crawley'. However, if the first of these two is accurate, it cannot refer to the present place, since any bridge between Charlwood and Crawley would have been north-west of Crawley, whereas the present Three Bridges is east of Crawley. The second reference, on the other hand, is valid, since Three Bridges is (roughly) between Worth (i.e. Worth Abbey) and Crawley. The 'three bridges' would have been over the river **Mole**, which rises at Crawley. Three Bridges was originally a separate village, but with the growth of Crawley after its designation as a new town in 1947, the village has become simply a district in a larger urban environment.

Three Cocks, village, Powys, Wales.

The name is that of an old coaching inn here. The Welsh name of the village is *Aberllynfi*, 'mouth [of the river] Llynfi'. The Llynfi flows into the Wye near the village.

Three Oaks, village, East Sussex, England.

The name was first recorded in 1543, as *le three Ok'*, with *Three Oakes* noted in 1640. Presumably there were three prominent oaks here at one time.

Three Rivers, administrative district, Hertfordshire, England.

The 'three rivers', all of which flow through the district, are the **Chess**, the Colne, and the **Gade**.

Thurne, river, Norfolk, England.

The name is a back formation from the village of the same name, just south of which the river flows into the **Bure**. The name was first recorded in 1577 as *Thurine*, with later documents noting it as *Thrin* 1622 and *Thyrn* 1724.

Tiptoe, village, Hampshire, England.

The earliest document to give the name is dated 1555, but some medieval deeds refer to the family of Tibetot with regard to Barton-on-Sea, the next parish, so the name may be not so recent as it appears.

Tobermory, town and port (Isle of Mull), Strathclyde, Scotland.

The town was founded in 1788 by the British Fisheries Society, with the name taken from a famous well here, *Tobar Mhoire*, 'Mary's well'.

Tollcross, district of Glasgow, Strathclyde, Scotland.

The district arose round an ironworks, and is named after Tollcross House, built here in the mid-17th century.

Torbay, administrative district, Devon, England.

The district was formerly a county borough including the towns of **Torquay**, Paignton, and Brixham, and deriving its name from Tor Bay, on the coast of which it is located. The 'Tor' of Tor Bay means 'hill' (see **Torquay**).

Torfaen, administrative district, Gwent, Wales.

The name seems to be an old Welsh one here, meaning 'stone gap', from *tor*, 'break', 'gap', and *maen*, 'stone'.

Torquay, town and resort, Devon, England.

The basic meaning of the name is 'quay at a place called Torre', the latter meaning 'hill' (modern 'tor'). The name was first recorded in 1591 as *Torrekay*, and a document of 1668 refers to the place as 'a small village called *Torkay*'. There may have been an earlier reference to the site in 1412, when a French ship carrying wine was captured and brought to Devon *'a un lieu appelle le Getee de Torrebaie'* ('to a place called the Jetty of Torrebay'). Originally the name was simply that of a jetty or landing stage here, perhaps built by the monks of Torre Abbey nearby, founded in 1196. By 1668 the name appears to have transferred to a settlement (see quotation above for this year), while the resort of Torquay arose mostly in the 19th century. At one time the settlement was known as 'Fleet', this name being recorded (as *Fleete*) in 1670. Johnston (1914) mistakenly derives the name from Celtic *tor cau*, 'hill hollow', and apparently on the basis that the present name of the town should be pronounced 'Torkay' rather than 'Torkey' adds, 'Of course, Torquay really has nothing to do with *quay*'. One of the present districts of Torquay is called Torre, thus preserving the origin of the name.

Torridge, administrative district, Devon, England.

The name derives from that of the river Torridge, which flows through the district, as well as that of Great Torrington, Little Torrington, and Black Torrington, all on the river here.

Tower Hamlets, borough, east London, England.

The borough was formed in 1965 from the former metropolitan boroughs of Bethnal Green, Stepney, and Poplar. These three outlying parishes or 'hamlets' had belonged since Norman times to the feudal estate of the Tower of London.

Tradeston, district of Glasgow, Strathclyde, Scotland.

The name derives from the Glasgow Trades House, who bought land here and laid out the district in 1790.

Tram Inn, village, Hereford and Worcester, England.

According to Bannister (1916): 'Before the railway was made a tram-line ran from Abergavenny to Hereford for conveying coal. On this was a public-house called Tram Inn. The Great Western Railway inexplicably called what should have been Dewchurch or Kilpeck Station Tram Inn.' Kilpeck and (Much) Dewchurch are villages near Tram Inn. The station is now closed, but Tram Inn is still a recognized Post Office name for the village here.

Trealaw, village, Mid Glamorgan, Wales.

The name, somewhat unusually, derives from the bardic name of David Williams (1809–63), a local coal owner and Welsh poet. This was Alaw Goch, said to mean 'red lily'. Williams bought land here in c.1853 and the village developed on it. Trealaw means 'village of Alaw'.

Tredegar, town, Gwent, Wales.

The present town arose in the 19th century as an industrial development and was named after Sir Charles Morgan Robinson Morgan, created Baron Tredegar in 1859, taking this title from the family seat at Tredegar, near Newport, Gwent. This original Tredegar means 'farm of ˙ Tegyr', the latter being a personal name. In the early 19th century, before its transfer to the Sirhowy valley by the Morgan landowners there, the name was recorded as *Tre Deg Erw*, popularly understood to mean 'ten acre farm' (Welsh *tre*, 'farm', *deg*, 'ten', *erw*, 'acre'). A further development from Tredegar was **New Tredegar**.

Trefecca, village, Powys, Wales.

The name is said to mean 'house of Rebecca', this being the name of Rebecca Prosser, who inherited land and built her home here in the second half of the 16th century.

Treharris, village, Mid Glamorgan, Wales.

The name is that of Frederick William Harris (d. 1917), who opened a large colliery here in 1873. The first coal was raised from the colliery, initially known as Harris's Navigation Pits, in 1879, by which time the name Treharris was already in use for the mining settlement that had begun to grow here. The Welsh name means 'village of Harris'.

Treherbert, village, Mid Glamorgan, Wales.

The village was so named in 1851 by the 2nd Marquis of Bute (see **Bute Town**). According to Morgan (1887), Herbert was a favourite name in the Bute family.

Trelawnyd, village, Clwyd, Wales.

The name has something of a complex history. In the 'Domesday Book' of 1086 it was recorded as *Rivelenoit*. This apparently means 'ford of Lyfnid' (Welsh *rhyd*, 'ford', plus a conjectured personal name). In 1652 the name was recorded as *Rhelofnoid*. Edward Lhuyd, in his *Parochialia* (1699), gives the name as either *Rhelownwyd* or *Trelawnwyd*, and says of these two names and their possible meanings: '. . . being formerly call'd by ye foregoing names supposed but erroneously because Lhawn o yd, for ye name in ancient writings is Rhyd y lwfnid, quasi Rhyd y Lhoffnayd, being a passage [i.e. a ford] in ye said par: below a mill call'd Velin issa ['lower mill'] which seems to be smoothed (llyfnwyd) or made passable by art . . .'. Shortly after this, in c.1700, an estate owner here, John Wynne of Gop, obtained a faculty to open a market in the village and hold an annual fair there, and he renamed the place *Newmarket*. This English name continued in sporadic use until 1954, when the Welsh name was established as Trelawnyd, as if understood as 'village of Lawnyd'.

Tremadoc (more correctly **Tremadog**), village, Gwynedd, Wales.

The village was developed in c.1805 by William Alexander Maddocks (1773–1828) soon after he had created **Portmadoc** one mile south of it, with both places thus named after him, Tremadoc meaning 'village of Maddocks'. This documented fact is not to the liking of Lewis (1849), who says that Tremadoc 'derives its name from a small rocky spot close by the town, called from time immemorial Ynys Madog or Madawg . . . Some persons, however, with a pardonable latitude, derive the name of the place from its patriotic and enterprising founder, the late William Alexander Madocks [*sic*], Esq.'.

Tremeirchion, village, Clwyd, Wales.

The village was originally called 'Dinmeirchion', with the 1086 'Domesday Book' recording the name as *Dinmersch*, 'fort of Meirchion' (the latter personal name being a form of Latin Marcianus). The substitution of *Tre-*, 'village', for *Din-* was apparently first recorded, or even actually made, by Thomas Pennant in his *Tour in Wales in 1773* (1883).

Tre Taliesin, village, Dyfed, Wales.

The original name of the village was *Cwmins-y-dafarn-fach*, 'commons of the little tavern'. This was changed in the 1820s to Tre Taliesin, since it apparently 'offended the strict observance of the local devout' (Thomas, 1977). The new name means 'village of Taliesin', the latter being a semi-legendary figure who has a burial stone (*Bedd Taliesin*) near here.

Tretomas, village (near Bedwas) Mid Glamorgan, Wales.

The name, meaning 'village of Thomas', apparently derives from that of W. J. Thomas, a coal owner here.

Triangle, village, West Yorkshire, England.

The name, today that of the industrial village here, originated from an inn called The Triangle after its location on an area of land between the turnpike to Lancashire and Oak Hill. The name was first recorded, for this inn, in 1777. In 1839 the location was described as a farmstead with five fields. Compare **Queensbury** (West Yorkshire).

Trossachs, The, mountains, Central, Scotland.

The name is said to be a Gaelic adaptation of the Welsh name *Trawsfynydd*, 'cross hills', or of part of this. It was first recorded in 1791. The actual Gaelic name for the mountains is *Na Trosaichen*. If this is the case, the Welsh name may have been taken generally, and not specifically from the village of Trawsfynydd, Gwynedd, whose own name may have derived from the old road that goes across the hills here from Dolgellau to Maentwrog.

Tufnell Park, district of north London, England.

The name comes from that of William Tufnell, lord of the manor of Barnsbury in 1753. An Act of Parliament of 1832 allowed the land to be used for building.

Tulse Hill, district of south London, England.

The name is that of the Tulse family, first recorded as living here in 1656. Sir Henry Tulse, Lord Mayor of London in 1683, was a landlord in the district.

Tumble, village, Dyfed, Wales.

The name derives from that of an inn here, the Tumble Inn. Apart from its punning connotation, the inn name could have been intended as an oblique reference to 'Tumbledown Dick', the nickname given to Oliver Cromwell's son Richard (who held the office of Protector for only seven months after his father's death, then 'tumbled down'). There was strong Royalist support in Wales, and it is possible that the disparaging nickname may have been seized on for convivial purposes.

Tunbridge Wells, town, Kent, England.

The name really means 'wells near Tonbridge', although the latter town is five miles to the north of modern Tunbridge Wells. The 'wells' are the famous mineral springs here, discovered in 1606 by Dudley North, 3rd Baron North (1581–1666), when staying at Lord Abergavenny's hunting seat at Eridge near here, with the aim of restoring his indifferent health. ('While returning to the metropolis, North noticed [. . .] a clear spring of water, which bore on its surface a shining scum, and left in its course down a neighbouring brook a ruddy, ochreous track. He tasted the water, at the same time sending one of his servants back to

Eridge for some bottles in which to take a sample to his London physician. A favourable judgment was pronounced upon the quality of the springs, which became known as Tunbridge Wells.' [*DNB*, 1885–1900]). Tonbridge was originally Tunbridge, but adopted the spelling with *o*, as in the 1086 'Domesday Book' record of the name (*Tonebrige*), to avoid confusion with Tunbridge Wells. The latter town was granted the prefix 'Royal' in 1909 as a result of a petition made to Edward VII by the Mayor and Burgesses in recognition of the many royal visitors to Tunbridge Wells.

Tyburnia see **Belgravia**.

Tylorstown, village, Mid Glamorgan, Wales.

The name derives from that of Alfred Tylor, who opened the first colliery here in 1873.

Tyne and Wear, metropolitan county, England.

The name links those of the two main rivers of the county, formed in 1974 to unify the urban complex of Newcastle-upon-Tyne, South Shields, Sunderland, and Tynemouth, each of which was formerly a county borough here.

Tyrrelspass, village, Westmeath, Ireland.

The name of the village refers to a passage through the bogs here where in 1597 Captain Richard Tyrrel and Piers Lacy ambushed and destroyed an English force led by Christopher Barnwell, son of Lord Trimleston. The village itself was laid out here in the late 18th century by the Countess of Belvedere. The Irish name has a similar meaning to the English, *Bealach an Tirialaigh*, 'road of Tyrrel'.

U

Union Canal, canal, Central/Lothian, Scotland.

The Canal runs west from Edinburgh to join the Forth and Clyde Canal south of Falkirk. Construction was begun in 1818, and the Canal opened in 1822 to complete the inland water link ('union') between Edinburgh and Glasgow. Commercial traffic ceased on the Canal in 1933 and it closed in 1965. In 1973, however, the stretch between Linlithgow and Winchburgh was reopened for recreational purposes.

Uplands, district of Stroud, Gloucestershire, England.

The district arose in 1901 when it was formed as a civil parish out of Stroud, subsequently becoming a ward in Stroud Urban District. The parish is in the north-east of the town on rising ground leading to the Cotswold Hills.

Uttlesford, administrative district, Essex, England.

The name is a revival of an old name here, apparently meaning 'Udel's ford'.

V

Valley, village, Gwynedd, Wales.

The name of the Anglesey village is first recorded in documents of 1825 concerning the licensing of a public house in the parish of Llanynghenedl, today a separate village two miles from Valley. At the time the Stanley Embankment had just been built to carry Telford's new road from Llanynghenedl across to Holy Island, and doubtless 'The Valley' was the name given by labourers to a cutting here during the construction of the embankment. A small group of houses grew up at the Llanynghenedl end of the embankment, and these came to be called either 'Embankment' or 'Valley', the latter from the cutting mentioned. The Ordnance Survey map of 1839 records the name as *The Valley*, and the name was adopted for the railway station built nearby in c.1847. In 1894 Valley Rural District Council came into being and the name was fully established from then on. With the siting of RAF Valley air base here in the 20th century the name gained even international status. The Welsh name of the village has not been consistently fixed. The name *Y Fali*, rendering the English, has been in use, and in 1980 an attempt was made to have the name *Dyffryn* ('valley') adopted.

Vauxhall, district of Birmingham, West Midlands, England.

The name derives from the London Vauxhall. Walter Showell's *Dictionary of Birmingham* (1855), quoting 'an old book descriptive of a tour through England' published in 1766, says that the name originates in 'a seat belonging to Sir Liston Holte, Bart., but now let out for a public house (opened June 4, 1758), where are gardens, &c., with an organ and other music, in imitation of Vauxhall, by which name it goes in the neighbourhood'. The place of amusement, regarded in its day as one of the best outside London, closed in 1850.

(The London Vauxhall amusement gardens opened in 1728 and closed in 1859.) The district name is still in use.

Ventnor, town and resort, Isle of Wight, England.

The resort grew up round the farm of a family named Vintner, with the farm's name recorded in this spelling in 1617. The earlier name of the location was 'Holeway' or 'Holloway', meaning 'hollow road'. However, the name may not be manorial in origin, and could be an early name based on a combination of Old English *finta*, 'tail', and *ōra*, 'shore', referring to the contour of the coastline here. Kökeritz (1940) says that a man named Will'us le Vyntener was recorded as living in nearby Bonchurch in c.1340. But he could have been an ancestor of the farmholder.

Via Devana, Roman road, East Anglia/North Wales, England/Wales.

The road ran from Colchester, Essex, through Cambridge and Godmanchester, Cambridgeshire across central England ultimately to Chester, Cheshire, and Holyhead, Gwynedd. The name is first recorded on an Ordnance Survey map dated 1825, and is now known to have been invented by Dr Mason, Woodwardian Professor of Geology at Cambridge University from 1734 to 1762. The name is based on the Roman name for Chester, *Deva*, to which it leads from Colchester (and Cambridge).

Via Gellia, road, Derbyshire, England.

The name is a mock Latin one designed to suggest a Roman road. The road, between Cromford near Wirksworth, and Grangemill, and now a section of the A5012, was constructed in the 19th century along a wooded ravine here by Philip Gell of Hopton Hall, Wirksworth, with its pseudo-Roman name apparently devised by Gell himself. The local pronunciation of the name is 'the Vi Jella' and, in an unexpected consequence, this was used as a basis for the trade name Viyella, the woven cloth produced at the factory of William Hollins which was located on the Via Gellia.

Vickerstown, town, Cumbria, England.
The town was built in 1901–4 as a 'marine garden city', modelled on **Port Sunlight** by Vickers Sons & Co. for their workers, following this company's purchase of Barrow Shipyard in 1896.

Victoria, district of south-west London, England.
The district centres on Victoria Station, which mainline terminus was opened on 1 October 1860 and named in honour of Queen Victoria. The name was reinforced for the district with the opening of Victoria Underground station in 1868 and further promoted with the opening of the Victoria Line on the Underground in 1968–9.

Victoria, village, Gwent, Wales.
The name originated with the opening of a coal mine here in 1837, the year of Queen Victoria's accession to the throne. Victoria was both the name of the mine and that of a street that led to it from **Ebbw Vale**. The former name of the site was *Troed-rhiw'r-clawdd*, '[place near a] dike at the foot of a hill'.

Vigo (Village), village, Kent, England.
The village arose as a new settlement at the foot of Vigo Hill here, near Meopham. The hill appears to have a commemorative name for the Spanish seaport of Vigo, captured by the British in 1719.

Virginia, town, Cavan, Ireland.
The town dates from the Plantation of Ulster in the first half of the 16th century, and although the town was founded in the reign of James I it was named in honour of his predecessor, Elizabeth I, the 'Virgin Queen'.

Virginia Water, residential district, Surrey, England.
The name derives from a large artificial lake here so called. This was made in 1746 by order of the newly appointed Ranger of Windsor Great Park, William Augustus, Duke of Cumberland (1721–65), who earlier had been Governor of Virginia in the United States. The future American state, when still unsettled, was given its name in 1584, in honour of Queen Elizabeth I, the 'Virgin Queen'. The transfer of an American name to England is unusual.

Vulcan Village, village, Merseyside, England.
The name derives from the Vulcan Works, founded by Robert Stephenson and Charles Tayleur in 1830. The village provided housing for their foundry workers.

W

Walkerburn, village (near Innerleithen), Borders, Scotland.

The village arose after 1854, when a noted local weaver, Henry Ballantyne (d. 1865), established a wool mill here with his sons. Before this year, the future textile manufacturing village 'consisted of two cots and a farmhouse', according to *Cassell* (1898). The 'burn' of the name is the river Tweed, on which the village stands; the first part of the name, according to Johnston (1934), refers to the *'wauking*, fulling or dressing of cloth' done in the river.

Wallacetown, district of Ayr, Strathclyde, Scotland.

The district arose as a village laid out in c.1760 on the land of Sir Thomas Wallace of Craigie. The village originally formed a single parish with Content, but separated from it in 1835.

Waltham Forest, borough of north London, England.

The borough was established in 1965 by the merging of the former boroughs of Chingford, Leyton, and Walthamstow, taking its name from the latter town and Epping Forest, which bounds it in the north east. The division of 'Walthamstow' before '-stow' is rather artificial, since this 'Waltham' is not a 'wood ham', like the many other places called Waltham (e.g. Great Waltham, Essex, and Bishops Waltham, Hampshire), but represents a personal name *Wilcume*, an abbess and queen who held land here. But what might have become 'Wilcumston' was doubtless influenced by Waltham Abbey, Essex, six miles to the north, to modify to Walthamstow.

Wandle, river, London, England.

The river name is a back formation of Wandsworth, through which it flows to join the Thames above Wandsworth Bridge. The name is first recorded in 1586, as *Vandalis riuulus*, with the form *Wandal* found in 1612. The former name of the river seems to have been 'Lidburn', recorded in 693 as *Hlidaburna*, this perhaps meaning 'stream of the slope'.

Ward End, district of Birmingham, West Midlands, England.

The district, formerly an ecclesiastical parish of Aston, was known in the 16th century as Little Bromwich, a name that is now restricted to a district of Birmingham closer to the city centre. The name Ward End may indicate the limit of a ward here, in the sense of an administrative district under the jurisdiction of an alderman.

Waringstown, village, Down, Northern Ireland.

The original name of the settlement was *Clanconnel*, said to indicate the 'clan' or people of Connell who lived here. The name was changed by an English settler William Waring, who made his home here in 1667 on land purchased by him from the dragoons of Cromwell's army. Samuel Waring introduced the manufacture of linen damask here in 1691. The Warings had been driven here from England in the 1550s at the time of the persecution of Protestants under Queen Mary. The Irish name of the village, with the same meaning as the English, is *Baile an Bhairínigh*.

Warrenpoint, town and resort, Down, Northern Ireland.

The site of the town, which in 1780 consisted of only two houses, is said to have derived its name from a rabbit warren here on the north shore of Carlingford Lough. The Irish name of the town is *An Pointe*, 'the point'.

Warwick Town, former district of Redhill, Surrey, England.

Warwick Town is described as a 'new town lying west of Redhill Junction

Station, towards Reigate' in *Black's Guide to the County of Surrey* (1887), and the district had apparently arisen some time before 1860 on land belonging to the Countess of Warwick, widow of the 4th Lord Monson. The name is no longer current for the district, although it is preserved in Warwick Road, **Redhill**.

Wash, river, Devon, England.

The name is a back formation of Washbourne, a village on the river, whose own name apparently means 'stream ('bourn') where sheep or clothes were washed'. The river is a tributary of the Harbourne.

Wash, The, arm of the North Sea, Lincolnshire/Norfolk, England.

The original name of the sea inlet was *The Washes*, referring to the sandbanks of land that were alternately covered and exposed by the sea ('washed' by it) to form two fords across between Lincolnshire and Norfolk. This form of the name is recorded (as *the wasshes*) before 1548, and also occurs in Shakespeare's *King John* (1595), where Philip the Bastard says that:

> '. . . half my power this night
> Passing these flats, are taken by the tide;
> These Lincoln Washes have devoured them.'

The plural form of the name was still in use in the 18th century, and was so mentioned by Defoe in 1722.

Waterloo, district of Crosby, Merseyside, England.

The district grew up round the Waterloo Hotel (originally the Royal Waterloo Hotel) founded here in 1815, the year of the victory at Waterloo, the final battle of the Napoleonic Wars. (Compare following entries.)

Waterloo, district of south-east London, England.

The name originated in the Waterloo Bridge over the Thames here, opened by the Prince Regent in 1817, two years after the victory at Waterloo, to replace the former Strand Bridge. The railway terminus of Waterloo Station was opened in 1848, taking its name from the bridge, and from this the name spread to the surrounding district. Waterloo Underground Station opened in 1906 to establish the name even more firmly, and the final element of the name was even used the following year, originally as a nickname, for the Bakerloo line on the Underground that ran, and still runs, from *Baker* Street to Water*loo*.

Waterloo, village (Isle of Skye), Highland, Scotland.

Over 1500 Skye men fought at the Battle of Waterloo (1815), and on their return many of them made their home here in this village near **Broadford**.

Waterloo, village (near Wishaw), Strathclyde, Scotland.

The name apparently derives from an inn here named after the Battle of Waterloo (1815).

Waterloo, village (near Dunkeld), Tayside, Scotland.

The name is said to have been given to a row of houses here soon after 1815 for veterans returning from the Battle of Waterloo that year.

Waterlooville, town, Hampshire, England.

The district grew up round an inn here built some time after 1815, the year of the victory at Waterloo, and called either the Waterloo Hotel or The Heroes of Waterloo. Inevitably, there are several local legends to explain the circumstances of the naming of the inn: one account tells of victorious troops resting here on their way back to barracks after landing at Portsmouth, another narrates that troops likewise stopped at the inn, as yet unnamed, and that it was named in their honour. The more prosaic truth is likely to be that the inn, in company with many others, was named commemoratively for the battle. The present public house, not the original, is simply named The Heroes. The original name of the location here was recorded in 1759 as *Whateland End*, in *c*.1825 as *Waitland End*, and in *c*.1840 as *Wheatland End*. All these variants seem to be a corruption of a farmhouse here in the 17th century known as Wait Lane End, after its location at the end of a lane on the land of a family named Wait or Wayte, who are known to have lived here from the 16th century. Today Waterlooville is virtually an inland extension of Portsmouth, and owes much of its expansion as a residential development to the importance of this city as a seaport and naval base and to its proximity to the holiday resort of **Southsea**. The name first appeared on Ordnance Survey maps of the mid-19th century as *Waterloo*, with *Waterloo Ville* given as a cross-referring variant of *Waterloo* in *Cassell* (1898).

Wattstown, village, mid Glamorgan, Wales.

The name derives from that of a former coal owner here, Edmund Watts.

Waveney, administrative district, Suffolk, England.

The name is that of the river Waveney, which forms the northern border of the district with Norfolk. The river name is an old one, perhaps meaning 'river by a quagmire'.

Waverley, administrative district, Surrey, England.

The name is that of Waverley Abbey in the district, south of Farnham, from which Walter Scott is said to have taken the title of his first novel. In 1974 Waverley district council superseded Godalming borough council, Farnham and Haslemere urban district council, and Hambledon rural district council.

Wealden, administrative district, East Sussex, England.

The name is that of The Weald, prominent here between the North and South Downs, and is based on an old form of the name such as *Waldan* (actually a dative plural), recorded in 1185.

Wealdstone, district of Harrow, London, England.

The name is first recorded in 1754, as *Weald Stone*. Although 'Stone' may be a family name, such as that of John atte Stone, known to have lived here in the 13th century, or John Stute de Stone, in the 16th century, it is more likely that the name refers to a boundary stone separating Harrow Weald (the former forest here) from the rest of the parish of Harrow. The district began to grow after the opening of the London and Birmingham Railway here in 1837, with Harrow station renamed Harrow and Wealdstone in 1897.

Wear Valley, administrative district, Durham, England.

The name refers both to the river Wear, which flows through the district from west to east, and to Weardale, its valley running east from Wearhead.

Wellington see **Egremont**.

Wellington Bridge, village, Wexford, Ireland.

The village grew up round a bridge here over the river Corock, with the bridge named after the Duke of Wellington, who was born in Dublin, and who held the family seat of Trim in the Irish parliament. The Irish name of the village is *Droichead Eoin*, 'John's bridge'.

Welsh Harp, district of West Hendon, London, England.

The name is popularly used for the Brent Reservoir, an artificial lake here formed in 1835–9 by the damming of the river Brent near its junction with the Silk stream. The origin of the name lies in the Old Welsh Harp, an inn on the main road here. This had tea gardens and was a popular resort of Londoners, especially on bank holidays.

Welshpool, town, Powys, Wales.

The original name of the settlement here was 'Pool', recorded as *Pola* 1253, *La Pole* 1278, and *Pool* 1411, with a late recording of *Poole Town* in 1719. At some time in the 15th century, or possibly earlier, the prefix 'Welsh' was added, giving *Walshe Pole* 1477, *Walshepole* 1478, and *Welshepoole* 1646. The popular explanation is that 'Welsh' was added to distinguish the place from Poole in Dorset. This seems unlikely, however, since the two towns are a long distance apart and even in different countries. More likely, the sense was 'pool on the Welsh side of the border', compared to some pool or lake that lay east of the town in England. (Welshpool is only three miles from the Shropshire border.) Similar names exist near the Welsh–English border, among them Welsh Newton, Hereford and Worcester (which must at one time have been in Wales), Welsh Frankton and English Frankton, both now in Shropshire but with the former village doubtless once in Wales, and similarly Welsh Bicknor, now in Hereford and Worcester, and English Bicknor, Gloucestershire. The Welsh name of the town is *Y Trallwng*, 'the marsh', 'the pool' (although also explained as *tra*, 'very', *llwng*, 'deep'). The 'pool' referred to is probably the lake below Powis Castle, south of Welshpool.

Welwyn Garden City, town, Hertfordshire, England.

The origin of the town lay in the artifically planned town begun here five miles south of Welwyn on a scheme by Ebenezer Howard. The city was completed under the New Towns Act of 1946 and officially designated a New Town on 20 May 1948. Residents of the town, many of whom commute daily to London to work, refer to the new town as 'Welwyn', but despite this the old town of Welwyn retains much of its identity, although close to the much larger Garden City.

Wendens Ambo, village, Essex, England.

The name was given to the village in 1662, when the two parishes of Great Wenden and Little Wenden (then known as Wenden Magna and Wenden Parva) were united. 'Ambo' is Latin for 'both', and occurs in some other place-names, such as Huttons Ambo, North Yorkshire, which is the united parish of High Hutton and Low Hutton.

Wentworth, residential district of Virginia Water, Surrey, England.

The land on which Wentworth House (now Wentworth Golf Club) stands was owned formerly by Mrs Elizabeth Wentworth (d. 1816), when it was known as *Wentworth's Waste*. The site was eventually acquired by Culling Charles Smith who built the present house in *c*.1800 and called it *Wentworth's*, which name lasted in this form until *c*.1855.

West End, district of west London, England.

According to the *Oxford English Dictionary* (1933), the West End is defined as 'that part of London lying westward of Charing Cross and Regent St. and including the fashionable shopping district, Mayfair, and the Parks'. The name seems to have been first recorded in 1807, and transferred to any town or city to mean 'fashionable quarter' by 1813. Compare **East End**. It was thus a geographical chance that made 'West End' have the connotation 'fashionable', 'rich', and 'East End' suggest 'artisan', 'poor'. Even so, it is notable that many towns and cities have a similar disposition of their 'rich' and 'poor' areas, so that Bristol, for example, has its university and fashionable Clifton in the west and docks and railways in the east, Cambridge has most of its colleges and gardens (The Backs) as well as its university library to the west and its railway station, cattle market and less affluent housing development to the east, and the oldest and most fashionable part of Shrewsbury lies to the west of the river Severn, rather than the east. But there are many exceptions, with Oxford, for example, having its colleges to the east and its poorer developments to the west, Manchester has its dockland in the west, and Margate has its fashionable residential area of **Cliftonville** to the east of the town centre, not the west. The influence that London's West End had on the subsequent development of 'West Ends' in other towns is therefore open to question, despite the several parallels.

West End, suburb of Southampton, Hampshire, England.

The name was recorded as *Westend* in 1607, but the district is actually north east of Southampton, so cannot refer to the city itself. Its name is too early to have been modelled on London's **West End**, so it must presumably have been named by contrast with some place east of it. It is not clear what this was.

West Lothian, administrative district, Lothian, Scotland.

The district corresponds to the old county of Linlithgow, whose alternative name was West Lothian. With the establishment of the region of Lothian in 1975, the name Linlithgow fell out of official use. See also **East Lothian** and **Midlothian**.

Westmeath, county, Ireland.

The county was created by statute in 1542, with the present boundaries established in *c.*1600. There is no 'East-meath': Westmeath is west of the county of Meath. The latter name means 'middle', since Meath was the fifth province of Ireland in the 13th century, with its territory much more extensive than that of the present county. (The other four provinces were Connaught, Leinster, Munster, and Ulster.)

West Midlands, metropolitan county, England.

The county came into being in 1974, established by the Local Government Act of 1972. The name had been in general use some time before this, as had 'East Midlands', for one of the two distinctive halves of the **Midlands**. Linguists, for example, had long distinguished the West Midland dialect of Middle English from the East Midland.

The metropolitan county of West Midlands centres on Birmingham and the nearby so-called 'Black Country' with its many industrial developments.

Westonville see **Cliftonville**.

Westport, town and port, Mayo, Ireland.

The village was planned by James Wyatt in *c.*1780 to establish a port for deep sea fishing here. The name of the village comes from Westport Bay near which it is situated. The bay's own name can be understood as 'west coast bay' since 'port' in Irish names has a wider sense than English 'port'. The Irish name of the village is *Cathair na Mart*, 'stone fort of the oxen'.

Westville, village, Lincolnshire, England.

The village was created as a township when a large area of fenland was drained here in 1812. Other townships established at the same time were **Carrington**, **Eastville**, **Frithville**, **Langriville**, **Midville**, and **Thornton-le-Fen**. Westville is in the West Fen, west of Midville and Eastville.

Westward Ho!, village and resort, Devon, England.

The resort is directly named after Charles Kingsley's novel, published in 1855. The previous year Kingsley, who had made his home at Eversley, Hampshire, took his wife to the already fashionable resort of **Torquay** for the benefit of her indifferent health. While there he began to write *Westward Ho!* and continued to write it when he and his wife moved on from south Devon to Bideford, north Devon, where the novel was completed. The book was published in August 1855 and became immensely popular, largely owing to the vivid and romantic descriptions of scenes in the Bideford area. In 1863 a group of local businessmen, realizing the potential of an area familiar to thousands of readers, and appreciating the natural attractions of the locality, formed a company to develop a resort

here. The company, named the North-
am Burrows (North Devon) Hotel and
Villa Building Company, had the Earl of
Portsmouth as its chairman and Lord
Fortescue as a patron. Two years later a
hotel had been built on the site two
miles from Bideford, and was officially
opened, as the Westward Ho! Hotel, by
the Countess of Portsmouth, wife of the
company's chairman. The name had
been proposed by a friend of Kingsley,
Dr W. H. Acland of Bideford, although
it appears that the author had not been
consulted and that the friendship between the two men was endangered for
a time. A church was built in 1870, and
by 1872 the resort proper had been
established. The hotel building still
exists: renamed first the Royal Hotel
(and so advertised in the Commercial
Directory and Gazetter (sic) of Devonshire [1870]), and then the Golden Bay
Hotel, it was converted into residential
apartments in 1963. The place-name is
unusual in its literary origin and its
punctuation mark (as in the title of the
novel). It appears to be merely a fortuitous coincidence that the name suggests a seaside location such as Plymouth Hoe, and that it agreeably echoes
the name of Mortehoe, another small
resort some ten miles to the north. It is
perhaps also a coincidence that it was
the westward journey of the Kingsleys
from Hampshire to Devon that inspired
the subject-matter, and title, of his most
successful novel.

Whale Island, island (Portsmouth Harbour), Hampshire, England.

The name was first so recorded in 1535,
with the name referring to the
appearance and contour of the island.

Whaley Bridge, town, Derbyshire, England.

The name was originally Whaley, so
recorded in 1842, from the nearby house
Whaley Hall. The 'Bridge' was added to
refer to the town's location on the river
Goyt.

Whitby Locks see **Ellesmere Port**.

Whitchurch, former name of Little Stanmore, district of Edgware, London,
England.

The name came into active use for a time
as an alternative to Little Stanmore, the
present name of the district. It is first
recorded in 1538, as *Whyzt Church*, with
a document of 1593 giving *Stanmer little
called also Whytechurch*. The reference
may have been to the colour of the walls
of the church here.

Whitehead, town and resort, Antrim,
Northern Ireland.

The location was originally called Castle
Chichester or Castle Chester, after the
castle built here in c.1604 by Sir Moyses
Hill. (The castle name appears to be
semi-arbitrary, designed to suggest an
English castle.) The name Whitehead
eventually prevailed for the town, with
this a translation of the Irish *An Ceann
Bán*, 'the white head', referring to a
nearby headland at the mouth of Belfast
Lough.

Whitehill, village, Gloucestershire, England.

The name seems to be modern, being
first recorded no earlier than 1830.
Presumably it refers to a 'white hill'
rather than a surname Whitehill. The
village is near Stroud.

Whiteley Village, village, Surrey, England.

The development arose as a model
village, laid out in 1911, and built in
1914–21 to the order of William
Whiteley, of Whiteley's Stores, London.
The designer of the village was Frank
Atkinson, who was also responsible for
Selfridge's store, London.

Whitemans Green, village, West Sussex, England.

The name appears to be a corruption of a
family named Sweetman who lived
here, since the place is recorded in 1520
as *Swetemannesgrene*. The present version of the name is first recorded in
1604, as *Whitman's Greene*.

Whyteleafe, residential district, Purley, Surrey, England.

The name seems to have originated as that of a field here, recorded in 1839 as *White Leaf Field*, with reference to the aspens that grew there. This field was bought by a Mr Glover in 1855 who built a house in what was then an almost deserted valley. The present affected spelling of the original name appears to have been introduced by the railway for its station here in the second half of the 19th century.

Wilsontown, village (near Carnwath), Strathclyde, Scotland.

The original name of the place was Forkens. This was changed in 1779 when three brothers named Wilson from London (according to Johnston [1934], two brothers) established the first ironworks in Lanarkshire here. The works closed in 1842.

Wilstead, village, Bedfordshire, England.

The name of the village had been *Wilshamstead* since at least the time of 'Domesday Book' (1086), where it is recorded as *Winessamestede*. At the same time, the pronunciation of the name had for many years been 'Wilstead', in 1978 the spelling of the name was modified to reflect this more accurately.

Windermere (Town), town, Cumbria, England.

The original name of the location here was *Birthwaite*, an old name meaning 'birch tree clearing'. In 1847 the railway came here and the name was changed to Windermere Town, for its location on the east side of Lake Windermere. Presumably the railway company, who were apparently responsible for the change of name, felt that the better-known name was more appropriate for the station of a budding resort.

Winton, district of Bournemouth, Dorset, England.

The name could have one of two possible origins. It may derive from *Winton*, the Latin abbreviation of the title of the bishop of Winchester (in full *Wintoniensis*, 'of Winchester'), since a bishop of Winchester was an ancestor of the Talbot family who owned an estate here (see **Talbot Village**). Alternatively, the name could refer to the title of another (Scottish) ancestor of the Talbot family, the Earl of Eglinton, who was created Earl of Winton in 1859. This was Archibald William Montgomerie, 13th Earl of Eglinton (1812–61).

Wood Green, district of north London, England.

The original village of Wood Green was at the edge of Enfield Chase, with its name recorded in 1502 as *Wodegrene*, 'green place by the wood'. Wood Green Underground station opened in 1932 to establish the name for the district.

Woodville, village, Derbyshire, England.

The place arose as a potters' village in the 19th century, and was originally called (or nicknamed) *Wooden-Box* or *The Box*. According to Reaney (1964), quoting an unidentified source, the name came from 'a hut set up there for a person to sit in to receive the toll at the turnpike . . . this box was originally a port wine butt from Drakelow Hall'. In 1845 the name was changed from Wooden-Box to Woodville, the latter suffix being regarded as more fitting for a residential community.

Woolpack, village, Kent, England.

The name was recorded in 1545 as *The Woolsack* (*sic*), and seems to have derived from an inn here called either the Woolsack or the Woolpack, with one or the other depicted on its sign.

Worcester Park, district of Kingston, London, England.

The name originated in the 17th century from Worcester House, the residence here of the Earl of Worcester, who was Keeper of the Great Park of Nonsuch in 1606.

Wormwood Scrubs, district of Hammersmith, London, England.

The old name of the place was 'Wormholt', recorded in 1189 as *Wormeholte*, this probably meaning 'holt (i.e. wood) infested with snakes'. This same wood is referred to as the 'Scrubs' of the name, with 'Wormholt', colloquially pronounced 'Wermet', altered to 'Wormwood'. The district became well known from its prison (popularly 'The Scrubs') built here in 1875.

Worth Matravers, village, Dorset, England.

The name is first recorded in this form (as *Worth Matrauers*) in 1664, but the name is almost certainly much older than this. 'Worth' occurs in the 'Domesday Book' of 1086 (as *Wirde*, meaning 'enclosure'). There was known to be a John Mautravers living here in 1335.

Wrexham Maelor, administrative district, Clwyd, Wales.

The first half of the name is that of the town, Wrexham, where the district has its administrative offices. The meaning of the second word is disputed. It may derive from *mael*, 'market', and *llawr*, 'ground', or *mai lawr*, 'plain land', or, most likely, but still not conclusively established, from *mael*, 'prince', and *llawr*, 'level floor of valley' so 'territory'.

Wychavon, administrative district, Hereford and Worcester, England.

The name is an artificial combination of the old name of Droit*wich*, recorded in 1347 as *Drihtwych* and in 1396 as *Dertwych*, and the river *Avon*. Droitwich is in the north of the district, and the Avon is in the south.

Wye, river, Buckinghamshire, England.

The name is a back formation from West Wycombe, now part of High Wycombe, where the river rises. The river is first so recorded in 1777, as *Wick*, with a document of 1810 calling it *The Wycombe stream*. Its earlier name seems to have been the 'Ise'. In *Records of Buckinghamshire* (1910–16) the river is referred to as 'the anonymous tributary stream, known as the Wycombe river (and said to have been named the Wye by the cadets of the Royal Military College at Great Marlow when map-making)'. This 'Royal Military College at Great Marlow' was the junior department of the present Royal Military Academy, Sandhurst, established at Great Marlow in 1802 but moving to Sandhurst in 1812.

Wyre, administrative district, Lancashire, England.

The name is that of the river Wyre, which flows through the district.

Y

Yar, river, Isle of Wight, England.

There are two rivers named Yar on the Isle of Wight. The first rises near Freshwater Bay on the south-west coast and flows north into the Solent at Yarmouth. The second rises at Niton near the south coast and flows into Brading Harbour west of Bembridge. The latter river may have a name that is a back formation from the small village of Yarbridge, located on it. But no early forms of the first river Yar have been found, and its name may be a back formation from Yarmouth. There seems to be no common link with the name of the river **Yare** in Norfolk.

Yare, river, Norfolk, England.

The name may be a back formation from Great Yarmouth, near where (at Gorles-ton) it flows into the North Sea. But the name was recorded as early as 150 by Ptolemy as *Gariennos*, and so could be traced back to this. On the other hand Yarmouth itself has no early recorded forms, and so could derive regularly from the river name.

York Town, district of Camberley, Surrey, England.

The name derives from Frederick, Duke of York, who was commander-in-chief of the British army when the Royal Military College (later the Royal Military Academy) moved to Sandhurst in 1812, this college having been founded by him. The Royal Military Academy is just to the east of **Camberley**. At first the new settlement here was called *New Town*.

'ROYAL' NAMES

BECAUSE of the many modern names beginning 'King-' (*King's County, King's Cross, Kingsgate, Kingstown,* and the like) or 'Queen-' (*Queensbury, Queen's County, Queensferry, Queenstown,* and so on), and because of the well-known modern towns and resorts of *Bognor Regis* and Royal *Tunbridge Wells,* it is often supposed that other places having these elements in their name are also modern. This is not so, and there are many places called Kingston, for example, whose name means simply 'manor held by the king', as well as places called Quinton (i.e. 'Queenstown') whose name similarly means that the manor there was held by the queen. Moreover, the majority of places whose names end in the detached suffix 'Regis' are not modern at all. The word, Latin for 'of the king', frequently denotes an early royal ownership or awarding of a royal charter.

To give a few specific examples, Kingsbridge, Devon, has a name that goes back to pre-Domesday days, with its name recorded in 962 as *Cinges bricg,* meaning that an Anglo-Saxon king held the bridge here. Among the many other places with similar names are Kingsbury, London (with a form of the name existing in 1044), Kingscote, Gloucestershire (1086), the three places Kingsdown in Kent (the village near Sittingbourne has a name that goes back to 850), Kingsland, Hereford and Worcester (1213, and compare the *Kingsland* in the Dictionary), Kingsteignton, Devon (recorded as held by the king in the 'Domesday Book' of 1086), and Kingswood, Gloucestershire (1166). And however much of a let-down it may be, some places beginning 'King-' have no royal connections at all, since the name is a distorted version of the original. Thus Kingsbury, Warwickshire, is named after a man called *Cyne,* and the two villages of High Kingthorpe and Low Kingthorpe, North Yorkshire, seem to have a name that is also derived from a personal name, perhaps originally one *Cyna.* Even Kingston-upon-Hull has an old name, although certainly a royal one. The original name of the settlement here was 'Hull', for its location on the river of this name, or 'Wike', meaning 'farm'. In 1292 the manor here came to Edward I and the place was given the name 'Kingston'.

Of well-known places beginning 'Queen-', apart from those in the Dictionary, we may mention North Queensferry, Fife, and South Queensferry, Lothian, as well as Queenborough, Kent. The two Scottish places have a common name dating back to the eleventh century when Queen Margaret of England, wife of the Scottish king Malcolm III, gave the inhabitants of the settlement the exclusive right of ferrying her across here. Queenborough received its name when it became a borough in 1367, with the royal honour paid to Queen Philippa of Hainault, wife of Edward III. Neither name is modern, therefore. (But compare the *Queensferry* in Clwyd, Wales.)

Almost all places whose names end in 'Regis' are of medieval origin, so that Lyme Regis, Dorset, was so named in 1285 when it received a royal charter from Edward I, and Bartley Regis, Hampshire, Grafton Regis, Northamptonshire, and Newton Regis, Warwickshire, were all 'owned' by the king just as Huish Episcopi, Somerset, belonged to a bishop, Cerne Abbas, Dorset, belonged to an abbot, and Zeal Monachorum, Devon, belonged to a community of monks. All have medieval Latin suffixes. Some 'Regis' names were earlier 'King-' names. Newton Regis was recorded as *Kyngesneweton* in 1285, and Wyke Regis, Dorset, was *Kingeswik* in 1242 (and Wyke Regis only in 1407). Similarly, Bere Regis, also in Dorset, was *Byre Regis* in 1495 but *Kingsbere* in 1280. The manor here was crown property.

Bognor Regis, therefore, is a special late use of the suffix—hence its inclusion in the Dictionary (despite the fact that 'Bognor' is an old name). The resort could well have been 'Royal Bognor', but apart from the unattractive sound of the name, doubtless 'Regis' was preferred for its classical associations and for its harmony with the three Dorset 'Regis' resorts further west along the south coast, with Lyme Regis being near the border with Devon, Wyke Regis located near Weymouth, and Wyke Regis an actual district of Weymouth, together with yet another 'royal' name, Melcombe Regis, also in Weymouth. (Bere Regis is inland, south of Blandford Forum.)

Thus 'Royal', used as a separate prefix (unlike, say, Farnham Royal, Berkshire), is the only genuine modern name element. It is perhaps more of a title than a name proper, and is certainly not used in everyday speech: an inhabitant of *Tunbridge Wells* will usually talk simply of 'Tunbridge'. (See the name for its acquisition of the title.) The only other 'Royal' town in Britain is Royal Leamington Spa, which received its title in 1838 from Queen Victoria, the year after she succeeded to the throne. (It was Victoria's visits to both Leamington and Tunbridge that led to the 'Royal' prefix in each case, although in the case of the latter town the award was not made until after her death.)

In conclusion, it should also be mentioned that four boroughs have been granted the 'Royal' title in modern times: the so-called Royal Boroughs of Kensington (and Chelsea), London, Kingston-upon-Thames, Greater London, and Windsor, Berkshire, in England, and the royal borough of Caernarfon in Wales. Kensington borough was granted the status of 'royal' in 1901 by Edward VII, in honour of Queen Victoria who died that year and who had been born at Kensington Palace.

Windsor was appointed a royal borough in 1922, the town having long had associations with the monarchs who had dwelt here at Windsor Castle. With Kingston-upon-Thames the royal associations go back a long way, and the settlement here was known as *Cyninges tun* in 838. In 1927, however, George V confirmed that the town had long enjoyed the status of a royal borough of Surrey, and in 1963 Kingston became a royal borough of London, with Caernarfon being granted the same status also this year. In 1965 Kensington amalgamated with Chelsea to form the Royal Borough of Kensington and Chelsea. In each of these cases, however, it is not the name that has acquired the title, but the status of each town as borough.

APPENDIX II
'SEASIDE' NAMES

OF the just over 550 seaside resorts listed in Harada (1979), 27 have a 'seaside' suffix. The majority of these are '-on-Sea' and run to 18 places: *Angmering-on-Sea*, Barton-on-Sea, Bigbury-on-Sea, Caister-on-Sea, Clacton-on-Sea, Frinton-on-Sea, Gorleston-on-Sea, *Greatstone-on-Sea*, Gwbert-on-Sea, *Highcliffe*-on-Sea, Holland-on-Sea, Leigh-on-Sea, *Littlestone-on-Sea*, Lydd-on-Sea, Middleton-on-Sea, *Milford-on-Sea*, *Southend-on-Sea*, and Sutton-on-Sea. Three places each are either '-by-Sea' or '-next-the-Sea': Goring-by-Sea (see *Ogwr*), Shoreham-by-Sea, Cley-next-the-Sea, Holme-next-the-Sea, and Wells-next-the-Sea. There is also Newbiggin-by-the-Sea. The two remaining resorts are *Lee-on-the-Solent* and Weston-super-Mare. To these names we can add others such as Leysdown-on-Sea, Westgate-on-Sea, the railway station of Durrington-on-Sea (a district of Worthing), and the two Northumberland villages of High Newton-by-the-Sea and Low Newton-by-the-Sea. Finally we must include the Essex village known variously as Bradwell-on-Sea, Bradwell-juxta-Mare, or Bradwell-near-the-Sea.

Most of these suffixes are recent ones, serving either to differentiate the place from another identically or similarly named, or to act as a kind of advertising tag to tempt visitors, house-buyers, and property-developers. After all, we do like to be beside the seaside.

Harada lists resorts right round the coasts of England, Scotland, and Wales, yet the majority of those with the 'seaside' suffix are in England, either on the coast of East Anglia or, as one might expect, along the south coast. Two, Gwbert-on-Sea and Ogmore-by-Sea, are in Wales, and the most northerly resorts of all are the two villages in Northumberland.

A few of the names have long had the suffix. Weston-super-Mare, with its Latin '-on-Sea', was so called as long ago as 1349. Here, obviously, the aim was to add a distinguishing suffix: 'Weston', the 'western village', is a very common name. Bradwell seems to have been '-juxta-Mare' or '-near-the-Sea' somewhat later, but also with the suffix to distinguish this 'broad stream' from others. (Doubtless one of them, not too far away, is Bradwell-juxta-Coggeshall.) With the possible exception of Gwbert-on-Sea and Frinton-on-Sea, it will in fact be noticed that almost all of the places have common names: Barton, Bigbury, Lee, Leigh, Newton, and Westgate are examples. In some cases, as we know, the suffix was given for a specific differentiation when a resort grew up near an existing village. Thus *Angmering-on-Sea* arose near Angmering, and Lydd-on-Sea, Kent, grew up two miles from Lydd. In some cases the suffix seems to have been influenced by other places nearby similarly named: both Goring-by-Sea and Durrington-by-Sea are districts of Worthing, West Sussex, with Angmering-on-Sea and Middleton-on-Sea a few miles away to the west, and Shoreham-by-Sea to the east. This could, of course, simply be because they are in a noted seaside county, 'Sussex by the Sea'. Yet further north we find a similar pattern in Clacton-on-Sea, Frinton-on-Sea, and Bradwell-on-Sea, all in Kent.

Ogmore-by-Sea, Mid Glamorgan, has a name to distinguish it from the nearby village of Ogmore, although Gwbert-on-Sea, Dyfed, appears to have no similarly named place near it. (Its name seems to derive from a *gwy-* root meaning 'water' and *pert*, 'pretty'.) Presumably the suffix is a 'recommendatory' one, as it is for *Milford-on-Sea*, Hampshire, which has no other Milford in its vicinity.

The 'seaside' suffix is not a peculiarly British phenomenon. If we cross the Channel to France (say, to Cherbourg) and work our way east, we will come to Villers-sur-Mer, Boulogne-sur-Mer and St. Pol-sur-Mer, among others. In Holland, further north, we find the resort of Katwijk-aan-Zee (linguistically nearer the English '-on-Sea'). (Surprisingly, there seem to be fewer resorts so designated in Spain, Portugal, and Italy. One finds Lloret de Mar and a few others in Spain, of course, and Francavilla al Mare in Italy, but the suffix is not nearly so abundant. Doubtless this is because these countries are full of resorts, whereas in Britain they are geographically and seasonally more restricted.

Wherever found, however, and whether used for distinction or recommendation, the 'seaside' suffix, whatever form it takes, is much more an integral part of the place-name than the 'royal' affixes mentioned in Appendix I. Indeed, where used for distinguishing purposes (Angmering-on-Sea, not Angmering), the words are essentially descriptive, and should not be omitted. In the cases of larger, well-known resorts, such as Southend-on-Sea and Clacton-on-Sea, the suffixes are not essential, but are usually retained as a traditional sign of respect for the importance of the place.

BIBLIOGRAPHY

THE Bibliography concentrates on works dealing with place-name origins, whether on a general or regional basis, together with authoritative gazetteers and guides that frequently themselves give the origins of names. The list is a fairly comprehensive one, but is not necessarily recommendatory. Some works, notably the EPNS publications, are obviously much more detailed and dependable than nineteenth-century topographical or discursive publications. Even so, almost every work below was used, wholly or partly, in the search for material for the Dictionary, and on that ground alone deserves to be included here. The titles may conceal the size of the work: the most voluminous is (apart from the *DNB* and *Oxford English Dictionary*) the four-part *Topographical Dictionary* of Lewis, the least weighty is the little 20-page 'occasional paper' *Place-Names of the Dacorum District*, by John Field, published by the Academic Board of Dacorum College, Hemel Hempstead, in 1977. Each, in its different approach and scope, is equally valuable. (The shortest publication of all, running to a mere nine pages, is the *Local Government Boundary Commission for England, Report No. 2*, which, however, deals not directly with place-name origins but local government legislation, albeit regarding the names of districts.)

It is hoped that the comprehensiveness of the Bibliography may make it equally valuable for readers interested in old place-names, as well as modern ones.

Six works are referred to by short titles in the text of the Dictionary.

AA England & Wales	Illustrated Road Book of England and Wales
AA Ireland	Road Book of Ireland
AA Scotland	Road Book of Scotland
Cassell	Cassell's Gazetteer of Great Britain and Ireland
DNB	Dictionary of National Biography
Postal Addresses	Postal Addresses and Index to Postcode Directories.

The first three of these were published by the Automobile Association, whose abbreviation (AA) is used to distinguish the works from others with similar titles.

The volume numbers of EPNS publications are given, for readers who may wish to consult them, and the short title of an EPNS volume, or volumes, devoted to a single county is given in the main text of the Dictionary as *'EPNS'* plus the name of the county, for example *'EPNS Surrey'* in the entry for *Raynes Park*.

The year of publication is given for each work. A year in square brackets is either the original date of publication of a reprinted work, or the precise or approximate year of publication of a work in which the actual publishing date was not stated (hence 'n.d.' for 'no date').

Adams, I. H., *The Making of Urban Scotland*, London, 1978
Addison, W., *Understanding English Place-Names*, London, 1979
Alexander, H., *The Place-Names of Oxfordshire*, Oxford, 1912
Alexander, W. M., *The Place-Names of Aberdeenshire*, Aberdeen, 1952
Anderson, J. P., *The Book of British Topography*, East Ardsley, 1976 [1881]
Anderson (later Arngart), O. S., *The English Hundred-Names*, Lund, 1934–6

Armstrong, A. M., Mawer, A., Stenton, F. M., and Dickins, B., *The Place-Names of Cumberland* (EPNS 20, 21, 22), Cambridge, 1950–2

Baddeley, W. St. C., *Place-Names of Gloucestershire: A Handbook*, Gloucester, 1913

Banks, F. R., *The Penguin Guide to London*, London, 1971

Bannister, A. T., *The Place-Names of Herefordshire: The Origin and Development*, Cambridge, 1916

Beach, R. P. O. (ed.), *Touring Guide to Ireland*, Basingstoke, 1976

Beach, R. P. O. (ed.), *Touring Guide to Scotland*, Basingstoke, 1981

Bebbington, G., *London Street Names*, London, 1972

Beveridge, E., *The 'Abers' and 'Invers' of Scotland*, Edinburgh, 1923

Blome, B., *The Place-Names of North Devonshire*, Uppsala, 1929

Booth, D., Perrott, D., *The Shell Book of the Islands of Britain*, London, 1981

Bourne, J., *Place-Names of Leicestershire and Rutland*, Leicester, 1981

Bowcock, E. W., *Shropshire Place Names*, Shrewsbury, 1923

Brabner, J. H. F. (ed.), *The Comprehensive Gazetteer of England and Wales*, London, 1894–5

Burton, N. (ed.), *The Historic Houses Handbook*, London, 1982

Butlin, R. A. (ed.), *The Development of the Irish Town*, London, 1977

Cameron, K., *English Place-Names*, London, 1969

Cameron, K., *The Place-Names of Derbyshire* (EPNS 27, 28, 29), Cambridge, 1959

Carter, H., *The Towns of Wales*, Cardiff, 1965

Cassell's Gazetteer of Great Britain and Ireland, London, 1893–8

Charles, B. G., *Non-Celtic Place-Names in Wales*, London, 1938

Clunn, H. P., *The Face of the Home Counties*, London, n.d. [c.1956]

Copley, G. J., *English Place-Names and their Origins*, Newton Abbot, 1971

Copley, G. J., *Names and Places*, London, 1963

Dalzell, W. R., *The Shell Guide to the History of London*, London, 1981

Darby, H. C. (ed.), *A New Historical Geography of England*, Cambridge, 1973

Darley, G., *Villages of Vision*, St. Albans, 1978

Dauzat, A., Rostaing, C., *Dictionnaire étymologique des noms de lieux en France*, Paris, 1978

Davies, C. S., Levitt, J., *What's in a Name?*, London, 1970

Davies, D., *Welsh Place-Names and Their Meanings*, Aberystwyth, n.d. [c.1975]

Davies, E., *Flintshire Place-Names*, Cardiff, 1959

Davies, E. (ed.), *A Gazetteer of Welsh Place-Names*, Cardiff, 1975

Davies, E. M., *Welsh Place-Names: Their Meanings Explained*, Swansea, 1978

Davies, E. T., *The Place Names of Gwent*, Risca, 1982

Delderfield, E., *Stories of Inns and Their Signs*, Newton Abbot, 1974

Dexter, T. F. G., *Cornish Names*, Truro, 1968 [1926]

Dictionary of National Biography, Oxford, 1975 [1885–1901]

Dodgson, J. McN., *The Place-Names of Cheshire* (EPNS 44, 45, 46, 47, 48, 54), Cambridge, 1970–81

Dorward, D., *Scotland's Place-Names*, Edinburgh, 1979

Duignan, W. H., *Notes on Staffordshire Place Names*, London, 1902

Duignan, W. H., *Warwickshire Place Names*, London, 1912

Duignan, W. H., *Worcestershire Place Names*, London, 1905

Dyson, T., *Place Names and Surnames—their origin and meaning: with special reference to the West Riding of Yorkshire*, Huddersfield, 1944

Edmunds, F., *Traces of History in the Names of Places*, London, 1872

Ekblom, E., *The Place-Names of Wiltshire*, Uppsala, 1917

Ekwall, E., *English River-Names*, Oxford, 1928

Ekwall, E., *Street-Names of the City of London*, Oxford, 1954

Ekwall, E., *The Concise Oxford Dictionary of English Place-Names*, Oxford, 1960

Ekwall, E., *The Place-Names of Lancashire*, Manchester, 1922

Elmes, J., *A Topographical Dictionary of London*, London, 1831

Encyclopaedia Britannica, 15th ed., Chicago, London, etc., 1976

Fägersten, A., *The Place-Names of Dorset*, East Ardsley, 1978 [1933]

Field, J., *Discovering Place-Names*, Princes Risborough, 1976

Field, J., *English Field-Names: A Dictionary*, Newton Abbot, 1982

Field, J., *Place Names of Dacorum District*, Hemel Hempstead, 1977

Field, J., *Place-Names of Great Britain and Ireland*, Newton Abbot, 1980

Field, J., *Place-Names of Greater London*, London, 1980

Forbes, A. R., *Place-Names of Skye and Adjacent Islands*, Paisley, 1923

Forster, K., *A Pronouncing Dictionary of English Place-Names*, London, 1981

Freeman-Grenville, G. S. P., *Atlas of British History*, London, 1979

Gambles, R., *Lake District Place-Names*, Clapham, 1980

Gazetteer of Great Britain, Southampton, 1975

Gelling, M., *Signposts to the Past*, London, 1978

Gelling, M., *Some notes on the place-names of Birmingham and the surrounding district*, Birmingham, 1954

Gelling, M., *The Place-Names of Berkshire* (EPNS 49, 50, 51), Cambridge, 1973–5

Gelling, M., *The Place-Names of Oxfordshire* (EPNS 23, 24), Cambridge, 1953–4

Gelling, M., Nicolaisen, W. F. H., Richards, M., *The Names of Towns and Cities in Britain*, London, 1970

Glover, J., *The Place Names of Kent*, London, 1976

Glover, J., *The Place Names of Sussex*, London, 1975

Gooch, E. H., *Place-Names of Lincolnshire*, Spalding, 1945

Goodall, A., *Place-Names of South-West Yorkshire*, Cambridge, 1913

Gould, N., *Looking at Place Names*, Havant, 1978

Gover, J. E. B., *Hampshire Place Names* (unpublished typescript), 1961

Gover, J. E. B., *The Place Names of Middlesex*, London, 1922

Gover, J. E. B., Mawer, A., Stenton, F. M., *The Place-Names of Devon* (EPNS 8, 9), Cambridge, 1931–2

Gover, J. E. B., Mawer, A., Stenton, F. M., *The Place-Names of Hertfordshire* (EPNS 15), Cambridge, 1938

Gover, J. E. B., Mawer, A., Stenton, F. M., *The Place-Names of Northamptonshire* (EPNS 10), Cambridge, 1933

Gover, J. E. B., Mawer, A., Stenton, F. M., *The Place-Names of Nottinghamshire* (EPNS 17), Cambridge, 1940

Gover, J. E. B., Mawer, A., Stenton, F. M., *The Place-Names of Wiltshire* (EPNS 16), Cambridge, 1939

Gover, J. E. B., Mawer, A., Stenton, F. M., in collaboration with Bonner, A., *The Place-Names of Surrey* (EPNS 11), Cambridge, 1934

Gover, J. E. B., Mawer, A., Stenton, F. M., in collaboration with Houghton, F. T. S., *The Place-Names of Warwickshire* (EPNS 13), Cambridge, 1936

Gover, J. E. B., Mawer, A., Stenton, F. M., with the collaboration of Madge, S. J., *The Place-Names of Middlesex (apart from the City of London)* (EPNS 18), Cambridge, 1942

Gray Jones, A., *The Place-Names of Ebbw Vale*, Llandyssul, n.d. [c.1935]

Groome, F. H. (ed.), *Ordnance Gazetteer of Scotland*, Edinburgh, 1882

Hadfield, J. (ed.), *The New Shell Guide to England*, London, 1981

Hadfield, J. (ed.), *The Shell Book of English Villages*, London, 1980

Harada, G. (ed.), *Around Britain's Seaside*, Basingstoke, 1979

Harben, H. A., *A Dictionary of London*, London, 1918

Harley, J. B. (ed.), *Ordnance Survey Maps: Reprints of the first edition of the one-inch Ordnance Survey of England and Wales*, Newton Abbot, 1980 [1805–73]

Harris, C. M., *What's in a Name?*, Speldhurst, 1977
Harris, P. V., *Pembrokeshire Place Names and Dialect*, Tenby, 1974
Harrison, H., *The Place-Names of the Liverpool District; or, The History and Meaning of the Local and River Names of South-west Lancashire and of Wirral*, London, 1898
Hill, J. S., *The Place-Names of Somerset*, Bristol, 1914
Hopwood, D., *The place-names of the county of Surrey including London in Surrey*, Cape Town, 1926
Horsley, J. W., *Place-Names in Kent*, Maidstone, 1921
Hoskins, W. G., *The Making of the English Landscape*, London, 1970
Hudson, E. (ed.), *Commercial Gazetteer of Great Britain*, London, n.d. [c.1960]
Illustrated Road Book of England and Wales, London, 1963
Inglis Ker, J., *Scotland for the Motorist*, London, 1927
The Irish Encyclopaedia, Dublin, 1968
Jackson, C. E., *The Place-Names of Durham*, London, 1916
Jakobsen, J., *The Place-Names of Shetland*, London, 1936
Johnson-Ferguson, E., *The Place-Names of Dumfriesshire*, Dumfries, 1935
Johnston, J. B., *Place-Names of Scotland*, East Ardsley, 1970 [1934]
Johnston, J. B., *The Place-Names of Berwickshire*, Edinburgh, 1940
Johnston, J. B., *The Place-Names of England and Wales*, London, 1914
Johnston, J. B., *The Place-Names of Stirlingshire*, Stirling, 1904
Jones, G. R., *Welsh Place Names*, Cardiff, 1979
Jones, H. C., *Place Names in Glamorgan*, Risca, 1976
Joyce, P. W., *Irish Local Names Explained*, Dublin, 1968 [c.1885]
Joyce, P. W., *The Origin and History of Irish Names of Places*, East Ardsley, 1972 [1875]
Kent, W. (ed.), revised by Thompson, G., *An Encyclopaedia of London*, London, 1970
Killanin, Lord, Duignan, M. V., *The Shell Guide to Ireland*, London, 1967
Kökeritz, H., *The Place-Names of the Isle of Wight*, Uppsala, 1940
Langenfelt, G., *Toponymics or derivations from local names in English*, Uppsala, 1920
Lewis, S., *A Topographical Dictionary of England*, London, 1849
Lewis, S., *A Topographical Dictionary of Ireland*, Port Washington, 1970 [1837]
Lewis, S., *A Topographical Dictionary of Scotland*, London, 1846
Lewis, S., *A Topographical Dictionary of Wales*, London, 1849
Lloyd Jones, J., *Enwau Lleoedd Sir Gaernarfon* ('Place Names of Caernarvonshire'), Cardiff, 1928
Local Government Boundary Commission for England, Report No. 1, London, 1972
Local Government Boundary Commission for England, Report No. 2, London, 1973
London Post Offices and Streets, London, 1978
MacBain, A., *Place-Names of the Highlands and Islands of Scotland*, Stirling, 1922
McClure, E., *British Place-Names in their Historical Setting*, East Ardsley, 1972 [1910]
McCormick, D., *Islands of England and Wales*, Reading, 1974
Macdonald, A., *The Place-Names of West Lothian*, Edinburgh, 1941
Macdonald, J., *Place-Names of West Aberdeenshire*, Aberdeen, 1899
MacGivney, J., *Place-Names of the County Longford*, Dublin, 1908
Mackenzie, W. C., *Scottish Place-Names*, London, 1931
Macnie, D. L., McLaren, M. (eds), *The New Shell Guide to Scotland*, London, 1977
Mason, O., *Bartholomew Gazetteer of Britain*, Edinburgh, 1977
Matthews, C. M., *Place-Names of the English-Speaking World*, London, 1972
Mawer, A., *Place-Names and History*, Liverpool, 1922
Mawer, A., Stenton, F. M., *Introduction to the Survey of English Place-Names* (EPNS 1), Cambridge, 1924

Mawer, A., Stenton, F. M., *The Place-Names of Bedfordshire and Huntingdonshire* (EPNS 3), Cambridge, 1926

Mawer, A., Stenton, F. M., *The Place-Names of Buckinghamshire* (EPNS 2), Cambridge, 1925

Mawer, A., *The Place-Names of Northumberland and Durham*, Cambridge, 1920

Mawer, A., Stenton, F. M., with the assistance of Gover, J. E. B., *The Place-Names of Sussex* (EPNS 6, 7), Cambridge, 1929–30

Mawer, A., Stenton, F. M., Houghton, F. T. S., *The Place-Names of Worcestershire* (EPNS 4), Cambridge, 1927

Maxwell, H., *The Place Names of Galloway*, Glasgow, 1930

Mills, A. D., *The Place-Names of Dorset* (EPNS 52, 53), Cambridge, 1977

Mills, D., *The Place Names of Lancashire*, London, 1976

Monkhouse, F. J. (ed.), *A Survey of Southampton and Its Region*, Southampton, 1964

Moore, W. G., *The Penguin Encyclopedia of Places*, London, 1978

Moorman, F. W., *The Place-Names of the West Riding of Yorkshire*, Leeds, 1910

Morgan, T., *Handbook of the Origin of Place-Names in Wales and Monmouthshire*, Merthyr Tydfil, 1887

Morris, R. W., *Yorkshire Through Place Names*, Newton Abbot, 1982

Munn, A., *Notes on the Place Names of the Parishes and Townlands of the County of Londonderry*, Derry, 1957

Munro, R. W. (revised), *Johnston's Gazetteer of Scotland*, Edinburgh, 1973

Mutschmann, H., *The Place-Names of Nottinghamshire*, Cambridge, 1913

Nicolaisen, W. F. H., *Scottish Place-Names*, London, 1979

O'Connell, J., *The Meaning of Irish Place Names*, Belfast, 1979

The Ordnance Survey Atlas of Great Britain, Southampton/Feltham, 1982

Osborn, F. J., Whittick, A., *New Towns: Their Origins, Achievements and Progress*, London, 1977

Owen, D. J., *The Origin and Development of the Ports of the United Kingdom*, London, 1939

Oxford English Dictionary, Oxford, 1971 [1933]

Parry, M. L., Slater, T. R. (eds), *The Making of the Scottish Countryside*, London, 1980

Passenger Timetable: Great Britain, London, 1982

Pierce, G. O., *The Place-Names of Dinas Powys Hundred*, Cardiff, 1968

Place Names on Maps of Scotland and Wales, Southampton, 1973

Pool, P. A. S., *The Place-Names of West Penwith*, Penzance, 1973

Postal Addresses and Index to Postcode Directories, London, 1976

Post Offices in the United Kingdom (Excluding the London Postal Area) and the Irish Republic, London, 1974

Potter, S., *Cheshire Place-Names*, Chester, 1954

Price, L., *The Place-Names of Co. Wicklow*, Dublin, 1945–67

Rawlings, G. B., *The Streets of London*, London, n.d. [c.1925]

Reaney, P. H., *The Origin of English Place-Names*, London, 1976

Reaney, P. H., *The Place-Names of Cambridgeshire and the Isle of Ely* (EPNS 19), Cambridge, 1943

Reaney, P. H., *The Place-Names of Essex* (EPNS 12), Cambridge, 1935

Richards, M., *An Atlas of Anglesey*, Llangefni, 1972

Richards, M., *Welsh Administrative and Territorial Units*, Cardiff, 1969

Richardson, A. E., *The Old Inns of England*, London, 1934

Rivet, A. L. F., Smith, C., *The Place-Names of Roman Britain*, London, 1981

Road Book of Ireland, Dublin, 1962

Road Book of Scotland, London, 1960

Roberts, R. G., *The Place-Names of Sussex*, Cambridge, 1914

Room, A., *Place-Names Changes Since 1900: A World Gazetteer*, London, 1980
Room, A., *Place-Names of the World*, Newton Abbot, 1974
Rostaing, C., *Les noms de lieux*, Paris, 1980
Schaffer, F., *The New Town Story*, London, 1970
Sedgefield, W. J., *The Place Names of Cumberland and Westmorland*, Manchester, 1915
Sephton, J., *A Handbook of Lancashire Place-Names*, Liverpool, 1913
Skeat, W. W., *The Place-Names of Bedfordshire*, Cambridge, 1906
Skeat, W. W., *The Place-Names of Berkshire*, Oxford, 1911
Skeat, W. W., *The Place-Names of Cambridgeshire*, Cambridge, 1904
Skeat, W. W., *The Place-Names of Hertfordshire*, Hertford, 1904
Skeat, W. W., *The Place-Names of Huntingdonshire*, Cambridge, 1904
Skeat, W. W., *The Place-Names of Suffolk*, Cambridge, 1913
Smith, A., *Dictionary of City of London Street Names*, Newton Abbot, 1970
Smith, A. H., *English Place-Name Elements* (EPNS 25, 26), Cambridge, 1956
Smith, A. H., *The Place-Names of Gloucestershire* (EPNS 38, 39, 40, 41), Cambridge, 1964–5
Smith, A. H., *The Place-Names of the East Riding of Yorkshire and York* (EPNS 14), Cambridge, 1937
Smith, A. H., *The Place-Names of the North Riding of Yorkshire* (EPNS 5), Cambridge, 1969
Smith, A. H., *The Place-Names of the West Riding of Yorkshire* (EPNS 30, 31, 32, 33, 34, 35, 36, 37), Cambridge, 1961–3
Smith, A. H., *The Place-Names of Westmorland* (EPNS 42, 43), Cambridge, 1967
Spaull, H., *New Place Names of the World*, London, 1970
Stenton, F. M., *The Place-Names of Berkshire*, Reading, 1911
Stokes, H. G., *English Place-Names*, London, 1948
Taylor, I., *Names and Their Histories*, London, 1896
Taylor, I., *Words and Places*, London, n.d. [1911]
The Geographical Digest, London, 1962– (annually)
The Ulster Guide, Belfast, 1949
Thomas, R., *South Wales*, Edinburgh, 1977
Thomas, R. J., *Enwau Afonydd a Nentydd Cymru* ('Names of Welsh Rivers and Streams'), Cardiff, 1938
Treharne, R. F., Fullard, H. (eds), *Muir's Historical Atlas*, London, 1973
Vale, E., *The Seas and Shores of England*, London, 1936
Vaughan-Thomas, W., Llewellyn, A., *The Shell Guide to Wales*, London, 1977
Walford, E., Thornbury, G. W., *Old and New London*, London, 1873
Walker, B., *The Place-Names of Derbyshire*, Derby, 1914–15
Wallenberg, J. K., *Kentish Place-Names*, Uppsala, 1931
Wallenberg, J. K., *The Place-Names of Kent*, Uppsala, 1934
Walsh, P., *The Placenames of Westmeath*, Dublin, 1915
Watson, G., *Goodwife Hot and Others: Northumberland's Past in its Place Names*, Newcastle upon Tyne, 1970
Watson, W. J., *The History of the Celtic Place-Names of Scotland*, Edinburgh, 1926
Watson, W. J., *Place-Names of Ross and Cromarty*, Inverness, 1904
Weekley, E., *The Romance of Names*, London, 1914
Wheatley, H. B., *London Past and Present: Its History, Associations, and Traditions Based upon The Handbook of London by the Late Peter Cunningham*, London, 1891
Where's Where: A Descriptive Gazetteer, London, 1974
Williams, I., *Enwau Lleoedd* ('Place Names'), Liverpool, 1945
Wyld, H. C., Oakes Hirst, T., *The Place Names of Lancashire*, London, 1911